The New
Nonprofit Almanac
and Desk Reference

The New Nonprofit Almanac and Desk Reference

The Essential Facts and Figures
for Managers, Researchers, and Volunteers

V408

Independent Sector

Murray S. Weitzman
Nadine T. Jalandoni

Urban Institute

Linda M. Lampkin
Thomas H. Pollak

JOSSEY-BASS
A Wiley Company
www.josseybass.com

Jossey-Bass books and products are available through most bookstores. To contact Jossey-Bass directly, call (888) 378-2537, fax to (800) 605-2665, or visit our web site at www.josseybass.com.

Substantial discounts on bulk quantities of Jossey-Bass books are available to corporations, professional associations, and other organizations. For details and discount information, contact the special sales department at Jossey-Bass.

We at Jossey-Bass strive to use the most environmentally sensitive paper stocks available to us. Our publications are printed on acid-free recycled stock whenever possible, and our paper always meets or exceeds minimum GPO and EPA requirements.

Library of Congress Cataloging-in-Publication Data
  The new nonprofit almanac and desk reference: the essential facts and figures for managers and volunteers/foreword by Sara Meléndez and Elizabeth Boris.—1st ed.
      p. cm.—(Jossey-Bass nonprofit and public management series)
  Includes bibliographical references and index.
  ISBN 0-7879-5726-7 (alk. paper)
    1. Nonprofit organizations—United States—Statistics. 2. Charities—Economic aspects—United States—Statistics. 3. Voluntarism—Economic aspects—United States—Statistics. I. Jossey-Bass Inc. II. Series.
    HD2769.2.U6 N47 2002
    361.7′63′0973021—dc21   2001008363

PB Printing   10 9 8 7 6 5 4 3 2 1   FIRST EDITION

The Jossey-Bass
Nonprofit and Public Management Series

Contents

List of Tables

List of Figures

Chapter 5

Resource B

Foreword

SINCE THE FIRST EDITION of the *Nonprofit Almanac* was published in 1984, the independent sector has grown considerably. Its growth is apparent in the increased number of organizations that comprise it, its vital role in providing key goods and services to American society, the rise in the resources with which it has been entrusted, and the higher expectations it has for accountability.

This growth has not gone unnoticed, as more nonprofit researchers, media reporters, policymakers, public officials, and corporate leaders, among others, have become interested in understanding the nature, scope, and dimensions of the sector. *The New Nonprofit Almanac and Desk Reference,* now in its sixth edition, has worked to sustain interest in the independent sector as well as to define and quantify the size, scope, and impact of the sector in American society.

We have learned much about the sector over the years, but we also are keenly aware that there is still much more to know and improve upon. A few trends we have identified that may likely affect the sector in the coming years include: the blurring of the boundaries between the nonprofit, for-profit, and government sectors; demographic changes; shifts in the national economy; new government policy initiatives and regulations affecting nonprofits; and developments in the field of information technology.

Nonprofit organizations have traditionally filled the gaps in social services unmet by government, but they now face competition from for-profit firms in areas such as health and education. In turn, nonprofit organizations have resorted to entrepreneurial strategies and have adopted marketing techniques to compete more effectively. Nonprofits face the challenge of competing with for-profit entities in the delivery of public services without losing sight of their primary reason for existence, that is, the public good.

The sector also will be affected by changes in the U.S. population. It will need to respond to the evolving needs and services required by an increasingly racially diverse and aging population.

The movements of the national economy will have a major impact on the independent sector. The robust economy of the mid- to late 1990s, which brought increased wealth, low unemployment, and low inflation rates, contributed to record levels of private charitable giving to the sector before the end of the twentieth century. The economy has since headed for a downturn, accompanied by a volatile stock market and dimming employment forecasts. A sustained economic slowdown will likely affect charitable giving levels.

In the policy arena, the administration of George W. Bush has proposed key initiatives, which will influence philanthropy and nonprofit activities in the coming years. These initiatives include a tax proposal that would extend the charitable contributions deduction to nonitemizers; allow donors over age fifty-nine-and-a-half to contribute their IRAs directly to charities without being taxed; change excise taxes paid by private foundations on their investment incomes to 1 percent from the current rate of 1 or 2 percent; and modify the estate tax. The administration also created a White House Office of Faith-Based and Community Initiatives mandated to work with faith-based and community problem solvers to make it easier for religious organizations with social service programs to obtain government grants.

Innovations in information technology may bring changes to the way the independent sector does business, with the advent of e-philanthropy, e-volunteering, and e-filing of IRS Form 990. A pilot project with twelve states to enable charities to electronically file a Form 990 and complete all state registration requirements is well underway. Electronic filing holds forth the promise of improved transparency while decreasing the reporting burden for nonprofits. Easy access will allow the data to be used to help inform management of nonprofits, increasing efficiency and effectiveness of sector activities as well as providing the public with information it needs to make wise giving decisions. There is increasing interest in electronic filing at the federal level as well, and it is our hope that the project with the states will ease the transition to a better national data system with electronic submission of information.

Increasing accountability and improving the quality of reported data can only strengthen the sector and its vital role in society.

January 2002

Sara Meléndez
President and CEO
INDEPENDENT SECTOR

Elizabeth Boris
Director, Center for Nonprofits and Philanthropy
The Urban Institute

Introduction

THIS BOOK is the sixth in a series of statistical digests on the independent sector of the United States. It combines in one compact publication aggregate national estimates compiled by the Research Program of INDEPENDENT SECTOR, summarized data from IRS Forms 990, and state profiles of the nonprofit sector developed by the National Center for Charitable Statistics of the Urban Institute.

This new edition likewise has taken intermediary steps to address some of our readers' concerns and suggestions to make the publication simpler and easier to use.

In June 2000 INDEPENDENT SECTOR convened a number of nonprofit researchers and practitioners in a focus group to listen to their comments and suggestions regarding the *Almanac*. Many of these suggestions have been taken into consideration. This edition has been produced in partnership with the National Center for Charitable Statistics, which moved to the Urban Institute from INDEPENDENT SECTOR in 1996. Further, INDEPENDENT SECTOR intends to provide interim data updates, as sources allow, via its Web site (http://www.IndependentSector.org).

This book is organized into two major parts. Part One includes the first four chapters of the book, which present estimates based on data collected from various government and private sources by INDEPENDENT SECTOR. It defines the size and scope of the independent sector and compares it with the other major sectors of the economy, namely, the business and government sectors. Part Two contains the fifth and final chapter. It presents detailed financial information on reporting 501(c)(3) organizations, or public charities, that file IRS Form 990, based on data processed and analyzed by the National Center for Charitable Statistics at the Urban Institute. Information is provided for the major types of organizations as classified by the

National Taxonomy of Exempt Entities—Core Codes (NTEE-CC) groupings as well as on a state and regional basis.

Chapter One provides an overview of the size, scope, and dimensions of the independent sector and its place in the U.S. economy. Major topics include national income originating from the independent sector, employment, the value of volunteers, earnings from work, and the number of organizations in the sector.

Chapter Two presents more detailed information on paid employment in the independent sector (without the added value of volunteers). Using employment statistics from the Bureau of Labor Statistics and the Bureau of Economic Analysis, the chapter presents information on the number of people employed by the independent sector and its subsectors, the independent sector's share of total wages and salaries in the economy, the general employment trends in the independent sector, and the demographic characteristics of independent sector employees.

Chapter Three focuses on private giving, one of the major sources of income for the independent sector. It provides an overview of the total private contributions to the sector from individuals, foundations, and corporations. Information and analyses are provided on giving trends, including the effects of tax laws and shifts in the economy on private giving and several insights from the survey on giving and volunteering in the United States conducted by INDEPENDENT SECTOR in 1999.

Chapter Four offers estimates on the income derived by the independent sector from three major sources: (1) private giving, (2) government payments, (3) and private payments (which include income resulting from the payment of dues and fees charged for services rendered). Other sources of income, such as endowment and investment income, are also included. Estimates are also provided on how organizations in the sector use the funds they receive.

Chapter Five reviews the financial conditions of 501(c)(3) organizations that file IRS Form 990. This is the first time that detailed financial information from the GuideStar-NCCS National Nonprofit Database on over 224,000 reporting charities is being presented. Tables and analyses are presented by type of organization categories and by state and regional groupings.

Four Resource sections provide additional assistance and background information to the reader. Resource A provides a simplified listing of the National Taxonomy of Exempt Entities classification system for the nonprofit sector. Developed by the National Center for Charitable Statistics over a period of time, the classification system is the basis for classifying the myriad nonprofits into categories. Resource B includes technical notes and discussions of the methodology used in arriving at estimates presented in this book as well as detailed definitions of data elements. Resource C lists the Web addresses of various organizations and government agencies that provide helpful information on various topics related to the nonprofit sector. Resource D is a glossary of terms used throughout this publication and in other research on the nonprofit sector.

The most current available data, which in some cases are for 1998, have been used in this edition of the *Almanac*. However, 1997 is the most recent year for which employment and payroll data for many tax-exempt organizations are available from the government offices concerned. For trend analyses and comparative purposes, most tables present a series of years, in most cases commencing from 1977 and ending in 1997 or 1998, a period of about twenty years.

We welcome comments and suggestions on how we can make the *Almanac* a better informative resource for our varied audience.

Acknowledgments

INDEPENDENT SECTOR wishes to express its appreciation to the following funders who provided generous support for this project.

The Atlantic Philanthropies

The Ford Foundation

The Robert Wood Johnson Foundation

The Ewing Marion Kauffman Foundation

The W. K. Kellogg Foundation

The Lilly Endowment, Inc.

The Charles Stewart Mott Foundation

And the corporate, foundation, and nonprofit members of
INDEPENDENT SECTOR

INDEPENDENT SECTOR also acknowledges the invaluable contributions of Dr. Virginia A. Hodgkinson, who pioneered and developed this series of statistical profiles on the independent sector and continues to lend her knowledge and expertise to this project.

INDEPENDENT SECTOR also would like to thank the following staff members for their assistance: Michael McCormack, director, technology; Kris Hammill, senior analyst; Keith Hume, analyst; and Patrick Rooney and Renu Poduval, research assistants.

Overview and Executive Summary

The State of the Independent Sector

THIS BOOK aspires to visibly portray the size, scope, and nature of the independent sector and its contributions to American society. It provides a current picture of the independent sector and its components and relates it with the other two major sectors of the economy, the business (for-profit) and government sectors. Defining the independent sector requires mentioning the wide range of organizations that it comprises. These include major hospitals and health care organizations, with their sizable revenue, as well as small community-based shelters or soup kitchens that rely mostly on donations to carry on their mission. Universities, churches and religious organizations, adult and day-care centers, environmental groups, libraries, humane societies, private foundations, museums, special Olympics, drug rehabilitation centers, international human rights organizations—these are but a few of the assorted types of organizations that make up the independent sector.

The independent sector is composed of two major groups of tax-exempt organizations: 501(c)(3) charitable organizations and religious congregations and organizations; and 501(c)(4) social welfare organizations.

Independent sector organizations are founded to serve a public purpose but are private and self-governing, nonprofit oriented and tax exempt, and some may receive tax-deductible contributions. Two other important features that make the independent sector unique are voluntarism and private philanthropy, which play critical roles in the sector. The sector is financed by three key sources, including private payments for dues and program services, government grants and contracts, and private charitable contributions in the form of time and money.

Size and Scope of the Independent Sector

- Almost 6 percent of all organizations in the United States belong to the nonprofit sector; 4.4 percent of all organizations belong specifically to the independent sector (see Figure ES.1). Independent Sector organizations constitute over 75 percent of the nonprofit sector.

- Between 1987 and 1997 the number of charitable organizations in the country increased at an annual rate of 5.1 percent as demand for their services increased. This was more than double the rate experienced by the business sector. The number of organizations in the independent sector now totals 1.2 million (and 1.6 million for the entire nonprofit sector).

- The independent sector's estimated share of national income in 1998 was 6.1 percent, or about $443.6 billion (including assigned values for volunteers), up from $325.0 billion in 1992. The entire nonprofit sector had a 6.7 percent share of national income, or a total of $485.5 billion. (See Figure ES.2.)

- Of those 501(c)(3) organizations that file Form 990 with the IRS, most are small organizations; 73 percent of them reported expenses of less than $500,000 in 1998.

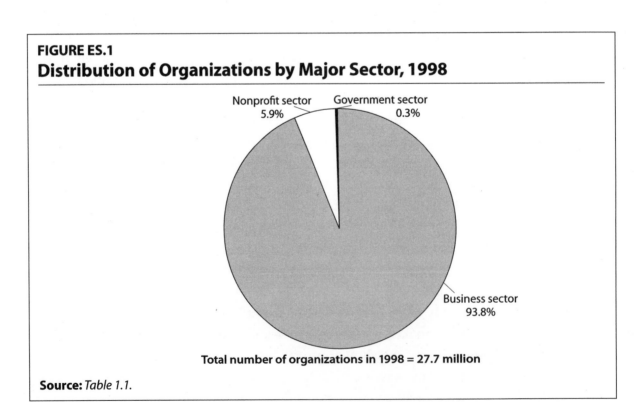

FIGURE ES.1
Distribution of Organizations by Major Sector, 1998

Nonprofit sector
5.9%

Government sector
0.3%

Business sector
93.8%

Total number of organizations in 1998 = 27.7 million

Source: *Table 1.1.*

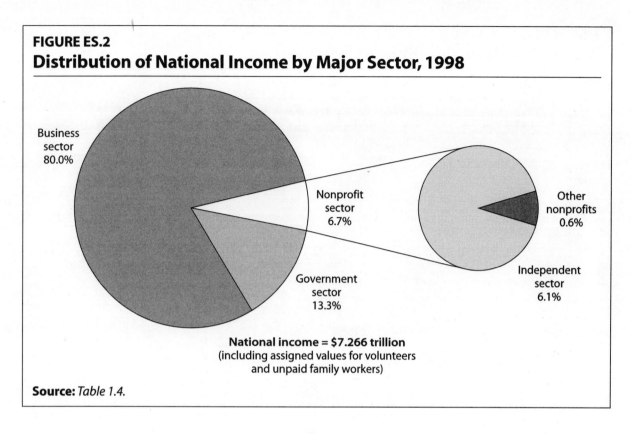

FIGURE ES.2
Distribution of National Income by Major Sector, 1998

Business
sector
80.0%

Nonprofit
sector
6.7%

Other
nonprofits
0.6%

Government
sector
13.3%

Independent
sector
6.1%

National income = $7.266 trillion
(including assigned values for volunteers
and unpaid family workers)

Source: *Table 1.4.*

- An estimated 89 percent of reporting independent sector organizations have been identified as "operating," that is, delivering information, products, and services to their members and the public. The remaining 11 percent are "support" organizations (such as United Ways and Catholic Charities USA), which collect funds and provide the financial support to operating organizations.

Paid and Voluntary Employment in the Independent Sector

- The independent sector employed an estimated 10.9 million paid employees in 1998. In addition, it benefited from the work contributed by another 5.8 million (full-time-equivalent) volunteers, who represented one-third of the total employment (both paid and unpaid) of the sector.

- Independent sector employees represented 7.1 percent of total U.S. employment, including both paid and voluntary.

- Among paid nonagricultural employees alone, independent sector employees represented 8.7 percent of all full- and part-time paid employees in the economy in 1998. The entire nonprofit sector represented 9.3 percent of all paid employees.

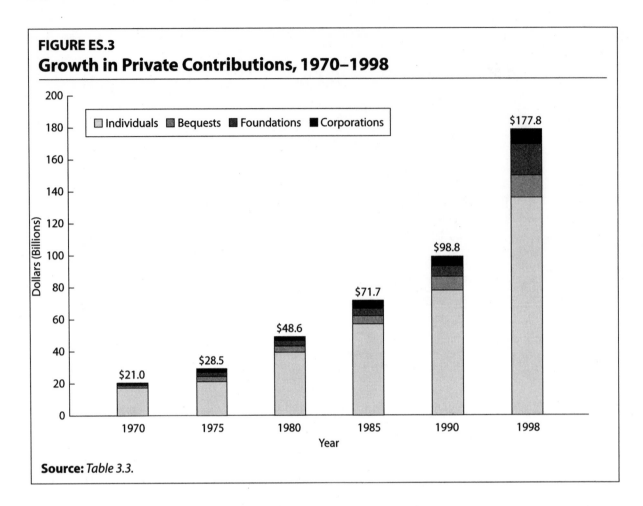

FIGURE ES.3
Growth in Private Contributions, 1970–1998

Source: *Table 3.3.*

- The nonprofit sector experienced its highest annual rate of growth in employment between 1987 and 1992—4.2 percent. In comparison, total nonagricultural employment grew by only 1.2 percent for the same period.

- The total assigned dollar value of volunteer time in 1998 reached almost $226 billion in all three major sectors combined. Voluntary employment represented one-third of the independent sector's national income.

Growth in Charitable Giving

- Preliminary estimates indicate that private charitable giving reached about $178 billion in 1998 and close to $190 billion in 1999. Gifts from individuals and their bequests accounted for 85 percent of all private giving. (See Figure ES.3.)

- Between 1995 and 1998, gifts from individuals increased by over $10 billion annually. This remarkable growth in charitable contributions was influenced by the growth in income and wealth of the population. The Council of Economic Advisers (2000) notes that during this same time period, unemployment and inflation rates were low, and the annual rate of growth of the economy was 4.1 percent. The strong stock market also had its effect on increasing both individual and foundation giving.

- In 1997 total private dollar contributions directed to the independent sector totaled $132 billion. Similarly, the total value of volunteer time given by individuals to the independent sector alone for the same year reached $134 billion. This clearly illustrates the equal importance of charitable contributions and volunteer time as crucial resources to the sector.

Revenue Sources for the Independent Sector

The revenue of the independent sector is generated from three major sources: private charitable contributions, government payments, and private payments received from dues and fees for program services and charges.

- Estimates for the total annual revenue of the independent sector in 1997 are $665 billion. Of this, 38 percent came from private payments for dues and services, 31 percent from government contracts and grants, 20 percent from private contributions, and 11 percent from other sources (including investments, interest, and dividends; see Figure ES.4).

- Although payments for dues and services continue to account for the largest share of independent sector revenue, their share has contracted over the years. Various factors may account for this shift, including increased competition from for-profits for services traditionally provided by nonprofits. The share of government payments has remained fairly constant from 1992 to 1997, after growing substantially from 1987 to 1992. The effect of the growth in private giving during the mid- to late 1990s is reflected in its increased share of total revenue, from 18.4 percent in 1992 to almost 20 percent by 1997.

- Independent sector total revenue is distributed somewhat disproportionately among its major subsectors (see Figure ES.5). In 1997 two subsectors, health services and education and research, shared 67 percent of the total annual revenue of the independent sector.

FIGURE ES.4
Independent Sector: Sources of Revenue, 1987 and 1997

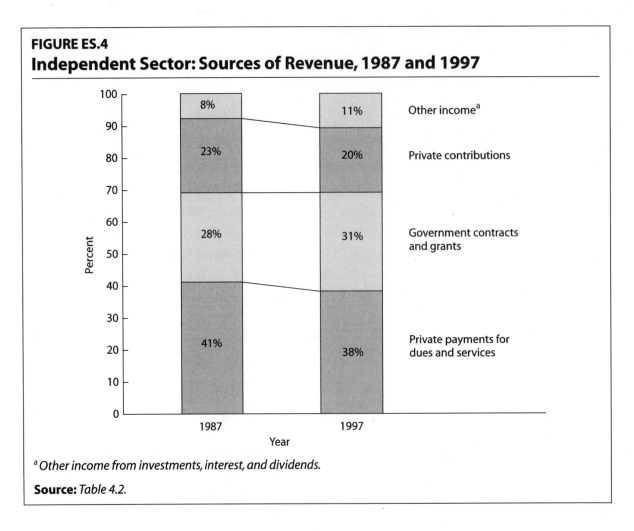

[a] *Other income from investments, interest, and dividends.*

Source: *Table 4.2.*

The remaining 33 percent was split among five subsectors: social and legal services (11.5 percent); religious organizations (11.5 percent); civic, social, and fraternal organizations (2.7 percent); arts and culture (2.3 percent); and foundations (5.0 percent).

Profile of the Major Subsectors of the Independent Sector

The diverse nature of the independent sector is reflected clearly among its subsectors. They vary not only in the size and type of organizations but also in the nature of their goals, missions, locations, and revenue sources.

Health Services

Health services dominates the independent sector in three ways: it has the largest total revenue of all the subsectors; it has the highest number of employees; and it has the largest share of total wages and salaries among the subsectors. Health services, although composed mostly of hospitals, also

FIGURE ES.5

Independent Sector: Distribution of Revenue by Subsector, 1997 Versus 1987

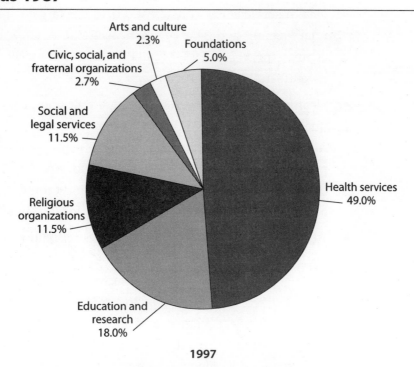

1997

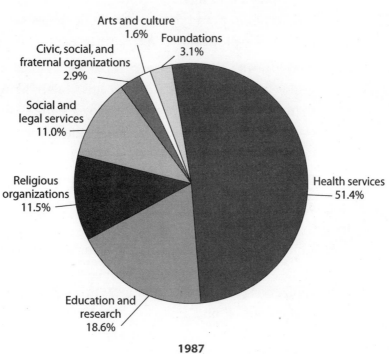

1987

Source: *Table 4.3.*

includes nursing and personal care facilities and other health services, such as specialized treatment facilities, home health care, outpatient services, and drug and alcohol treatment centers.

- Health services has consistently held the largest share of total annual revenue of the independent sector since 1977. In 1997 its total estimated revenue of $326 billion accounted for 49 percent of total revenue in the entire sector.

- Health services has been receiving a growing proportion of its annual funds from government payments. In 1997, 42 percent of its funds came from government payments, 47 percent from private payments, 4 percent from private contributions, and 7 percent from other sources. In comparison, in 1977 government payments only accounted for 32 percent of total funds for the subsector.

- About 43 percent of all independent sector paid workers worked in health services in 1998, down from 47 percent in 1992. Among the various components of this subsector, hospitals employed 72 percent of all workers. From 1992 to 1997 the rate of growth in employment for health services was at a low of 1.7 percent. This was probably the result of several factors, including limits imposed by the government and managed care organizations on hospital charges and admissions and the number of hospitals switching from nonprofit to for-profit status in recent years.

- In 1998 health services earned 54 percent of total wages and salaries in the independent sector, with hospitals making up the largest share. As with the number of employees, the share of hospitals has been declining since 1992, whereas the other components of this subsector have been growing.

- Health services received the second largest share of foundation grants in 1998 (after education and research), receiving 16.5 percent of all funds given by foundations.

- Among the major subsectors reporting to the IRS in 1998, health services was found to have the smallest increase in the number of organizations; it had minimal growth in total revenue, public support, expenses, and assets between 1992 and 1998.

Education and Research

The education and research subsector comprises colleges and universities, preschool, elementary, secondary, and correspondence schools, libraries, and other educational and research institutions.

- In 1997 education and research had $119 billion of total revenue. Private payments from dues, tuition, and services made up 56 percent of total funds. Government payments contributed 19 percent, private contributions accounted for 13 percent, and the remaining 11 percent came from other sources.

- Although education and research has the second largest annual revenue among the subsectors, its share of total revenue in the independent sector has declined from a high of 25 percent in 1977 to 18 percent in 1997.

- In 1998 the education and research subsector had 22 percent of all paid workers in the independent sector. More than half of all these employees were concentrated in higher education institutions. Similarly, its share of total wages and salaries in the independent sector was 21 percent.

- Education received the largest share of all foundation giving (24 percent) in 1998 in terms of both dollars and number of grants.

- The number of education organizations reporting to the IRS grew by 53 percent between 1992 and 1998. This was accompanied by the 80 percent growth in the number of student services organizations. Higher education grew by 20 percent, and elementary and secondary institutions increased by 26 percent.

Social and Legal Services

Organizations that make up the social and legal services subsector include individual and family services, legal aid groups providing pro bono services, child day-care, residential care, job-training and related services, and youth and housing development.

- Employment in social and legal services grew at a faster rate than in any other subsector. Its share of total employment in the independent sector grew from 13.0 percent in 1977 to 17.5 percent in 1998, reflecting the increase in demand for the services this subsector provides. Consequently, its share of total wages and salaries in the independent sector also grew from 9.2 percent in 1977 to 12.1 percent by 1998.

- This subsector had an 11.5 percent share of total revenue in the independent sector in 1997. Total revenue in the social and legal services subsector reached $76.7 billion. Between 1987 and 1997 its total revenue had an annual growth rate of 6.3 percent, with most of the growth (8.8 percent) occurring between 1987 and 1992.

- In 1997 government payments made up 52 percent of total revenue received by social and legal services. It is the most reliant on government support among the subsectors and therefore is the most sensitive to public policy changes. Private contributions accounted for 20 percent of revenue, private payments accounted for 19 percent, and 9 percent came from other sources.

Religious Organizations

Religious organizations (including religious congregations of all faiths) had estimated revenue of $76.3 billion in 1997. This subsector is unique in that private contributions account for most of its funds.

- In 1997 private contributions of $73 billion accounted for 95 percent of the total revenue of religious organizations. The annual rate of change in this subsector's total revenue between 1987 and 1997 was 2.7 percent, with most of the growth taking place in the last five years.

- Among all independent sector entities, religious organizations receive the largest share of funds from total private giving (individual, foundation, and corporate)—44 percent in 1998. This may be the result of the religious commitment of many Americans in supporting their churches as well as a perception that religious institutions are generally trustworthy in using the donations for the public good. However, estimates show that religious organizations' share of private contributions has decreased from the 53 percent share it enjoyed in 1995 to 44 percent in 1998.

- In 1998 religious organizations' share of independent sector employment was 11.6 percent.

Arts and Culture

Included in the arts and culture subsector are museums, orchestras, botanical and zoological gardens, performing arts groups, ballet groups, nonprofit radio and television, literary organizations, and other humanities-oriented organizations.

- In 1997 the arts and culture subsector represented just over 2 percent of total funds in the independent sector. It had total revenue of about $15.4 billion, growing substantially from its 1992 revenue of $8.5 billion. This subsector had the highest annual growth rate for total revenue (7.0 percent) between 1987 and 1997 and grew the most (10.4 percent) over the last five years (1992–1997).

- Private contributions made up the largest share of this subsector's total funds (44 percent), followed by private payments (28 percent), payments from other sources (19 percent), and government payments (10 percent).

Geographical and State Trends

The number of reporting public charities and their distribution by region and state closely mirror the distribution of the total U.S. population among the states.

- The ten states with the largest number of charitable organizations in 1998 (excluding religious congregations and smaller organizations) were California, New York, Texas, Pennsylvania, Ohio, Illinois, Florida, Massachusetts, Michigan, and New Jersey.

- Wyoming, Nevada, Idaho, and Delaware reported the smallest number of public charities .

- The South had 28 percent of reporting organizations, followed by the Midwest (24 percent), the Northeast (23 percent), and the West (22 percent).

- Between 1992 and 1998 the number of reporting charitable organizations grew by 50 percent in the Mountain region, compared with 39 percent nationally. Six of the eight states constituting this region also experienced large population increases between 1990 and 2000, including Nevada (66 percent), Arizona (40 percent), and Colorado (31 percent).

- Revenue growth rates for reporting public charities were highest in the East South Central region and lowest in the Pacific region. Among states, North Dakota and Oregon led with the highest revenue growth rates.

- The South led in the growth of public support, which increased by 77 percent for the period between 1992 and 1998. The region also led in the growth of total assets for charitable organizations, recording an 89 percent growth rate from 1992 to 1998.

Reference

Council of Economic Advisers, Office of the President. *Philanthropy in the American Economy.* Washington, D.C.: Author, 2000.

Part One

The Size of the Independent Sector

THE OBJECTIVE of this section is to present a cohesive and coherent set of data elements for selected years that summarizes the dimensions of the independent sector. This framework, which was developed by INDEPENDENT SECTOR, allows for comparison with the two other major sectors of the economy, the business (for-profit) and government sectors. To achieve this goal, INDEPENDENT SECTOR has compiled, estimated, and analyzed a wide variety of information, including data originating from the government and business sectors, as well as the nonprofit sector.

The following are some of the government departments that provide significant amounts of valuable data:

- U.S. Department of the Treasury (for information on tax-exempt organizations' tax returns and private contributions)

- U.S. Department of Commerce (for information on the census of service industries, population data, and national income accounts)

- U.S. Department of Labor (for information on employment and wages)

- U.S. Department of Education (for general statistics and special studies)

- U.S. Department of Health and Human Services (for general and social statistics)

Other important sources of information include such institutions as the following:

- National Council of the Churches of Christ in the USA
- AAFRC Trust for Philanthropy
- Foundation Center
- American Hospital Association
- Council for Aid to Education

All of the organizations just listed, both government and private, as well as surveys sponsored by INDEPENDENT SECTOR, provide the necessary information for the estimates presented in Part One. The principal questions that these estimates attempt to answer are:

- How does the independent sector compare with the other sectors of the economy in terms of number of entities, number of paid and volunteer employees, wages and salaries, and national income?

- What is the level of activity among the various subsectors of the independent sector as measured by employment, wages, and salaries?

- Within each subsector, what are the proportions of revenue that stem from various sources, such as private contributions, government grants, fees for services, and investment income, and how are these revenues expended?

As the word *estimates* denotes, these numbers are educated approximations; although we have aimed for it, we cannot claim complete accuracy. However, it is believed that the approach taken in developing the estimates—that is, placing the independent sector within the context of the American economy—avoids egregious errors in measuring the dimensions of the independent sector.

Chapter 1

Defining the Independent Sector and Its Place in the National Economy

THE INDEPENDENT SECTOR, which constitutes the largest share of the non-profit (or "voluntary") sector, has been described as diverse, disparate, and a challenge to define. Similar to the associations referred to by Alexis de Tocqueville 165 years ago, the institutions that make up the sector are of "a thousand other kinds—religious, moral, serious, futile, very general or restricted, enormous or diminutive" (Tocqueville, 1999 [1835], p. 106). Among the many, varied organizations that make up the independent sector are religious organizations, private colleges and schools, foundations, hospitals, day-care centers, environmental organizations, museums, symphony orchestras, youth organizations, advocacy groups, and neighborhood organizations, to name a few. What is common among them all is their mission to serve a public purpose, their voluntary and self-governing nature, and their exclusion from being able to distribute profits to stockholders (Boris and Steuerle, 1998, p. 3).

This chapter provides an overview of the independent sector in the context of the U.S. economy. Specifically, it examines how many organizations belong to the independent sector; how much of the national income is generated by the sector; and how many people it employs and their share of the total wages and salaries in the economy. Trends are also provided to compare the size of the independent sector to that of the other major sectors of the national economy, namely, the business and government sectors.

In brief, the independent sector:

- Includes two major groups of tax-exempt organizations: 501(c)(3) charitable organizations and 501(c)(4) social welfare organizations and all religious organizations and congregations.

- Comprises 1.2 million organizations—or 1.6 million if all nonprofit organizations are included (see Table 1.1)

TABLE 1.1

Number of Organizations in the United States by Major Sector and Selected Components, 1977–1998

	1977		1982	
	Number (Thousands)	**Percent**	**Number (Thousands)**	**Percent**
Total	15,944	100.0	18,209	100.0
Nonprofit sector total	1,123	7.0	1,180	6.5
Independent sector organizations	739	4.6	793	4.4
Total 501(c)(3) and 501(c)(4) organizations reported by the IRS	406	2.5	454	2.5
501(c)(3) organizations reported by the IRS	276	1.7	322	1.8
501(c)(4) organizations reported by the IRS	130	0.8	132	0.7
Church congregations	333	2.1	339	1.9
Other nonprofit organizations exempt from federal income tax	384	2.4	387	2.1
Business (for-profit) sector total	14,741	92.5	16,947	93.1
Farm	2,456	15.4	2,401	13.2
Nonfarm	12,285	77.1	14,546	79.9
Government sector total[a]	80	0.5	82	0.5
Local	80	0.5	82	0.5

[a] For federal and state government, for all years shown, the number is less than 500, and the percentage is less than 0.05 percent.

[b] The National Center for Charitable Statistics identified over 81,000 churches in the 1997 IRS Business Master File of Tax-Exempt Organizations, resulting in possible double-counting of some churches in this table. The number was retained for purposes of comparison with earlier years.

Sources: Internal Revenue Service, Data Book, various years; Internal Revenue Service, Statistics of Income Bulletin, various years; Lindner, various years; U.S. Bureau of the Census, 1999.

1987		1992		1997		1998	
Number (Thousands)	**Percent**	**Number (Thousands)**	**Percent**	**Number (Thousands)**	**Percent**	**Number (Thousands)**	**Percent**
21,867	100.0	24,468	100.0	27,586	100.0	27,692	100.0
1,285	5.9	1,426	5.8	1,586	5.8	1,627	5.9
907	4.1	1,030	4.2	1,188	4.3	1,228	4.4
561	2.6	689	2.8	835	3.0	874	3.2
422	1.9	546	2.2	693	2.5	734	2.7
139	0.6	143	0.6	142	0.5	140	0.5
346	1.6	341	1.4	353[b]	1.3	354	1.3
378	1.7	396	1.6	398	1.4	399	1.4
20,499	93.7	22,957	93.8	25,913	93.9	25,977	93.8
2,213	10.1	2,108	8.6	2,191	7.9	2,191	7.9
18,286	83.6	20,849	85.2	23,722	86.0	23,785	85.9
83	0.4	85	0.3	88	0.3	88	0.3
83	0.4	85	0.3	87.5	0.3	87.5	0.3

TABLE 1.2

Active Entities on IRS Business Master File of Tax-Exempt Organizations, 1987–1998

Tax Code Number	Type of Tax-Exempt Organization	1987	1992	1996	1997	1998[b]
501(c)(1)	Corporations organized under an act of Congress	24	9	20	27	14
501(c)(2)	Title-holding companies	5,977	6,529	7,100	7,113	7,125
501(c)(3)	Religious, charitable, and similar organizations[a]	422,103	546,100	654,186	692,524	733,790
501(c)(4)	Social welfare organizations	138,485	142,673	139,512	141,776	139,533
501(c)(5)	Labor and agricultural organizations	75,238	71,012	64,955	64,902	64,804
501(c)(6)	Business leagues	59,981	70,871	77,274	78,406	79,864
501(c)(7)	Social and recreational clubs	60,146	64,681	60,845	66,387	66,691
501(c)(8)	Fraternal beneficiary societies	98,979	93,544	91,972	87,990	84,507
501(c)(9)	Voluntary employees' beneficiary societies	10,927	14,986	14,486	14,464	14,240
501(c)(10)	Domestic fraternal beneficiary societies	17,813	21,415	20,925	20,954	21,962
501(c)(11)	Teachers' retirement fund	11	10	13	13	13
501(c)(12)	Benevolent life insurance associations	5,572	6,103	6,343	6,368	6,423
501(c)(13)	Cemetery companies	7,942	9,025	9,562	9,646	9,792
501(c)(14)	Credit unions	6,652	5,559	5,157	4,959	4,378
501(c)(15)	Mutual insurance companies	950	1,157	1,212	1,206	1,251
501(c)(16)	Corporations to finance crop operation	18	23	23	25	25
501(c)(17)	Supplemental unemployment benefit trusts	728	625	565	542	533
501(c)(18)	Employee-funded pension trusts	5	8	2	1	1
501(c)(19)	War veterans' organizations	24,749	28,096	31,464	31,961	35,682
501(c)(20)	Legal services organizations	210	217	131	92	56
501(c)(21)	Black lung trusts	21	23	25	27	28
501(c)(23)	Veterans' associations founded prior to 1880		2	2	2	2
501(c)(24)	Trusts described in section 4049 of ERISA[c]		1	1	1	1
501(c)(25)	Holding companies for pensions and so on		290	794	908	1,017
501(d)	Religious and apostolic organizations	88	92	113	115	118
501(e)	Cooperative hospital service organizations	80	68	54	50	43
501(f)	Cooperative service organizations of operating educational organizations	1	1	1	1	1
521	Farmers' cooperatives	2,405	2,086	1,773	1,754	1,442
	Total exempt organizations	939,105	1,085,206	1,188,510	1,232,214	1,273,336

Note: All figures are for the fiscal year ended September 30.

[a] Not all 501(c)(3) organizations are included because certain organizations, such as churches, integrated auxiliaries, subordinate units, and conventions or associations of churches, need not apply for recognition of exemption unless they desire a ruling.

[b] Excludes state-sponsored high-risk health insurance organizations and worker's compensation reinsurance organizations, which were categories added to 1998 data. Figures are preliminary.

[c] ERISA = Employee Retirement Income Security Act.

Source: Internal Revenue Service, Data Book, various years.

- Accounts for 4.4 percent of all identified institutions in the United States—or 5.9 percent if all nonprofit organizations are included (see Table 1.1)

- Grew in number of organizations by 31 percent between 1987 and 1997, surpassing the growth rate of both the business and government sectors

- Accounts for 6.1 percent of total national income

- Employs 10.9 million paid employees and 5.8 million volunteers

- Represents 7.1 percent of total paid employment

- Covers nearly 5.4 percent of total actual earnings from work

- Provides an important share of the goods and services consumed by the population

What Is the Independent Sector?

There are twenty-five different categories of tax-exempt organizations under the U.S. tax code (see Table 1.2), all of which receive exemption from federal income taxes and, at the discretion of local authorities, from property tax. Two major groups of tax-exempt organizations as defined under U.S. tax code constitute the independent sector: *501(c)(3) charitable organizations* and *501(c)(4) social welfare organizations.* However, 501(c)(3) charitable institutions are the only group of tax-exempt organizations that can receive tax-deductible contributions from individuals and corporations. They include organizations that serve religious, educational, charitable, scientific, and literary purposes. They also include organizations testing for the public safety, fostering certain national and international sports competitions, or working to prevent cruelty to children and animals, as well as private and corporate foundations. Charitable organizations are not allowed to distribute their excess revenue to individuals or other stakeholders as in business organizations. Charitable organizations are limited with regard to legislative lobbying. In general, 501(c)(3) and 501(c)(4) organizations serve a much wider variety of population groups than other categories of tax-exempt organizations that require their members to be of a particular status, profession, or occupation—such as professional societies, labor unions, or bar associations, among others.

The second group of organizations included in the independent sector—501(c)(4) social welfare organizations—likewise work for the public benefit. They have no restrictions on their lobbying activities to promote the public good. These organizations, composed mainly of civic and social welfare groups and local associations of employees, may lobby to promote community welfare and undertake charitable, educational, or recreational activities. (See Figure B.1 in Appendix B for a graphic representation of the components of the independent sector.)

Growth in the Number of Organizations Among the Major Sectors

Measuring the number of organizations in the independent sector is a complex activity, largely because of the diversity of its components. The IRS Business Master File of Tax-Exempt Organizations lists the number of organizations registered with the IRS. Excluded from this list, however, are many congregations, conventions, or associations with religious affiliations and numerous community organizations with less than $5,000 in gross revenue, which need not register with the IRS. Trends from available data nevertheless indicate that the independent sector grew significantly from 1977 to 1998 (see Figure 1.1).

- Of the 27.7 million operating organizations in the United States in 1998, approximately 1.6 million were nonprofit organizations. Over

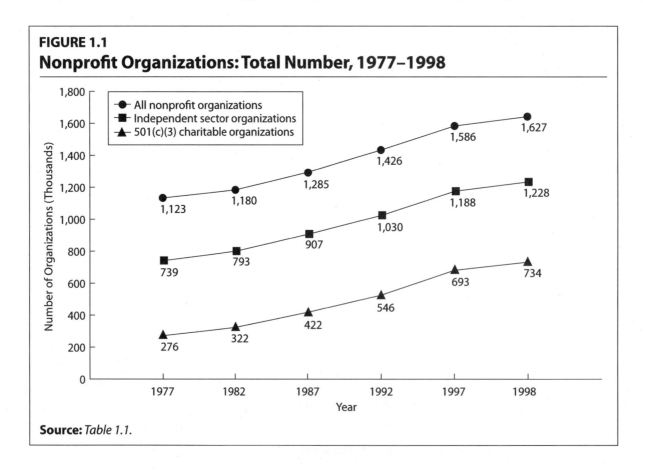

FIGURE 1.1
Nonprofit Organizations: Total Number, 1977–1998

Legend:
- All nonprofit organizations
- Independent sector organizations
- 501(c)(3) charitable organizations

All nonprofit organizations: 1,123 (1977), 1,180 (1982), 1,285 (1987), 1,426 (1992), 1,586 (1997), 1,627 (1998)

Independent sector organizations: 739 (1977), 793 (1982), 907 (1987), 1,030 (1992), 1,188 (1997), 1,228 (1998)

501(c)(3) charitable organizations: 276 (1977), 322 (1982), 422 (1987), 546 (1992), 693 (1997), 734 (1998)

Y-axis: Number of Organizations (Thousands)
X-axis: Year

Source: *Table 1.1.*

75 percent of all nonprofits, or 1.2 million organizations, belonged to the independent sector. (See Table 1.1.)

- The IRS reported 733,790 charitable and religious [501(c)(3)] organizations and 139,533 social welfare [501(c)(4)] organizations in its 1998 Business Master File of Tax-Exempt Organizations. Other types of nonprofit organizations numbered about 400,000. (See Table 1.2.)

- Churches, subordinate units, and conventions or associations of churches, although qualifying as 501(c)(3) entities, are not required to register with the IRS and are largely undercounted in this category. About 354,000 churches and analogous religious congregations, such as temples or mosques, can be identified. (See Table 1.3.)

- The entire nonprofit sector made up 5.9 percent of all organizations in the country in 1998, whereas the independent sector represented 4.4 percent of all existing organizations. The business sector dominated, with 93.8 percent of all organizations, and the government sector comprised 0.3 percent of all organizations. (See Table 1.1.)

- The number of independent sector organizations grew at an annual rate of 2.7 percent between 1987 and 1997, surpassing its growth rate in the previous decade (2.1 percent). This expansion was caused by the increase in the number of 501(c)(3) charitable organizations that were formed, which grew at an annual rate of 5.1 percent, or more than double the rate of the business sector. Figure 1.2 compares annual rates of change among major and selected sectors over three time periods.

- Between 1987 and 1997 the number of organizations in the independent sector increased by 31 percent, growing from 907,000 to almost 1.2 million. This was largely accounted for by the 64 percent increase in the number of charitable 501(c)(3) organizations between 1987 and 1997. In comparison, the number of businesses grew by only 26 percent and government by 5 percent over the same time period. (See Figure 1.3.)

Share of National Income Among the Major Sectors

The U.S. Bureau of Economic Analysis defines *national income* as the "total net income earned in production." "It differs from gross domestic product [GDP] mainly in that it excludes depreciation charges and other allowances for business and institutional consumption of durable capital goods and indirect business taxes" (Council of Economic Advisers, 2000, p. 336).

TABLE 1.3

Number of Churches Reported

Religious Body	Year	Churches Reported
Advent Christian Church	1998	305
African Methodist Episcopal Church	1999	6,200
African Methodist Episcopal Zion Church	1998	3,098
American Baptist Association	1998	1,760
American Baptist Churches in the USA	1998	3,800
Apostolic Episcopal Church	1999	225
Assemblies of God	1998	11,937
Associated Reformed Presbyterian	1997	238
Association of Free Lutheran Congregations	1997	243
Baptist General Conference	1998	876
Baptist Missionary Association of America	1999	1,334
Brethren in Christ Church	1998	210
Christian and Missionary Alliance	1998	1,964
Christian Brethren (a.k.a. Plymouth Brethren)	1997	1,150
Christian Church (Disciples of Christ)	1997	3,818
Christian Churches and Churches of Christ	1988	5,579
Christian Congregation, Inc.	1997	1,438
Christian Methodist Episcopal Church	1983	2,340
Christian Reformed Church in North America	1998	733
Church Christ in Christian Union	1998	226
Church of Christ, Scientist	1998	2,200
Church of God (Anderson, IN)	1998	2,353
Church of God (Cleveland, TN)	1995	6,060
Church of God in Christ	1991	15,300
Church of God Prophecy	1997	1,908
Church of Jesus Christ of Latter-Day Saints	1997	10,811
Church of the Brethren	1997	1,095
Church of the Nazarene	1998	5,101
Church of the United Brethren in Christ	1997	228
Churches of Christ	1999	15,000
Churches of God, General Conference	1998	339
Conservative Baptist Association of America	1998	1,200
Conservative Congregational Christian Conference	1998	236
Cumberland Presbyterian Church	1998	774
Episcopal Church	1996	7,390
Evangelical Covenant Church	1998	628
Evangelical Free Church of America	1995	1,224
Evangelical Lutheran Church in America	1998	10,862
Fellowship of Grace Brethren Churches	1997	260
Free Methodist Church of North America	1998	990
Friends General Conference	1998	620
Friends United Meeting	1997	501
Full Gospel Fellowship of Churches and Ministers International	1999	896
General Association of General Baptists	1997	790
General Association of Regular Baptist Churches	1998	1,415
General Conference Mennonite Brethren Churches	1996	368
Greek Orthodox Archdiocese of America	1998	523
Hutterian Brethren	1997	428
Independent Fundamental Churches of America	1999	659
International Baptist Bible Fellowship	1997	4,500
International Church of the Foursquare Gospel	1998	1,851

TABLE 1.3 (continued)

Number of Churches Reported

Religious Body	Year	Churches Reported
International Council of Community Churches	1998	150
International Pentecostal Holiness Church	1998	1,716
Jehovah's Witnesses	1999	11,064
Korean Presbyterian Church in America	1992	203
Lutheran Church—Missouri Synod	1997	6,218
Mennonite Church	1998	926
Mennonite Church, General Conference	1998	313
Missionary Church	1998	335
National Association of Free Will Baptists	1998	2,297
National Baptist Convention of America, Inc.	1987	2,500
National Baptist Convention, USA, Inc.	1992	33,000
National Congregational Christian Churches	1998	416
National Organization of the New Apostolic Church of North America	1998	401
North American Baptist Conference	1997	268
Old Order Amish Church	1993	898
Open Bible Standard Churches, Inc.	1998	386
Orthodox Church in America	1998	625
Pentecostal Assemblies of the World, Inc.	1998	1,750
Pentecostal Church of God	1998	1,237
Presbyterian Church in America	1998	11,260
Presbyterian Church (USA)	1997	1,340
Progressive National Baptist Convention, Inc.	1995	2,000
Reformed Church in America	1998	902
Religious Society of Friends (Conservative)	1994	1,200
Reorganized Church of Jesus Christ of Latter-Day Saints	1998	1,236
Roman Catholic Church	1998	19,584
Salvation Army	1998	1,388
Seventh-Day Adventist Church	1998	4,405
Southern Baptist Convention	1998	40,870
Sovereign Grace Believers	1998	300
United Church of Christ	1998	6,017
United Methodist Church	1998	36,170
United Pentecostal Church International	1995	3,790
Universal Fellowship of Metropolitan Community Churches	1998	300
Wesleyan Church (USA)	1998	1,590
Wisconsin Evangelical Lutheran Synod	1997	1,240
Number of churches 200 or more		343,050
Plus number of churches less than 200		6,456
Total		349,506
Plus:		
Synagogues	1999	2,900
Mosques	1999	1,200
Total number of churches reported		353,606

Note: *Religious bodies that have 200 or more churches are identified in this table.*

Sources: *Lindner, 2000; estimates received from the Council on American-Islamic Relations and the United Jewish Communities. Used by permission of the Yearbook of American and Canadian Churches.*

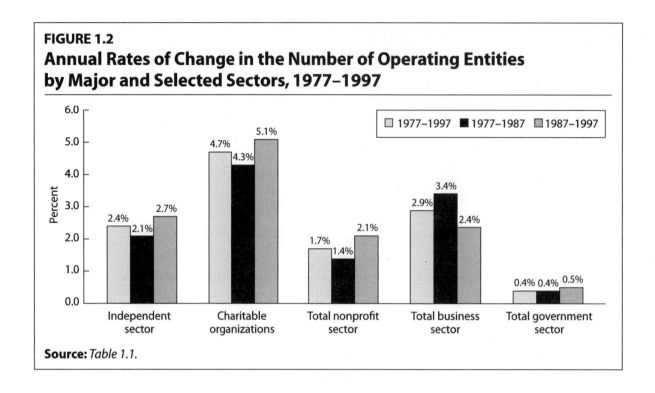

FIGURE 1.2

Annual Rates of Change in the Number of Operating Entities by Major and Selected Sectors, 1977–1997

Source: *Table 1.1.*

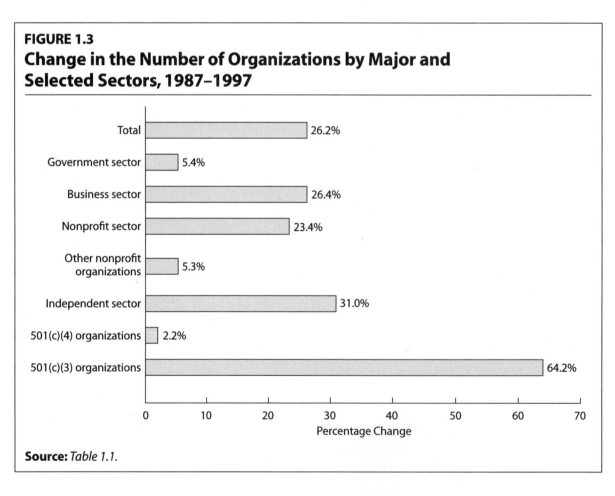

FIGURE 1.3

Change in the Number of Organizations by Major and Selected Sectors, 1987–1997

Source: *Table 1.1.*

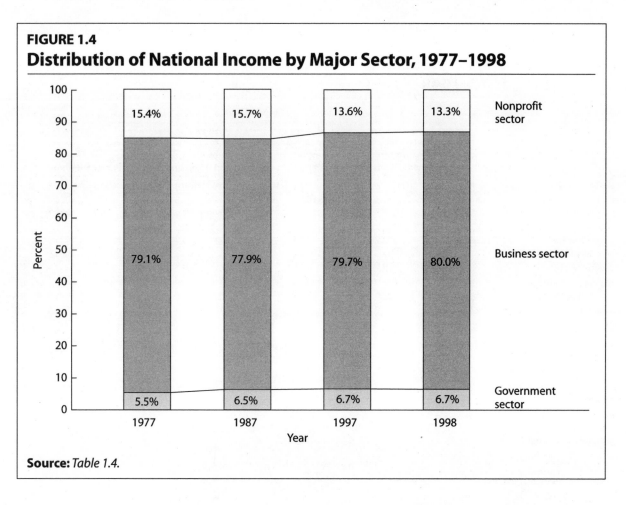

FIGURE 1.4

Distribution of National Income by Major Sector, 1977–1998

Source: *Table 1.4.*

National income is about 80 percent of GDP. National income is largely made up of compensation of employees (70 percent); the rest includes proprietors' income, rental income, corporate profits, and net interest.

In estimating the share of national income for nonprofit and government organizations, only the compensation of employees and employer supplements to salaries (such as contributions for social insurance, pension plans, and health insurance) are included. Returns of capital are included only for the business (for-profit) sector.

- In 1997 and 1998 total national income was $6.86 trillion and $7.27 trillion, respectively. This amount includes the assigned, or imputed, value for volunteer time and unpaid family workers. For 1997 and 1998 the independent sector's share of national income was 6.1 percent, and the total nonprofit sector's share was 6.7 percent. The business sector's share of national income, in comparison, increased from 79.7 percent in 1997 to 80.0 percent in 1998. The government sector's share decreased slightly from 13.6 to 13.3 percent for the same period. (See Table 1.4 and Figure 1.4.)

TABLE 1.4

National Income by Major Sector, Including Values for Volunteers, 1977–1998

	Current Dollars										
	1977		1982		1987		1992		1997		1998	
	Amount (Billions)	Percent	Amount (Billions)	Percent	Amount (Billions)	Percent	Amount (Billions)	Percent	Amount (Billions)	Percent	Amount (Billions)	Percent
Total, including assigned values	1,687.1	100.0	2,673.6	100.0	3,830.4	100.0	5,180.3	100.0	6,856.1	100.0	7,266.5	100.0
Total, excluding assigned values	1,635.4	96.9	2,601.9	97.3	3,802.0	99.3	4,993.7	96.4	6,634.9	96.8	7,036.4	96.8
Assigned values, total	51.7	3.1	98.7	3.7	156.4	4.1	186.6	3.6	221.2	3.2	230.1	3.2
Assigned values for volunteers	46.0	2.7	92.2	3.4	149.8	3.9	179.4	3.5	216.5	3.2	225.9	3.1
Assigned values for unpaid family workers[a]	5.7	0.3	6.5	0.2	6.6	0.2	7.2	0.1	4.7	0.1	4.2	0.1
Private nonprofit sector	93.6	5.5	171.9	6.4	247.1	6.5	354.7	6.8	460.8	6.7	485.5	6.7
Excluding assigned values	57.3	3.4	99.2	3.7	145.8	3.8	232.0	4.5	312.8	4.6	331.0	4.6
Assigned values	36.3	2.2	72.7	2.7	101.3	2.6	122.7	2.4	148.1	2.2	154.6	2.1
Independent sector	84.4	5.0	155.7	5.8	219.8	5.7	325.0	6.3	421.5	6.1	443.6	6.1
Excluding assigned values	517	3.1	90.2	3.4	133.3	3.5	214.2	4.1	287.5	4.2	303.8	4.2
Assigned values	32.7	1.9	65.5	2.4	86/5	2/3	110.8	2.1	134.0	2.0	139.8	1.9
Other nonprofit organizations	9.2	0.5	16.1	0.6	27.3	0.7	29.7	0.6	39/3	0.6	41.9	0.6
Excluding assigned values	5.6	0.3	8.9	0.3	12.5	0.3	17.8	0.3	25.2	0.44	27.1	0.4
Assigned values	3.6	0.2	7.2	0.3	14.8	0.4	11.9	0.2	14.1	0.2	14.8	0.2
Business (for-profit) sector	1,334.1	79.1	2,101.4	78.6	2,983.0	77.9	4,025.8	77.7	5,461.2	79.7	5,812.2	80.0
Excluding assigned values	1,327.1	78.7	2,106.9	78.8	3,097.4	80.9	4,008.7	77.4	5,444.6	79.4	5,795.5	79.8
Assigned values, total	7.0	0.4	9.2	0.3	13.6	0.4	17.1	0.3	16.6	0.2	16.6	0.2
Assigned values for volunteers	1.3	0.1	2.7	0.1	7.0	0.2	9.9	0.2	11.9	0.2	12.4	0.2
Assigned values for unpaid family workers[a]	5.7	0.3	6.5	0.2	66	0.2	7.2	0.1	4.7	0.1	4.2	0.1
Government sector	259.4	15.4	400.3	15.0	600.3	15.7	799.8	15.4	934.1	13.6	968.8	13.3
Excluding assigned values	251.0	14.9	395.8	14.8	558.8	14.6	753.0	145	877.5	12.8	909.9	12.5
Assigned values	8.4	0.5	16.8	0.6	41.5	1.1	46.8	0.9	56.6	0.8	58.9	0.8

Note: National income *is the total net income earned in production. Unlike GDP, it excludes depreciation and other allowances for business and institutional consumption of durable goods and indirect business taxes. Constant 1997 dollars are derived using the Consumer Price Index.*

[a] Unpaid family workers *are persons working without pay in a business operated by a member of the household to whom they are related by birth or marriage.*

Sources: *U.S. Department of Commerce, various years; Hodgkinson, Weitzman, and the Gallup Organization,* Giving and Volunteering, *various years; U.S. Department of Labor, various years; Council of Economic Advisers, 2000.*

- Modifying the national income account to include the assigned, or imputed, value of volunteer time underscores the significance that volunteer activity has on the independent sector and on American society. The value of volunteer time is calculated by taking the average hourly wage for nonagricultural workers and increasing it by 12 percent to estimate fringe benefits. In 1997 and 1998 the value of volunteer time accounted for approximately one-third of the independent sector's total national income (see Table 1.4).

- In 1998 the assigned value for volunteer activities added another $225.9 billion to total national income (Saxon-Harrold and others, 1999). Figure 1.5 traces the dollar value of volunteer time from 1977

	Constant 1997 Dollars										
1977		1982		1987		1992		1997		1998	
Amount (Billions)	Percent	Amount (Billions)	Percent	Amount (Billions)	Percent	Amount (Billions)	Percent	Amount (Billions)	Percent	Amount (Billions)	Percent
4,468.3	100.0	4,491.7	100.0	5,592.6	100.0	5,926.1	100.0	6,830.4	100.0	7,111.4	100.0
4,331.4	96.9	4,327.5	96.3	5,371.7	96.0	5,712.7	96.4	6,609.2	96.8	6,885.5	96.8
136.9	3.1	164.2	3.7	221.0	4.0	213.5	3.6	221.2	3.2	225.9	3.2
121.8	2.7	153.3	3.4	211.6	3.8	205.2	3.5	216.5	3.2	221.8	3.1
15.1	0.3	10.8	0.2	9.3	0.2	8.2	0.1	4.7	0.1	4.1	0.1
247.9	5.5	285.9	6.4	349.1	6.2	405.8	6.8	460.9	6.7	476.6	6.7
151.8	3.4	165.0	3.7	206.0	3.7	265.4	4.5	312.8	4.6	324.9	4.6
96.1	2.2	120.9	2.7	143.1	2.6	140.4	2.4	148.1	2.2	151.8	2.1
223.5	5.0	259.0	5.8	310.5	5.6	371.8	6.3	421.5	6.2	435.5	6.1
136.9	3.1	150.0	3.3	188.3	3.4	245.0	4.1	287.5	4.2	298.3	4.2
86.6	1.9	108.9	2.4	122.2	2.2	126.8	2.1	134.0	2.0	137.2	1.9
24.4	0.5	26.8	0.6	38.6	0.7	34.0	0.6	39.3	0.6	41.2	0.6
14.8	0.3	14.8	0.3	17.7	0.3	20.4	0.3	25.2	0.4	26.6	0.4
9.5	0.2	12.0	0.3	20.9	0.4	13.6	0.2	14.1	0.2	14.5	2.3
3,533.4	79.1	3,519.5	78.4	4,395.4	78.6	4,605.4	77.7	5,435.5	79.6	5,683.8	79.9
3,514.8	78.7	3,504.2	78.0	4,376.2	78.2	4,585.9	77.4	5,418.9	79.3	5,667.5	79.7
18.5	0.4	15.3	0.3	19.2	0.3	19.6	0.3	16.6	0.2	16.3	0.2
3.4	0.1	4.5	0.1	9.9	0.2	11.3	0.2	11.9	0.2	12.2	0.2
15.1	0.3	10.8	0.2	9.3	0.2	8.2	0.1	4.7	0.1	4.1	0.1
687.0	15.4	686.2	15.3	848.1	15.2	915.0	15.4	934.1	13.7	951.0	13.4
664.8	14.9	658.3	14.7	789.5	14.1	861.4	14.5	877.5	12.8	893.2	12.6
22.2	0.5	27.9	0.6	58.6	1.0	53.5	0.9	56.6	0.8	57.8	0.8

to 1998 in both current dollars and constant 1997 dollars. Using constant 1997 dollars to control for inflation, the dollar value of volunteer time has increased from $121.8 billion in 1977 to $221.8 billion in 1998, an increase of 82 percent.

- Excluding the assigned value for volunteers, the annual percentage increase in national income for the independent sector from 1977 to 1997 was 3.8 percent, compared with 2.2 percent for business and 1.4 percent for government (see Table 1.5). Since 1992 the trend has altered, with the business sector surpassing the growth rate of the independent sector.

TABLE 1.5

Annual Rates of Change in National Income by Major Sector, 1977–1998

	1977	1977	1977	1977
Beginning Year	**1977**	**1977**	**1977**	**1977**
Ending Year	**1982**	**1987**	**1992**	**1997**
Number of Years	**5**	**10**	**15**	**20**
	(Percent)	(Percent)	(Percent)	(Percent)
Total	0.0	2.2	1.9	2.1
Assigned values, total	3.7	4.9	3.0	2.4
Assigned values for volunteers	4.7	5.7	3.5	2.9
Assigned values for unpaid family workers[a]	(6.5)	(4.7)	(4.0)	(5.7)
Private nonprofit sector	2.9	3.5	3.3	3.1
Excluding assigned values	1.7	3.1	3.8	3.7
Assigned values	4.7	4.1	2.6	2.2
Independent sector	3.0	3.3	3.4	3.2
Excluding assigned values	1.8	3.2	4.0	3.8
Assigned values	4.7	3.5	2.6	2.2
Other nonprofit organizations	1.9	4.7	2.2	2.4
Excluding assigned values	0.0	1.8	2.1	2.7
Assigned values	4.7	8.2	2.4	2.0
Business (for-profit) sector	(0.1)	2.2	1.8	2.2
Excluding assigned values	(0.1)	2.2	1.8	2.2
Assigned values, total	(3.8)	0.4	0.4	(0.6)
Assigned values for volunteers	5.5	11.1	8.3	6.4
Assigned values for unpaid family workers[a]	(6.5)	(4.7)	(4.0)	(5.7)
Government sector	0.0	2.1	1.9	1.5
Excluding assigned values	(0.2)	1.7	1.7	1.4
Assigned values	4.7	10.2	6.0	4.8

Note: *Percentage changes are based on constant 1997 dollars.*

[a] Unpaid family workers *are persons working without pay in a business operated by a member of the household to whom they are related by birth or marriage.*

Source: *Table 1.4.*

1982 1987 5	1982 1992 10	1982 1997 15	1987 1992 5	1987 1997 10	1992 1997 5	1997 1998 1
(Percent)	(Percent)	(Percent)	(Percent)	(Percent)	(Percent)	(Percent)
4.4	2.8	2.9	1.2	2.1	3.0	4.2
6.1	2.7	2.0	(0.7)	0.0	0.7	2.1
6.7	3.0	2.3	(0.6)	0.2	1.1	2.4
(2.9)	(2.7)	(5.4)	(2.5)	(6.6)	(10.6)	(12.3)
4.1	3.6	3.2	3.1	2.8	2.6	3.4
4.5	4.9	4.4	5.2	4.3	3.3	3.9
3.4	1.5	1.4	(0.4)	0.3	1.1	2.5
3.7	3.7	3.3	3.7	3.1	2.5	3.3
4.7	5.0	4.4	5.4	4.3	3.3	3.7
2.3	1.5	1.4	0.7	0.9	1.1	2.4
7.6	2.4	2.6	(2.5)	0.2	3.0	4.7
3.6	3.2	3.6	2.9	3.6	4.4	5.6
11.8	1.3	1.1	(8.2)	(3.9)	0.7	3.0
4.5	2.7	2.9	0.9	2.1	3.4	4.6
4.5	2.7	2.9	0.9	2.2	3.4	4.6
4.7	2.5	0.5	0.4	(1.5)	(3.2)	(1.8)
17.1	9.7	6.7	2.7	1.9	1.0	2.3
(2.9)	(2.7)	(5.4)	(2.5)	(6.6)	(10.6)	(12.3)
4.3	2.9	2.1	1.5	1.0	0.4	1.8
3.7	2.7	1.9	1.8	1.1	0.4	1.8
16.0	6.7	4.8	(1.8)	(0.4)	1.1	2.2

FIGURE 1.5
Assigned Dollar Value of Volunteer Time, 1977–1998

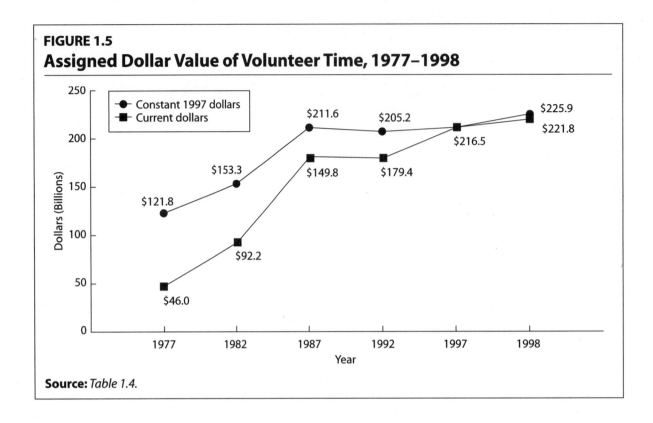

Source: *Table 1.4.*

Employment in the Major Sectors

Included in the estimates for employment are all paid full-time or part-time employees, self-employed workers, and persons working without pay, including volunteers and family workers.

- An estimated 153.6 million people worked in 1998, and 144.1 million of them (94.0 percent) received pay. Volunteers constitute 6.1 percent of all workers and numbered over 9.3 million in 1998. (See Table 1.6.)

- The independent sector's share of total paid employment rose from 5.3 percent in 1977 to 7.1 percent in 1998. In actual number of employees, the figure nearly doubled, from 5.5 million in 1977 to 10.9 million in 1998 (see Figure 1.6).

- In comparison, the number of paid employees in the business sector increased by 50 percent, from 66.3 million employees in 1977 to 100.0 million employees in 1998; the number of paid employees in the government sector increased by 20 percent, from 18.5 million to 22.2 million.

- In 1998 one out of every twelve paid employees in the United States worked in the nonprofit sector.

- In 1998 about 5.7 million individuals, or 62 percent of all volunteers, worked in the independent sector. The government sector benefited

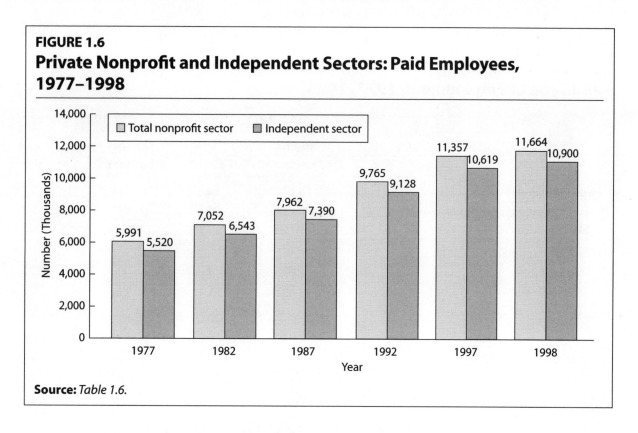

FIGURE 1.6

Private Nonprofit and Independent Sectors: Paid Employees, 1977–1998

Source: *Table 1.6.*

from the services of over 2.4 million volunteers, or 26 percent of total volunteer employment; half a million individuals volunteered for the business sector. (See Figure 1.7.)

- Volunteers represented 35 percent of total employment in the independent sector in 1998. When their numbers are combined with paid employment, the independent sector's share of total national employment increases from 7.1 percent to 10.8 percent.

Earnings from Work in the Major Sectors

In 1998 Americans' actual earnings from paid work (wages and salaries and self-employment income, excluding fringe benefits) reached $4.8 trillion. About 5.9 percent of total actual earnings originated from the nonprofit sector. Businesses accounted for 79.7 percent of actual earnings, and 14.4 percent was generated by the government sector. (See Figure 1.8.)

- When the total value of volunteer employment and unpaid family work is added into the equation, total earnings from work increases by $206 billion, reaching $5 trillion. In essence, volunteer employment contributed over $200 billion in unpaid human resources to the economy. (See Table 1.7.)

TABLE 1.6

Estimated Employment in the United States by Major Sector and Type of Employment, 1977–1998

	1977		1982	
	Number (Thousands)	**Percent**	**Number (Thousands)**	**Percent**
Paid employment	98,492	94.8	106,755	93.9
Full-time and part-time employees	90,734	87.3	97,832	86.0
Self-employed	7,758	7.5	8,923	7.8
Unpaid employment	5,441	5.2	6,962	6.1
Volunteers	4,600	4.4	6,300	5.5
Family workers[a]	841	0.8	662	0.6
Total	103,933	100.0	113,717	100.0
Private nonprofit sector	9,620	9.3	12,023	10.6
Full-time and part-time employees	5,991	5.8	7,052	6.2
Volunteers	3,629	3.5	4,971	4.4
Independent sector	8,791	8.5	11,024	9.7
Full-time and part-time employees	5,520	5.3	6,543	5.8
Volunteers	3,271	3.1	4,481	3.9
Other nonprofit organizations	829	0.8	999	0.9
Full-time and part-time employees	471	0.5	509	0.4
Volunteers	358	0.3	490	0.4
Business (for-profit) sector	74,994	72.2	81,062	71.3
Full-time and part-time employees	66,262	63.8	71,294	62.7
Self-employed	7,758	7.5	8,923	7.8
Unpaid family workers[a]	841	0.8	662	0.6
Volunteers	133	0.1	183	0.2
Government sector	19,319	18.6	20,632	18.1
Full-time and part-time employees	18,482	17.8	19,485	17.1
Volunteers	837	0.8	1,147	1.0
Total	103,933	100.0	113,717	100.0

[a] Unpaid family workers *are persons working without pay in a business operated by a member of the household to whom they are related by birth or marriage.*

Sources: *U.S. Department of Commerce, various years; Hodgkinson, Weitzman, and the Gallup Organization,* Giving and Volunteering, *various years; Kirsch, Hume, and Jalandoni, 2001; U.S. Department of Labor, various years.*

1987		1992		1997		1998	
Number (Thousands)	Percent	Number (Thousands)	Percent	Number (Thousands)	Percent	Number (Thousands)	Percent
120,479	92.9	128,142	93.3	141,161	93.7	144,149	93.9
110,798	85.5	118,102	86.0	130,617	86.7	133,917	87.2
9,681	7.5	10,040	7.3	10,544	7.0	10,232	6.7
9,172	7.1	9,246	6.7	9,431	6.3	9,435	6.1
8,759	6.8	8,901	6.5	9,260	6.1	9,294	6.1
413	0.3	345	0.2	171	0.1	141	0.1
129,651	100.0	137,388	100.0	150,592	100.0	153,584	100.0
13,899	10.7	15,853	11.5	17,691	11.7	18,021	11.7
7,962	6.1	9,765	7.1	11,357	7.5	11,664	7.6
5,927	4.6	6,088	4.4	6,334	4.2	6,357	4.1
12,459	9.6	14,628	10.6	16,343	10.9	16,645	10.8
7,390	5.7	9,128	6.6	10,619	7.1	10,900	7.1
5,059	3.9	5,500	4.0	5,724	3.8	5,745	3.7
1,440	1.1	1,225	0.9	1,348	0.9	1,376	0.9
572	0.4	637	0.5	738	0.5	764	0.5
868	0.7	588	0.4	610	0.4	612	0.4
92,391	71.3	96,349	70.1	108,450	72.0	110,922	72.2
81,889	63.2	85,474	62.2	97,226	64.6	100,038	65.1
9,681	7.5	10,040	7.3	10,544	7.0	10,232	6.7
413	0.3	345	0.2	171	0.1	141	0.1
408	0.3	490	0.4	509	0.3	511	0.3
23,361	18.0	25,186	18.3	24,451	16.2	24,641	16.0
20,938	16.1	22,863	16.6	22,034	14.6	22,215	14.5
2,423	1.9	2,323	1.7	2,417	1.6	2,426	1.6
129,651	100.0	137,388	100.0	150,592	100.0	153,584	100.0

TABLE 1.7

Earnings from Work by Major Sector and Type of Employment, 1977–1998

	1977		1982	
	Amount (Billions)	Percent	Amount (Billions)	Percent
Total actual earnings and assigned values	1,193.7	100.0	1,851.7	100.0
Actual earnings, total	1,146.9	96.1	1,762.9	95.2
Earnings from wages and salaries	994.0	83.3	1,587.4	85.7
Earnings from self-employment	152.9	12.8	175.5	9.5
Assigned values, total	46.8	3.9	88.8	4.8
Assigned values for volunteers	41.1	3.4	82.3	4.4
Assigned values for unpaid family workers[a]	5.7	0.5	6.5	0.4
Nonprofit sector	84.2	7.1	153.6	8.3
Wages and salaries	51.8	4.3	88.7	4.8
Assigned values for volunteers	32.4	2.7	64.9	3.5
Independent sector	75.9	6.4	139.2	7.5
Wages and salaries	46.7	3.9	80.7	4.4
Assigned values for volunteers	29.2	2.4	58.5	3.2
Other nonprofit organizations	8.3	0.7	14.4	0.8
Wages and salaries	5.1	0.4	8.0	0.4
Assigned values for volunteers	3.2	0.3	6.4	0.3
Business (for-profit) sector	899.6	75.4	1,375.9	74.3
Wages and salaries	739.8	62.0	1,191.5	64.3
Self-employment	152.9	12.8	175.5	9.5
Assigned values, total	6.9	0.6	8.9	0.5
Assigned values for volunteers	1.2	0.1	2.4	0.1
Assigned values for unpaid family workers[a]	5.7	0.5	6.5	0.4
Government sector	209.9	17.6	322.2	17.3
Wages and salaries	202.4	17.0	307.3	16.5
Assigned values for volunteers	7.5	0.6	14.9	0.8
Total for all sectors	1,193.7	100.0	1,851.7	100.0

[a] Unpaid family workers *are persons working without pay in a business operated by a member of the household to whom they are related by birth or marriage.*

Sources: *U.S. Department of Commerce, various years; Hodgkinson, Weitzman, and the Gallup Organization,* Giving and Volunteering, *various years; Kirsch, Hume, and Jalandoni, 2001; U.S. Department of Labor, various years.*

1987		1992		1997		1998	
Amount (Billions)	Percent	Amount (Billions)	Percent	Amount (Billions)	Percent	Amount (Billions)	Percent
2,703.8	100.0	3,541.2	100.0	4,666.4	100.0	5,006.8	100.0
2,563.4	94.8	3,373.9	95.3	4,468.3	95.8	4,800.9	95.9
2,250.5	83.2	2,955.2	83.5	3,889.7	83.4	4,194.8	83.8
312.9	11.6	418.7	11.8	578.6	12.4	606.1	12.1
140.4	5.2	167.3	4.7	198.1	4.2	205.9	4.1
133.8	4.9	160.1	4.5	193.4	4.1	201.7	4.0
6.6	0.2	7.2	0.2	4.7	0.1	4.2	0.1
217.3	8.0	309.0	8.7	397.7	8.5	419.8	8.4
126.9	4.7	199.5	5.6	265.5	5.7	281.9	5.6
90.4	3.3	109.5	3.1	132.2	2.9	137.9	2.8
193.2	7.1	283.1	8.0	363.7	7.8	383.5	7.7
116.0	4.3	184.2	5.2	244.1	5.2	258.8	5.2
77.2	2.9	98.9	2.8	119.6	2.6	124.7	2.5
24.1	0.9	25.9	0.7	34.1	0.7	36.3	0.7
10.9	0.4	15.3	0.4	21.4	0.5	23.1	0.5
13.2	0.5	10.6	0.3	12.7	0.3	13.2	0.3
2,027.2	75.0	2,622.7	74.1	3,553.7	76.2	3,841.5	76.7
1,701.4	62.9	2188	61.8	2,959.8	63.4	3,220.1	64.3
312.9	11.6	418.7	11.8	578.6	12.4	606.1	12.1
12.9	0.5	16.0	0.5	15.3	0.3	15.3	0.3
6.3	0.2	8.8	0.2	10.6	0.2	11.1	0.2
6.6	0.2	7.2	0.2	4.7	0.1	4.2	0.1
459.3	16.9	609.5	17.2	714.9	15.3	745.4	14.9
422.2	15.5	567.7	16.0	664.4	14.2	692.8	13.8
37.1	1.4	41.8	1.2	50.5	1.0	52.6	1.1
2,703.8	100.0	3,541.2	100.0	4,666.4	100.0	5,006.8	100.0

FIGURE 1.7

Distribution of Full-Time Volunteers by Major Sector, 1977, 1987, and 1998

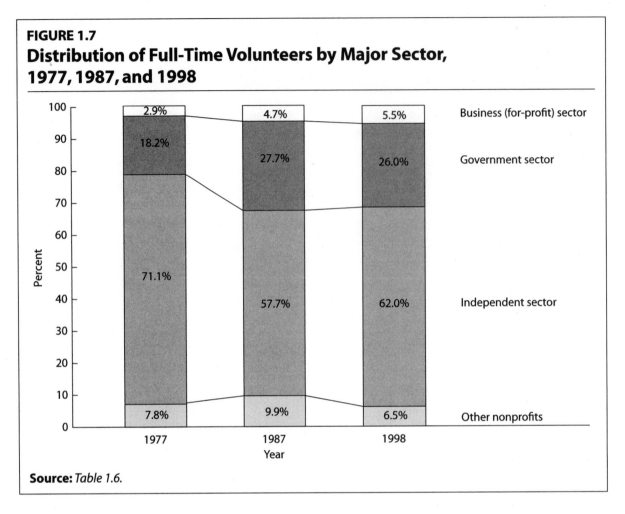

Source: *Table 1.6.*

FIGURE 1.8

Distribution of Paid Earnings by Major Sector, 1998

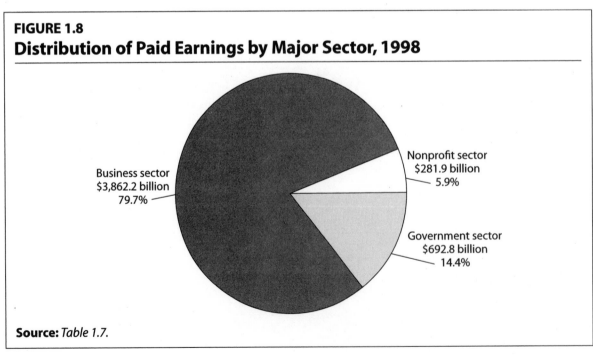

Source: *Table 1.7.*

- In 1998 the assigned value of volunteer labor in the independent sector alone reached nearly $125 billion, or about one-third of total earnings in the sector. This ratio was slightly higher for other nonprofits, for which it represented 36 percent of total earnings. (See Table 1.7.)

Relationship Between Expenditures of the Independent Sector and the American Population

A quantitative indicator of the independent sector's contribution to improving quality of life can be conceived as the relationship between its total current operating expenditures and the total American population. Data on current operating expenditures are not available solely for the independent sector but refer to all private nonprofit organizations. However, approximately 90 percent of both employment and earnings from work in all private nonprofit organizations can be attributed to the independent sector.

- In 1999 current operating expenditures for all nonprofit organizations were estimated at $784.6 billion. Over a forty-year period, in constant 1996 dollars, these expenditures increased from $172.2 billion in 1959 to $723.4 billion in 1999. (See Table 1.8.)

- Again using constant 1996 dollars, the amount expended by nonprofit organizations for every man, woman, and child in the United States rose from $972 in 1959 to $1,595 in 1979, reaching $2,649 by 1999 (see Figure 1.9).

Independent Sector's Share of Total Services and Personal Consumption

Personal consumption expenditures refers to the total amount of goods (durable and nondurable) and services purchased by the resident population of the United States. Although most of the goods and services purchased by individuals are from businesses, goods and services may also originate from the government, from overseas, or from nonprofit institutions.

- The current operating expenditures of nonprofit organizations as a percentage of both total services and personal consumption expenditures peaked in 1993 at 22.3 percent and 12.9 percent, respectively. It has declined slightly since then, settling at 21.5 percent of services and 12.5 percent of personal consumption expenditures in 1999. (See Table 1.9.)

TABLE 1.8

Nonprofit Organizations: Estimated Current Operating Expenditures,* 1959–1999

Year	Total (Billions) Current Dollars Amount	Total (Billions) Constant 1996 Dollars Amount	Total (Billions) Constant 1996 Dollars Index 1959 = 100	Per Capita Constant 1996 Dollars Amount	Per Capita Constant 1996 Dollars Index 1959 = 100	Population (Midyear, in Millions)
1959	17.8	172.2	100.0	972.3	100.0	177.1
1960	20.2	188.2	109.3	1,040.9	107.1	180.8
1961	21.4	192.2	111.6	1,046.3	107.6	183.7
1962	23.6	202.0	117.3	1,082.5	111.3	186.6
1963	25.6	209.4	121.6	1,106.2	113.8	189.3
1964	28.0	217.8	126.5	1,135.0	116.7	191.9
1965	30.6	230.0	133.6	1,183.7	121.7	194.3
1966	34.4	243.0	141.1	1,236.0	127.1	196.6
1967	38.4	252.6	146.7	1,270.6	130.7	198.8
1968	43.4	264.4	153.5	1,317.4	135.5	200.7
1969	50.0	277.4	161.1	1,368.5	140.7	202.7
1970	55.8	277.4	161.1	1,352.5	139.1	205.1
1971	62.0	286.6	166.4	1,379.9	141.9	207.7
1972	68.6	297.2	172.6	1,415.9	145.6	209.9
1973	76.4	306.4	177.9	1,446.0	148.7	211.9
1974	85.2	314.2	182.5	1,468.9	151.1	213.9
1975	94.6	327.6	190.2	1,516.7	156.0	216.0
1976	103.2	330.8	192.1	1,516.7	156.0	218.1
1977	112.8	340.8	197.9	1,547.0	159.1	220.3
1978	126.4	346.6	201.3	1,557.1	160.1	222.6
1979	141.8	359.0	208.5	1,594.8	164.0	225.1
1980	162.0	374.0	217.2	1,642.5	168.9	227.7
1981	182.8	385.2	223.7	1,674.8	172.2	230.0
1982	204.0	398.0	231.1	1,714.0	176.3	232.2
1983	225.8	407.6	236.7	1,739.7	178.9	234.3
1984	247.8	415.2	241.1	1,756.3	180.6	236.4
1985	267.2	429.4	249.4	1,800.4	185.2	238.5
1986	292.0	451.0	261.9	1,873.7	192.7	240.7
1987	331.2	475.2	276.0	1,956.4	201.2	242.9
1988	373.6	509.6	295.9	2,079.2	213.8	245.1
1989	411.4	537.2	312.0	2,171.4	223.3	247.4
1990	457.2	560.2	325.3	2,240.8	230.5	250.0
1991	496.8	580.8	337.3	2,298.4	236.4	252.7
1992	538.8	594.6	345.3	2,328.1	239.4	255.4
1993	572.6	616.0	357.7	2,386.7	245.5	258.1
1994	604.4	638.2	370.6	2,449.0	251.9	260.6
1995	636.8	658.6	382.5	2,503.2	257.4	263.1
1996	673.0	673.0	390.8	2,534.8	260.7	265.5
1997	708.2	697.4	405.0	2,602.2	267.6	268.0
1998	743.2	711.4	413.1	2,629.0	270.4	270.6
1999	784.6	723.4	420.1	2,648.8	272.4	273.1

*Current operating expenditures are estimated by doubling the reported GDP for nonprofit institutions. Constant 1996 dollars represent a "chain-type" price index prepared by the Bureau of Economic Analysis.

Source: Council of Economic Advisers, 2000.

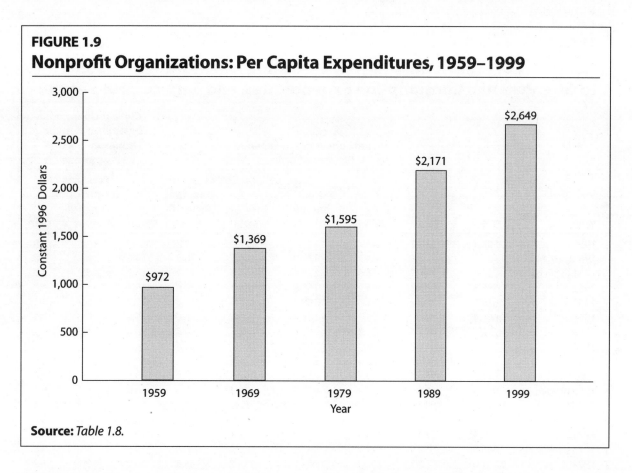

FIGURE 1.9
Nonprofit Organizations: Per Capita Expenditures, 1959–1999

Source: *Table 1.8.*

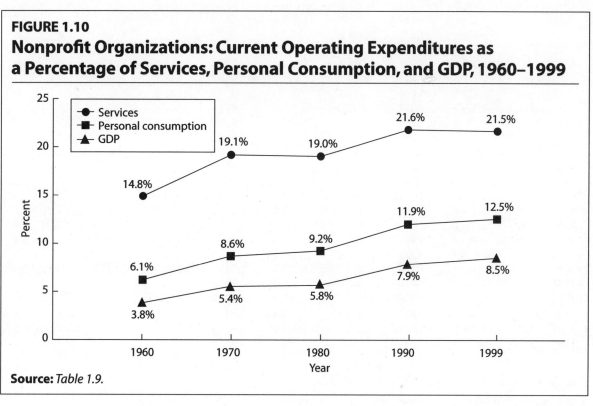

FIGURE 1.10
Nonprofit Organizations: Current Operating Expenditures as a Percentage of Services, Personal Consumption, and GDP, 1960–1999

Source: *Table 1.9.*

TABLE 1.9

Nonprofit Organizations: Current Operating Expenditures Related to GDP, Personal Consumption Expenditures, and Services, 1959–1999

| Year | GDP | Personal Consumption Expenditures (Billions of Dollars) | | | | Current Operating Expenditures | Current Operating Expenditures in the Nonprofit Sector as a Percentage of: | | |
		Total	Durable Goods	Non-durable Goods	Services Total		Services	Personal Consumption Expenditures	GDP
1959	507.4	318.2	42.7	148.5	127.0	17.8	14.0	5.6	3.5
1960	527.4	332.3	43.3	152.9	136.1	20.2	14.8	6.1	3.8
1961 (T) Feb.	545.7	342.7	41.8	156.6	144.3	21.4	14.8	6.2	3.9
1962	586.5	363.8	46.9	162.8	154.1	23.6	15.3	6.5	4.0
1963	618.7	383.2	51.6	168.2	163.4	25.6	15.7	6.7	4.1
1964	664.4	411.8	56.7	178.7	176.4	28.0	15.9	6.8	4.2
1965	720.1	444.4	63.3	191.6	189.5	30.6	16.1	6.9	4.2
1966	789.3	481.8	68.3	208.8	204.7	34.4	16.8	7.1	4.4
1967	834.1	508.7	70.4	217.1	221.2	38.4	17.4	7.5	4.6
1968	911.5	558.8	80.8	235.7	242.3	43.4	17.9	7.8	4.8
1969 (P) Dec.	985.3	605.5	85.9	253.2	266.4	50.0	18.8	8.3	5.1
1970 (T) Nov.	1,039.7	649.0	85.0	272.0	292.0	55.8	19.1	8.6	5.4
1971	1,128.6	702.4	96.9	285.5	320.0	62.0	19.4	8.8	5.5
1972	1,240.4	770.7	110.4	308.0	352.3	68.6	19.5	8.9	5.5
1973 (P) Nov.	1,385.5	852.5	123.5	343.1	385.9	76.4	19.8	9.0	5.5
1974	1,501.0	932.3	122.3	384.5	425.5	85.2	20.0	9.1	5.7
1975 (T) Mar.	1,635.2	1,030.3	133.5	420.7	476.1	94.6	19.9	9.2	5.8
1976	1,823.9	1,149.8	158.9	458.3	532.6	103.2	19.4	9.0	5.7
1977	2,031.4	1,278.4	181.2	497.2	600.0	112.8	18.8	8.8	5.6
1978	2,295.9	1,430.3	201.7	550.2	678.4	126.4	18.6	8.8	5.5
1979	2,566.4	1,596.2	214.4	624.4	757.4	141.8	18.7	8.9	5.5
1980 (P) Jan.	2,795.6	1,763.0	214.2	696.1	852.7	162.0	19.0	9.2	5.8
1981	3,131.3	1,944.2	231.3	758.9	954.0	182.8	19.2	9.4	5.8
1982 (T) Nov.	3,259.2	2,079.3	240.2	787.6	1,051.5	204.0	19.4	9.8	6.3
1983	3,534.9	2,286.4	281.2	831.2	1,174.0	225.8	19.2	9.9	6.4
1984	3,932.7	2,498.5	326.9	884.7	1,286.9	247.8	19.3	9.9	6.3
1985	4,213.0	2,712.7	363.3	928.8	1,420.6	267.2	18.8	9.8	6.3
1986	4,452.9	2,895.2	401.3	958.5	1,535.4	292.0	19.0	10.1	6.6
1987	4,742.5	3,105.3	419.7	1,015.3	1,670.3	331.2	19.8	10.7	7.0
1988	5,108.3	3,356.6	450.2	1,082.9	1,823.5	373.6	20.5	11.1	7.3
1989	5,489.1	3,596.7	467.8	1,165.4	1,963.5	411.4	21.0	11.4	7.5
1990 (P) July	5,803.2	3,831.5	467.6	1,246.1	2,117.8	457.2	21.6	11.9	7.9
1991 (T) Mar.	5,986.2	3,971.2	443.0	1,278.8	2,249.4	496.8	22.1	12.5	8.3
1992	6,318.9	4,209.6	470.8	1,322.9	2,415.9	538.8	22.3	12.8	8.5
1993	6,642.3	4,454.7	513.4	1,375.2	2,566.1	572.6	22.3	12.9	8.6
1994	7,054.3	4,716.4	560.8	1,438.0	2,717.6	604.4	22.2	12.8	8.6
1995	7,400.5	4,969.0	589.7	1,497.3	2,882.0	636.8	22.1	12.8	8.6
1996	7,813.2	5,237.6	616.5	1,574.1	3,047.0	673.0	22.1	12.8	8.6
1997	8,300.8	5,524.4	642.9	1,641.7	3,239.8	708.2	21.9	12.8	8.5
1998	8,759.9	5,848.6	698.2	1,708.9	3,441.5	743.2	21.6	12.7	8.5
1999	9,248.4	6,254.9	758.1	1,841.1	3,655.7	784.6	21.5	12.5	8.5

Note: *(P) = peak in business cycle; (T) = trough in business cycle.*

Sources: *See NPA Table 1.8 for current operating expenditure estimates; U.S. Department of Commerce, various years; Council of Economic Advisers, various years.*

- Over the forty-year period from 1959 to 1999, the current operating expenditures of nonprofit institutions as a percentage of personal consumption expenditures were on an upward trend (see Figure 1.10). This indicates that nonprofit institutions were providing an increasing share of goods and services to the population.

- As a percentage of GDP, current operating expenditures of nonprofits peaked at 8.6 percent in 1993 through 1996, decreasing slightly to 8.5 percent in recent years (see Table 1.9).

References

Boris, E. T., and Steuerle, C. E. (eds.). *Nonprofits and Government: Collaboration and Conflict.* Washington, D.C.: Urban Institute Press, 1998.

Council of Economic Advisers, Office of the President. *Economic Report of the President.* Washington, D.C.: U.S. Government Printing Office, various years.

Hodgkinson, V. A., Weitzman, M. S., and the Gallup Organization. *Giving and Volunteering in the United States.* (Various editions.) Washington, D.C.: INDEPENDENT SECTOR, various years.

Internal Revenue Service. *Data Book.* (Various editions.) Washington, D.C.: U.S. Government Printing Office, various years.

Internal Revenue Service. *Statistics of Income Bulletin.* (Various editions.) Washington, D.C.: U.S. Government Printing Office, various years.

Kirsch, A. D., Hume, K., and Jalandoni, N. T. *Giving and Volunteering in the United States: Findings from a National Survey.* (1999 edition.) Washington, D.C.: INDEPENDENT SECTOR, 2001.

Lindner, E. W. (ed.). *Yearbook of American and Canadian Churches.* (68th ed.) Nashville, Tenn.: Abingdon Press, 2000.

Saxon-Harrold, S.K.E., and others. *Giving and Volunteering in the United States, 1999—Executive Summary.* Washington, D.C.: INDEPENDENT SECTOR, 1999.

Tocqueville, Alexis de. *Democracy in America, Vol. II.* New York: Knopf, 1999.

U.S. Bureau of the Census. *Statistical Abstract of the United States.* (119th ed.) Washington, D.C.: U.S. Government Printing Office, 1999.

U.S. Department of Commerce, Bureau of Economic Analysis. *Survey of Current Business.* (Various editions.) Washington, D.C.: U.S. Government Printing Office, various years.

U.S. Department of Labor, Bureau of Labor Statistics. *Employment and Earnings.* (Various editions.) Washington, D.C.: U.S. Government Printing Office, various years.

Chapter 2

Employment Trends in the Independent Sector

THE PRIMARY PURPOSE of this chapter is to present periodic estimates of employment and total wages and salaries for the independent sector and its key subsectors. Comparisons are also made of the demographic characteristics of independent sector employees with those of the business and government sectors. The sources of data from which the estimates are derived include those of both government and private organizations.

There are limitations in estimating employment in the independent sector. Numbers of employees and their wages and salaries have been estimated almost entirely from data produced by government agencies using the Standard Industrial Classification (SIC) system. The census of service industries, held every five years, has served as a primary benchmark in preparing estimates. Statistics from the Bureau of Labor Statistics, the American Hospital Association (2000), and the National Center for Education Statistics have also been used to fill in data gaps and help compensate for limitations.

Estimating employment in the independent sector has been made even more difficult by the government's change from using the SIC system to using the North American Industry Classification System (NAICS). Future attempts at estimating employment in the independent sector will require accommodating the changes between the two classification systems.

In brief, employment trends in the independent sector indicate the following:

- In 1998, 9.3 percent of all nonagricultural employees in the economy worked in the nonprofit sector, and 8.7 percent were employed specifically in the independent sector. Government employed 15.7 percent, and 75.0 percent worked for businesses.

- From 1987 to 1992, while the rest of the economy experienced modest growth, the nonprofit sector experienced its highest annual rate of increase in employment (4.2 percent). Comparative data for the business sector for the same period show that the rate of increase in employment was 0.7 percent.

- Over a twenty-one-year period the number of employees in the independent sector nearly doubled, from 5.5 million in 1977 to 10.9 million in 1998; there was similar growth in the number of employees in the entire nonprofit sector.

- The independent sector's share of total wages and salaries in the economy in 1998 was 6.3 percent ($259 billion), with an annual average wage and salary estimate of $23,743, compared with $33,232 for all other nonagricultural employees.

- Although the health services subsector continues to be the sector's largest employer, the social and legal services group has increased its share of total employment more than any other subsector since 1977.

- There is a higher proportion of females (71 percent) and African Americans (14 percent) employed in the independent sector than in either the government or private sector. Female employees are especially predominant in the health services and social and legal services subsectors.

Employment Patterns in the Independent Sector

This series differs from the expanded estimates of employment presented in Chapter One, which include paid employees, the self-employed, unpaid family workers, and volunteers. Data presented in this chapter pertain only to full- and part-time paid employees in the major nonagricultural sectors of the economy.

- Paid employees in the entire nonprofit sector in 1998 represented 9.3 percent of all paid employees in the economy. The independent sector, with 10.9 million paid employees, comprised 8.7 percent of all workers. In comparison, government employed 15.7 percent, and the business sector employed 75.0 percent, of all workers. (See Table 2.1 and Figure 2.1.)

- Employment in the nonprofit sector grew at an annual rate of 3.2 percent from 1977 to 1997. This was higher than the annual growth rate of both the government sector (1.3 percent) and the business sector (2.0 percent). Services, a major component of the business sector, grew at 3.0 percent, slightly lower than the rate of growth for the nonprofit sector. (See Table 2.2.)

TABLE 2.1

Nonprofit, Business, and Government Sectors: Number of Workers* Employed, Selected Years, 1977–1998

	1977		1982		1987	
	Number (Thousands)	Percent	Number (Thousands)	Percent	Number (Thousands)	Percent
Total	82,471	100.0	89,566	100.0	102,310	100.0
Nonprofit sector	5,991	7.3	7,052	7.9	7,962	7.8
Independent sector	5,520	6.7	6,543	7.3	7,390	7.2
Other	471	0.6	509	0.6	572	0.6
Business (for-profit) sector	61,353	74.4	66,677	74.4	77,333	75.6
Goods	24,346	29.5	23,813	26.6	24,784	24.2
Services	37,007	44.9	42,864	47.9	52,549	51.4
Government sector	15,127	18.3	15,837	17.7	17,015	16.6
Federal (civilian)	2,727	3.3	2,739	3.1	2,943	2.9
State	3,377	4.1	3,640	4.1	3,963	3.9
Local	9,023	10.9	9,458	10.6	10,109	9.9

*This table includes only nonagricultural wage and salary workers.

Sources: U.S. Department of Labor, various years; Hodgkinson and Weitzman, Nonprofit Almanac, 1996; authors' estimates.

FIGURE 2.1

Nonprofit, Business, and Government Sectors: Percentage of Total Paid Employment, 1977–1998

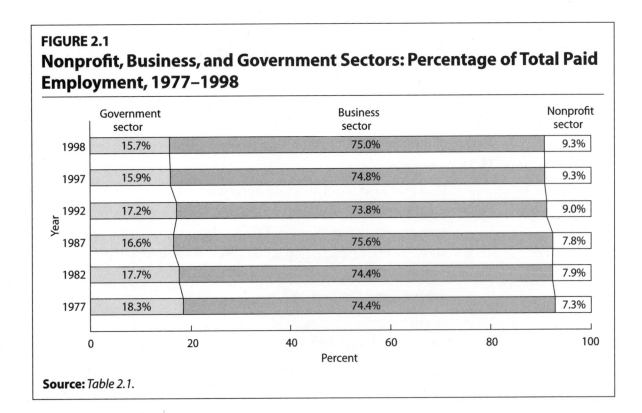

Source: Table 2.1.

1992		1994		1996		1997		1998	
Number (Thousands)	Percent	Number (Thousands)	Percent	Number (Thousands)	Percent	Number (Thousands)	Percent	Number (Thousands)	Percent
108,603	100.0	114,034	100.0	119,523	100.0	122,690	100.0	125,826	100.0
9,765	9.0	10,329	9.1	10,959	9.2	11,357	9.3	11,664	9.3
9,128	8.4	9,656	8.5	10,237	8.6	10,619	8.7	10,900	8.7
637	0.6	673	0.6	722	0.6	738	0.6	764	0.6
80,194	73.8	84,588	74.2	89,117	74.6	91,776	74.8	94,343	75.0
23,231	21.4	23,913	21.0	24,431	20.4	24,962	20.3	25,347	20.1
56,963	52.5	60,675	53.2	64,686	54.1	66,814	54.5	68,996	54.8
18,644	17.2	19,117	16.8	19,447	16.3	19,557	15.9	19,819	15.7
2,969	2.7	2,870	2.5	2,757	2.3	2,699	2.2	2,686	2.1
4,408	4.1	4,562	4.0	4,624	3.9	4,582	3.7	4,612	3.7
11,267	10.4	11,685	10.2	12,066	10.1	12,276	10.0	12,521	10.0

- The nonprofit sector experienced its highest annual rate of growth in employment (4.2 percent) between 1987 and 1992. The government sector also experienced a higher annual growth rate (1.8 percent) between 1987 and 1992 when compared with other time periods. (See Figure 2.2.)

- In contrast, the annual growth rate of total nonagricultural employment between 1987 and 1992 was 1.2 percent, lower than any period since 1977. The employment growth rate was depressed largely by the 0.7 percent growth of the business sector (a combined result of a positive rate for the services component and a negative rate for the goods component). (See Table 2.2.)

- The number of paid employees in all nonprofit organizations nearly doubled, from 6.0 million to 11.7 million, between 1977 and 1998 (see Table 2.3). Employment in the independent sector increased from 5.5 million in 1977 to 10.9 million in 1998, with the greatest expansion in employment occurring between 1987 and 1992 (see Figure 2.3).

- In 1998 the independent sector's share of total nonagricultural wages and salaries was 6.3 percent ($259 billion), significantly lower than its share of total paid employment (8.7 percent; see Table 2.4). This is further reflected in the 1998 annual average wage and salary estimate of $23,743 for independent sector entities, compared with $33,253 for other nonagricultural workers (see Table 2.5).

FIGURE 2.2

Nonprofit, Business, and Government Sectors: Annual Rates of Change in Employment, 1977–1997

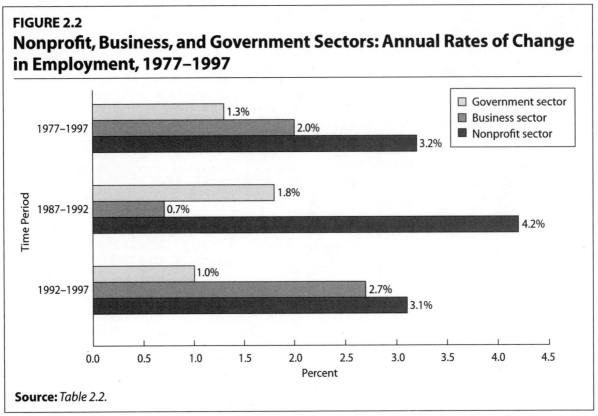

Source: *Table 2.2.*

FIGURE 2.3

Nonprofit and Independent Sectors: Growth of Employment, 1977–1998

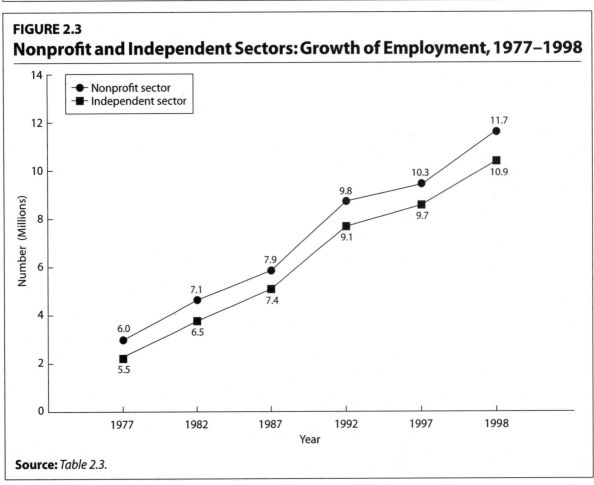

Source: *Table 2.3.*

TABLE 2.2

Independent and Other Nonagricultural Sectors: Annual Rates of Change in Employment, 1977–1997

	1977	1977	1977	1977	1982	1982	1982	1987	1987	1992
Beginning Year:	1977	1977	1977	1977	1982	1982	1982	1987	1987	1992
Ending Year:	1982	1987	1992	1997	1987	1992	1997	1992	1997	1997
Number of Years:	5	10	15	20	5	10	15	5	10	5
All sectors										
Percentage change	108.6	124.1	131.7	148.8	114.2	121.3	137.0	106.2	119.9	113.0
Annual rate of change	1.7	2.2	1.9	2.0	2.7	1.9	2.1	1.2	1.8	2.5
Nonprofit sector										
Percentage change—overall	117.7	132.9	163.0	189.6	112.9	138.5	161.0	122.6	142.6	116.3
Annual rate of change—overall	3.3	2.9	3.3	3.2	2.5	3.3	3.2	4.2	3.6	3.1
Percentage change—other than independent sector	108.1	121.4	135.2	156.7	112.4	125.1	145.0	111.4	129.0	115.9
Annual rate of change— other than independent sector	1.6	2.0	2.0	2.3	2.4	2.3	2.5	2.2	2.6	3.0
Percentage change— independent sector	118.5	133.9	165.4	192.4	112.9	139.5	162.3	123.5	143.7	116.3
Annual rate of change— independent sector	3.5	3.0	3.4	3.3	2.5	3.4	3.3	4.3	3.7	3.1
Business sector										
Percentage change—overall	108.7	126.0	130.7	149.6	116.0	120.3	137.6	103.7	118.7	114.4
Annual rate of change—overall	1.7	2.3	1.8	2.0	3.0	1.9	2.2	0.7	1.7	2.7
Percentage change—goods component	97.8	101.8	95.4	102.5	104.1	97.6	104.8	93.7	100.7	107.5
Annual rate of change— goods component	(0.4)	0.2	(0.3)	0.1	0.8	(0.2)	0.3	(1.3)	0.1	1.4
Percentage change—service component	115.8	142.0	153.9	180.5	122.6	132.9	155.9	108.4	127.1	117.3
Annual rate of change— service component	3.0	3.6	2.9	3.0	4.2	2.9	3.0	1.6	2.4	3.2
Government sector										
Percentage change—overall	104.7	112.5	123.2	129.3	107.4	117.7	123.5	109.6	114.9	104.9
Annual rate of change— overall	0.9	1.2	1.4	1.3	1.4	1.6	1.4	1.8	1.4	1.0
Percentage change— federal (civilian)	100.4	107.9	108.9	99.0	107.4	108.4	98.5	100.9	91.7	90.9
Annual rate of change— federal (civilian)	0.1	0.8	0.6	(0.1)	1.4	0.8	(0.1)	0.2	(0.9)	(1.9)
Percentage change—state	107.8	117.4	130.5	135.7	108.9	121.1	125.9	111.2	115.6	103.9
Annual rate of change— state	1.5	1.6	1.8	1.5	1.7	1.9	1.5	2.2	1.5	0.8
Percentage change—local	104.8	112.0	124.9	136.1	106.9	119.1	129.8	111.5	121.4	109.0
Annual rate of change— local	0.9	1.1	1.5	1.6	1.3	1.8	1.8	2.2	2.0	1.7

Note: *The formula for annual rate of change is: {EXP[LN(ending year value/beginning year value)/t] – 1} × 100*

Source: *Table 2.1.*

TABLE 2.3

Nonprofit Sector: Paid Employment, Selected Years, 1977–1998

	1977 Number (Thousands)	1977 Percent	1982 Number (Thousands)	1982 Percent	1987 Number (Thousands)	1987 Percent	1992 Number (Thousands)	1992 Percent	1997 Number (Thousands)	1997 Percent	1998 Number (Thousands)	1998 Percent
All sectors	82,471.0	n/a	89,566.0	n/a	102,310.0	n/a	108,604.0	n/a	122,690.0	n/a	125,826.0	n/a
Nonprofit sector	5,990.8	100.0	7,052.1	100.0	7,961.7	100.0	9,765.1	100.0	11,356.5	100.0	11,663.9	100.0
Independent sector [a]	5,519.5	92.1	6,543.0	92.8	7,389.9	92.8	9,128.3	93.5	10,618.9	93.5	10,900.1	93.5
Other nonprofit organizations, total [b]	471.3	7.9	509.1	7.2	571.8	7.2	636.8	6.5	737.6	6.5	763.8	6.5
Business associations	77.2	1.3	54.5	0.8	92.3	1.2	101.5	1.0	107.8	0.9	108.7	0.9
Professional membership organizations	31.4	0.5	35.9	0.5	44.1	0.6	52.7	0.5	59.1	0.5	61.5	0.5
Labor unions and similar organizations	141.0	2.4	144.1	2.0	132.1	1.7	141.3	1.4	142.3	1.3	142.9	1.2
Political and membership organizations n.e.c. [c]	61.9	1.0	65.1	1.0	94.4	1.2	89.0	0.9	118.0	1.0	126.6	1.1
Hotels and other lodging places	16.4	0.3	18.8	0.3	18.8	0.2	17.6	0.2	16.6	0.1	16.6	0.1
Membership, sports, and recreation clubs	94.4	1.6	107.2	1.6	125.7	1.6	140.0	1.4	173.7	1.5	181.8	1.6
Commercial research and development testing laboratories	35.6	0.6	40.1	0.6	47.0	0.6	73.2	0.7	88.5	0.8	92.5	0.8
Management consulting and public relations services	13.4	0.2	13.4	0.2	17.4	0.2	21.5	0.2	31.6	0.3	33.2	0.3

Note: n.e.c. = not elsewhere classified.

[a] Detailed in Table 2.6.

[b] Total of all nonprofit organizations listed other than independent sector.

[c] Political and membership organizations n.e.c. include political organizations and clubs and such organizations as farm bureaus, farm groups, Christian Science reading rooms, and automobile associations.

Sources: U.S. Department of Labor, various years; U.S. Bureau of the Census, Census of Service Industries, various years; authors' estimates.

TABLE 2.4

Nonprofit Sector: Wages and Salaries, Selected Years, 1977–1998

	1977		1982		1987		1992		1997		1998[c]	
	Amount (Billions)	Percent	Amount (Billions)	Percent	Amount (Billions)	Percent	Amount (Billions)	Percent	Amount (Billions)	Percent	Amount (Billions)	Percent
All sectors	942.9	100.0	1,504.9	100.0	2,168.6	100.0	2,873.3	100.0	3,780.6	100.0	4,079.9	100.0
Business and government sectors	891.1	94.5	1,416.2	94.1	2,041.7	94.1	2,673.8	93.1	3,515.1	93.0	3,798.0	93.1
Nonprofit sector	51.8	5.5	88.7	5.9	126.9	5.9	199.5	6.9	265.5	7.0	281.9	6.9
Independent sector	46.7	5.0	80.7	5.4	116.0	5.3	184.2	6.4	244.1	6.5	258.8	6.3
Other nonprofit organizations, total [a]	5.1	0.5	8.0	0.5	10.9	0.5	15.3	0.5	21.4	0.6	23.1	0.6
Business associations	0.9	0.1	1.5	0.1	2.2	0.1	3.2	0.1	4.1	0.1	4.2	0.1
Professional membership organizations	0.4		0.6		1.0		1.6	0.1	2.3	0.1	2.5	0.1
Labor unions and similar organizations	1.7	0.2	2.6	0.2	3.0	0.1	3.7	0.1	4.2	0.1	4.4	0.1
Political and membership organizations n.e.c [b]	0.5	0.1	0.8	0.1	1.4	0.1	1.4	0.1	2.2	0.1	2.6	0.1
Hotels and other lodging places	0.1		0.2		0.2		0.2		0.2		0.2	
Membership, sports, and recreation clubs	0.7	0.1	1.1	0.1	1.4	0.1	2.2	0.1	3.7	0.1	4.0	0.1
Commercial research development testing laboratories	0.6	0.1	1.0	0.1	1.2	0.1	2.3	0.1	3.4	0.1	3.7	0.1
Management consulting and public relations services	0.2		0.2		0.5		0.7		1.3		1.5	

Note: *n.e.c. = not elsewhere classified. Percentages less than 0.1 percent are omitted from the table.*

[a] *Total of all nonprofit organizations listed other than independent sector.*

[b] *Political and membership organizations n.e.c. include political organizations and clubs and such organizations as farm bureaus, farm groups, Christian Science reading rooms, and automobile associations.*

[c] *Figures are preliminary.*

Source: *U.S. Department of Labor, various years.*

TABLE 2.5

Independent Sector: Employment and Total Wages and Salaries, Selected Years, 1977–1998

Nonagricultural Employees	Employment		Total Wages and Salaries		Annual Average Wages and Salaries[a]	
	Number (Thousands)	Percent	Amount (Billions)	Percent	Dollars	All
	(1)	(2)	(3)	(4)	(5)	(6)
1977						
All	82,471	100.0	943	100.0	11,433	100.0
All except nonprofit sector	76,480	92.7	891	94.5	11,651	101.9
All except independent sector	76,951	93.3	896	95.0	11,646	101.9
Nonprofit sector	5,991	7.3	52	5.5	8,646	75.6
Independent sector	5,520	6.7	47	5.0	8,460	74.0
1982						
All	89,566	100.0	1,505	100.0	16,802	100.0
All except nonprofit sector	82,514	92.1	1,416	94.1	17,163	102.1
All except independent sector	83,023	92.7	1,424	94.6	17,154	102.1
Nonprofit sector	7,052	7.9	89	5.9	12,578	74.9
Independent sector	6,543	7.3	81	5.4	12,334	73.4
1987						
All	102,310	100.0	2,169	100.0	21,196	100.0
All except nonprofit sector	94,348	92.2	2,042	94.1	21,640	102.1
All except independent sector	94,920	92.8	2,053	94.7	21,625	102.0
Nonprofit sector	7,962	7.8	127	5.9	15,938	75.2
Independent sector	7,390	7.2	116	5.3	15,697	74.1
1992						
All	108,604	100.0	2,873	100.0	26,457	100.0
All except nonprofit sector	98,839	91.0	2,674	93.1	27,052	102.2
All except independent sector	99,476	91.6	2,689	93.6	27,033	102.2
Nonprofit sector	9,765	9.0	200	6.9	20,430	77.2
Independent sector	9,182	8.5	184	6.4	20,061	75.8
1997						
All	122,690	100.0	3,781	100.0	30,814	100.0
All except nonprofit sector	111,333	90.7	3,515	93.0	31,573	102.5
All except independent sector	112,071	91.3	3,537	93.5	31,556	102.4
Nonprofit sector	11,357	9.3	266	7.0	23,378	75.9
Independent sector	10,619	8.7	244	6.5	22,987	74.6
1998						
All	125,826	100.0	4,080	100.0	32,410	100.0
All except nonprofit sector	114,162	90.7	3,798	93.1	33,253	102.6
All except independent sector	114,926	91.3	3,821	93.7	33,232	102.5
Nonprofit sector	11,664	9.3	282	6.9	24,160	74.5
Independent sector	10,900	8.7	259	6.3	23,743	73.3

[a] Annual average wages and salaries are determined by dividing total wages (column 3) by employment (column 1).

Sources: See Table 2.1. for employment estimates (authors' estimates); U.S. Department of Labor, various years; Hodgkinson and Weitzman, Nonprofit Almanac, 1996; U.S. Department of Commerce, various years.

Employment Trends by Subsector

Employment estimates are derived from various government and private organizations. Principal sources are the *Census of Service Industries* (U.S. Bureau of the Census, various years) and *Employment and Earnings* (U.S. Department of Labor, various years). Until recently the SIC system was the basis for grouping data. U.S. government agencies are gradually adopting NAICS as their standard for publishing more recent data. Some industry groupings between the SIC system and NAICS correspond directly, but most of the higher-level groupings do not. This has affected and will affect the process of compiling nonprofit employment estimates. Although every effort has been made to make 1997 and 1998 figures compatible with earlier years, future versions of these employment tables may change to accommodate differences between the classification systems.

- The health services subsector continued to be the dominant employer in the independent sector, employing 43 percent of all paid workers in 1998. This share has decreased since 1992, when health services employed nearly 47 percent of all workers. (See Table 2.6.)

- In the health services subsector, 72 percent of all workers were employed in hospitals in 1998, down from 86 percent in 1977. Hospitals' increasing reliance on outside organizations to deliver emergency medical care and on clinics to perform routine medical services has affected employment distribution in the health services subsector. Other contributing factors include government and private insurers' placing limits on payments and hospital stays, plus hospital cost-cutting initiatives. The annual rate of change in employment for hospitals from 1977 to 1997 was 2.2 percent, relatively low when compared with the rates for nursing and personal aid facilities (5.2 percent) and for the entire health services subsector (3.2 percent). From 1992 to 1997 the rate of employment growth in this subsector declined significantly to 1.7 percent, with hospitals recording a scant increase of 0.3 percent. (See Table 2.7.)

- The education and research subsector had a 21.6 percent share of all independent sector employees in 1998, down slightly from 23.2 percent in 1977 (see Figure 2.4). The percentages have remained fairly steady since 1996. From 1977 to 1998, more than one-half of all employment in this subsector was concentrated in higher education institutions (that is, colleges and universities). Employment in private elementary and secondary schools also increased at an annual rate of 3.4 percent for the period 1977 to 1997, doubling in actual number of employees from 428,000 in 1977 to 854,000 in 1997 (see Tables 2.6 and 2.7).

TABLE 2.6

Independent Sector: Employment by Subsector, Selected Years, 1977–1998

	SIC Code	1977 Number (Thousands)	Percent	1982 Number (Thousands)	Percent
Total for independent sector		5,519.5	100.0	6,543.0	100.0
Health services	80	2,458.7	44.5	3,074.9	47.0
Nursing and personal care facilities	805	206.4	3.7	288.2	4.4
Hospitals	806	2,121.1	38.4	2,593.7	39.6
Other health services	808, 809	131.2	2.4	193	2.9
Clinics of doctors of medicine and dentists[a]	8011				
Education and research	82, 873	1,279.7	23.2	1,442.9	22.1
Private colleges and universities	822	702.6	12.7	753.2	11.5
Private elementary and secondary schools	821	427.7	7.7	527.9	8.1
Selected educational services	823, 824, 829	49.4	0.9	53.5	0.8
Noncommercial research	873[b]	100.0	1.8	108.3	1.7
Social and legal services	81, 83	715.1	13.0	921.4	14.1
Legal services	81	12.4	0.2	14.5	0.2
Social services, total	83	702.7	12.7	906.9	13.9
Individual and family services, and social services n.e.c.	832, 839[b]	290.3	5.3	413.5	6.3
Job training and related services	8331	129.6	2.3	171.3	2.6
Child day-care services	8351	141.3	2.6	149.7	2.3
Residential care	8361	141.5	2.6	172.4	2.6
Religious organizations	866	678.5	12.3	691.2	10.6
Civic, social, and fraternal organizations	864	305.4	5.5	305.1	4.7
Arts and culture	483, 79, 84	65.7	1.2	89.1	1.4
Radio and television broadcasting	483	9.6	0.2	11.6	0.2
Producers, orchestras, entertainers, and fairs	792, 7999	27.2	0.5	41.6	0.6
Museums, and botanical and zoological gardens	84	28.9	0.5	35.9	0.5
Foundations	6732	16.4	0.3	18.4	0.3

Note: *n.e.c. = not elsewhere classified; SIC = Standard Industrial Classification. Owing to rounding, percentage figures may not total 100.*

[a] *No estimates provided for 1977, 1982, or 1987.*

[b] *Estimates prepared for years prior to 1988 are based on the 1972 SIC codes. In 1987 revised SIC codes were published by the Office of Management and Budget. Although various government agencies adopted the*

	1987		1992		1997		1998	
	Number (Thousands)	Percent	Number (Thousands)	Percent	Number (Thousands)	Percent	Number (Thousands)	Percent
	7,389.9	100.0	9,128.4	100.0	10,618.9	100.0	10,900.1	100.0
	3,367.0	45.6	4,250.3	46.6	4,617.6	43.5	4,681.0	42.9
	347.8	4.7	497.9	5.5	570.8	5.4	572.5	5.3
	2,664.8	36.1	3,252.0	35.6	3,304.2	31.1	3,347.2	30.7
	354.4	4.8	342.6	3.8	546.4	5.1	557.3	5.1
			157.8	1.7	196.2	1.8	204.0	1.9
	1,666.3	22.5	1,878.3	20.6	2,294.9	21.6	2,349.8	21.6
	907.8	12.3	1,000.3	11.0	1,225.6	11.5	1,248.8	12.2
	565.5	7.7	674.0	7.4	827.8	7.8	853.6	8.3
	68.2	0.9	63.0	0.7	81.8	0.8	83.0	0.8
	124.8	1.7	141.0	1.5	159.7	1.5	164.4	1.6
	1,196.2	16.2	1,428.2	15.6	1,825.3	17.2	1,910.9	17.5
	14.5	0.2	21.3	0.2	22.0	0.2	22.0	0.2
	1,181.7	16.0	1,406.9	15.4	1,803.3	17.0	1,888.9	17.3
	514.2	7.0	632.6	6.9	787.9	7.4	828.5	7.6
	213.1	2.9	270.5	3.0	352.8	3.3	367.2	3.4
	200.9	2.7	185.2	2.0	238.5	2.2	250.4	2.3
	253.5	3.4	318.6	3.5	424.1	4.0	442.8	4.1
	650.2	8.8	960.3	10.5	1,206.5	11.4	1,266.4	11.6
	366.3	5.0	420.9	4.6	443.2	4.2	455.2	4.2
	121.7	1.6	165.4	1.8	199.4	1.9	204.8	1.9
	19.0	0.3	20.0	0.2	20.0	0.2	20.0	0.2
	54.3	0.7	79.1	0.9	94.0	0.9	96.8	0.9
	48.4	0.7	66.3	0.7	85.4	0.8	88.0	0.8
	22.2	0.3	25.0	0.3	32.0	0.3	32.0	0.3

1987 SIC revision at different times, the impact on estimates of employment and wages and salaries for the independent sector and other nonprofits was minimal. Further changes were made with the adoption of NAICS in 1999, which will have an impact on future estimates of nonprofit employment.

Sources: *U.S. Bureau of the Census,* Economic Census, *1997; U.S. Department of Labor, various years.*

TABLE 2.7

Independent Sector: Annual Rates of Change in Employment by Subsector, 1977–1997

	Beginning Year:	1977	1977	1977	1977	1982	1982	1982	1987	1987	1992
	Ending Year:	1982	1987	1992	1997	1987	1992	1997	1992	1997	1997
	Number of Years:	5	10	15	20	5	10	15	5	10	5
Independent sector											
Percentage change—overall		118.5	133.9	165.4	192.4	112.9	139.5	162.3	123.5	143.7	116.3
Annual rate of change—overall		3.5	3.0	3.4	3.3	2.5	3.4	3.3	4.3	3.7	3.1
Health services											
Percentage change—overall		125.1	136.9	172.9	187.8	109.5	138.2	150.2	126.2	137.1	108.6
Annual rate of change—overall		4.6	3.2	3.7	3.2	1.8	3.3	2.7	4.8	3.2	1.7
Percentage change—nursing and personal aid		139.6	168.5	241.2	276.6	120.7	172.8	198.1	143.2	164.1	114.6
Annual rate of change— nursing and personal aid		6.9	5.4	6.0	5.2	3.8	5.6	4.7	7.4	5.1	2.8
Percentage change— hospitals		122.3	125.6	153.3	155.8	102.7	125.4	127.4	122.0	124.0	101.6
Annual rate of change— hospitals		4.1	2.3	2.9	2.2	0.5	2.3	1.6	4.1	2.2	0.3
Education and research											
Percentage change—overall		112.8	130.2	146.8	179.3	115.5	130.2	159.0	112.7	137.7	122.2
Annual rate of change— overall		2.4	2.7	2.6	3.0	2.9	2.7	3.1	2.4	3.3	4.1
Percentage change— private elementary and secondary schools		123.4	132.2	157.6	193.5	107.1	127.7	156.8	119.2	146.4	122.8
Annual rate of change— private elementary and secondary schools		4.3	2.8	3.1	3.4	1.4	2.5	3.0	3.6	3.9	4.2
Percentage change— colleges and universities		107.2	129.2	142.4	174.4	120.5	132.8	162.7	110.2	135.0	122.5
Annual rate of change— colleges and universities		1.4	2.6	2.4	2.8	3.8	2.9	3.3	2.0	3.0	4.1
Social and legal services											
Percentage change—overall		128.8	167.3	199.7	255.3	129.8	155.0	198.1	119.4	152.6	127.8
Annual rate of change—overall		5.2	5.3	4.7	4.8	5.4	4.5	4.7	3.6	4.3	5.0
Religious organizations											
Percentage change—overall		101.9	95.8	141.5	177.8	94.1	138.9	174.6	147.7	185.6	125.6
Annual rate of change—overall		0.4	(0.4)	2.3	2.9	(1.2)	3.3	3.8	8.1	6.4	4.7
Civic, social, and fraternal organizations											
Percentage change—overall		99.9	119.9	137.8	145.1	120.1	138.0	145.3	114.9	121.0	105.3
Annual rate of change—overall		0.0	1.8	2.2	1.9	3.7	3.3	2.5	2.8	1.9	1.0
Arts and culture											
Percentage change—overall		135.6	185.2	251.8	303.5	136.6	185.6	223.8	135.9	163.8	120.6
Annual rate of change—overall		6.3	6.4	6.3	5.7	6.4	6.4	5.5	6.3	5.1	3.8
Foundations											
Percentage change—overall		112.2	135.4	152.4	195.1	120.7	135.9	173.9	112.6	144.1	128.0
Annual rate of change—overall		2.3	3.1	2.9	3.4	3.8	3.1	3.8	2.4	3.7	5.1

Source: *Table 2.6.*

FIGURE 2.4

Independent Sector: Distribution of Employment by Subsector, 1977, 1987, and 1998

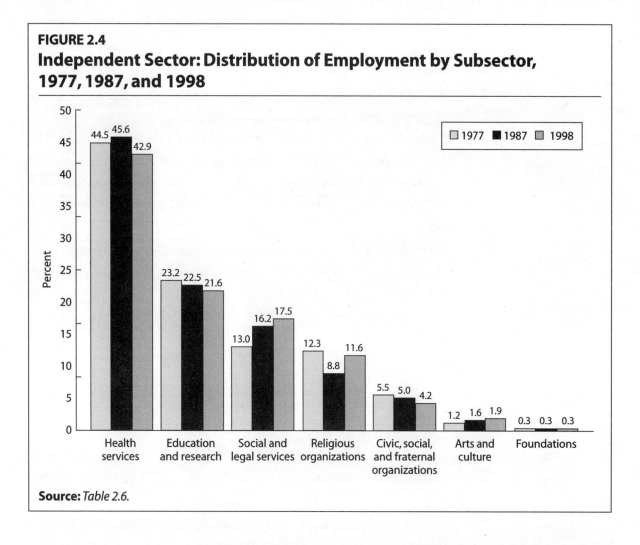

Source: *Table 2.6.*

- Social and legal services' share of independent sector employment grew more than that of any other subsector. From 1977 to 1998 its share increased from 13.0 percent to 17.5 percent (see Figure 2.4). This increase reflects the escalating demand for the type of services this subsector provides. Other establishments included in this group are those providing free legal assistance as well as social and rehabilitation services for the physically challenged and disadvantaged. The annual rate of change in employment for this subsector from 1977 to 1997 was 4.8 percent, the highest rate among all the major groups (see Table 2.7).

- In 1998 religious organizations' share of independent sector employment reached 11.6 percent, nearly reaching its highest recorded share of 12.3 percent in 1977 (see Figure 2.4). The annual rate of change in employment for the group was 2.9 percent for the twenty-year period from 1977 to 1997, but its highest annual rate of employment growth occurred from 1987 to 1992, when it was recorded at 8.1 percent (see Table 2.7).

- From 1977 to 1997 employment in the arts and culture subsector had a threefold increase. Its share of total employment increased from 1.2 percent in 1977 to 1.9 percent in 1998 (see Figure 2.4).

- The share of employment represented by civic, social, and fraternal organizations (alumni associations, scout organizations, veterans' and university clubs, and citizens' and youth associations) declined from 5.5 percent in 1977 to 4.2 percent in 1998 (see Figure 2.4). The number of establishments in this subsector also declined, from 42,000 in 1992 to 36,000 in 1997, which may account for the slower rate of employment growth in this subsector.

- Employment in private foundations and charitable trusts as a share of total independent sector employment remained steady at 0.3 percent between 1977 and 1998 (see Figure 2.4). Employment in this subsector doubled from 16,000 in 1977 to 32,000 in 1998 (see Table 2.6).

Trends in Wages and Salaries by Subsector

Wages and salaries in the independent sector grew at a faster rate than the nonagricultural economy as a whole from 1977 to 1998. The data shown in Table 2.8 reveal the following major trends in wages and salaries during that period:

- Total wages and salaries in the independent sector expanded more than fivefold from an estimated $47 billion in 1977 to $259 billion by 1998.

- In 1998 the health services subsector earned 54 percent ($141 billion) of total wages and salaries in the independent sector, down from a high of 58 percent in 1992. Hospitals in 1998 represented 42 percent of total wages and salaries, the lowest estimate for this group since 1977. Wages and salaries of hospitals represented 77 percent of the total health services subsector in 1998, declining steadily from 89 percent since 1977. Other health services and nursing and personal care facilities, in comparison, have increased their share of wages and salaries in this subsector.

- The education and research subsector's share of total wages and salaries in 1998 was 21 percent, up slightly from 1992. From 1977 to 1992, there was a downward trend for this subsector's share of wages and salaries, but it stabilized over the last six years. This trend is largely influenced by trends in private colleges and universities, which cover the largest share of wages and salaries (56 percent) in the education and research group. The U.S. Department of Education (2000) projects stability in current expenditures in higher education, of which 47 to 62 percent are for salaries and wages, through the end of the 1990s and most of 2000.

- The social and legal services subsector has undergone a steady and marked increase in its share of wages and salaries since 1977. Its share went from a low of 9.2 percent in 1977 to 12.1 percent in 1998. Growth was primarily caused by increased employment in all its component areas, including individual and family services, job training, child day care, and residential care services.

- Religious organizations' share of total wages and salaries in the independent sector was 8.8 percent in 1998, mirroring the record high first set in 1977.

- Civic, social, and fraternal organizations' share of total wages and salaries declined from 3.2 percent in 1977 to 2.1 percent in 1998.

- Arts and culture, as well as foundations, have largely maintained their share of total wages and salaries for the period under study.

Employment Trends by Gender, Race, and Ethnicity in the Independent Sector

The demographic composition of paid employment varies by sector of the economy. Historically, the independent sector has served as a sector of access for women and African Americans. The independent sector has a much higher proportion of females and African Americans, and a smaller proportion of employees of Hispanic origin, than other sectors.

- In 1998 female employees constituted 71 percent of all paid employees in the independent sector (see Figure 2.5), compared with 46 percent in all sectors of the economy (see Table 2.9).

- Females represented from 50 to over 80 percent of all employees in all of the major subsectors. In 1998 social and legal services and health services had the highest rate of female employment, whereas the religious organizations and arts and culture subsectors had the lowest. (See Table 2.10.)

- African Americans constituted 14 percent of all employees in the independent sector in 1998, compared with 11 percent in all sectors of

TABLE 2.8

Independent Sector: Wages and Salaries by Subsector, Selected Years, 1977–1998

	SIC Code	1977 Amount (Billions)	Percent	1982 Amount (Billions)	Percent
Total for independent sector		46.7	100.0	80.7	100.0
Health services	80	22.8	48.8	44.4	55.0
Nursing and personal care facilities	805	1.2	2.6	2.6	3.2
Hospitals	806	20.3	43.5	39.2	48.6
Other health services	808, 809	1.3	2.8	2.6	3.2
Clinics of doctors of medicine and dentists[a]	8011	0.0	0.0	0.0	0.0
Education and research	82, 873	13.2	28.3	18.2	22.6
Private colleges and universities	822	3.2	6.9	5.1	6.3
Private elementary and secondary schools	821	8.3	17.8	10.3	12.8
Selected educational services	823, 824, 829	0.4	0.9	0.5	0.6
Noncommercial research	873, (892)[b]	1.3	2.8	2.3	2.9
Social and legal services	81, 83	4.3	9.2	7.8	9.7
Legal services	81	0.2	0.4	0.3	0.4
Social services, total	83	4.1	8.8	7.5	9.3
Individual and family services, and social services n.e.c.	832, 839[b]	2.0	4.3	4.1	5.1
Job training and related services	8331	0.5	1.1	0.9	1.1
Child day-care services	8351	0.7	1.5	1.0	1.2
Residential care	8361	0.9	1.9	1.5	7.9
Religious organizations	866	4.1	8.8	6.8	8.4
Civic, social, and fraternal organizations	864	1.5	3.2	2.1	2.6
Arts and culture	483, 79, 84	0.6	1.3	1.1	1.4
Radio and television broadcasting	483	0.1	0.2	0.2	0.2
Producers, orchestras, entertainers, and fairs	792, 7999	0.3	0.6	0.5	0.6
Museums, and botanical and zoological gardens	84	0.2	0.4	0.4	0.5
Foundations	6732	0.2	0.4	0.3	0.4

Note: *n.e.c. = not elsewhere classified; SIC = Standard Industrial Classification. Owing to rounding, percentage figures may not total 100.*

[a] *Figures are preliminary.*

[b] *Estimates prepared for years prior to 1988 are based on the 1972 SIC codes. In 1987 revised SIC codes were published by the Office of Management and Budget. Although various government agencies adopted the*

	1987		1992		1997		1998[a]	
	Amount (Billions)	Percent	Amount (Billions)	Percent	Amount (Billions)	Percent	Amount (Billions)	Percent
	116.0	100.0	184.2	100.0	244.1	100.0	258.8	100.0
	61.5	53.0	106.4	57.8	134.0	54.9	140.5	54.3
	3.8	3.3	7.6	4.1	10.3	4.2	10.9	4.2
	51.8	44.7	87.1	47.3	103.4	42.4	108.2	41.8
	5.9	5.1	6.4	3.5	12.2	5.0	12.7	4.9
	0.0	0.0	5.3	2.9	8.1	3.3	8.7	3.4
	28.3	24.4	36.4	19.8	50.8	20.8	53.9	20.8
	7.3	6.3	10.6	5.8	13.7	5.6	14.8	5.7
	16.7	14.4	19.8	10.7	28.7	11.8	30.2	11.7
	1.0	0.9	1.0	0.5	1.5	0.6	1.6	0.6
	3.3	2.8	5.0	2.7	6.9	2.8	7.3	2.8
	13.1	11.3	19.9	10.8	28.8	11.8	31.2	12.1
	0.3	0.3	0.6	0.3	0.6	0.2	0.7	0.3
	12.8	11.0	19.3	10.5	28.2	11.6	30.5	11.8
	6.7	5.8	10.0	5.4	14.0	5.7	15.2	5.9
	1.5	1.3	2.6	1.4	4.0	1.6	4.3	1.7
	1.7	1.5	1.9	1.0	2.9	1.2	3.1	1.2
	1.9	2.9	2.5	4.8	2.6	7.3	3.0	3.1
	7.5	6.5	14.0	7.6	20.7	8.5	22.8	8.8
	3.2	2.8	4.2	2.3	5.2	2.1	5.5	2.1
	2.0	1.7	2.9	1.6	4.0	1.6	4.2	1.6
	0.4	0.3	0.5	0.3	0.5	0.2	0.5	0.2
	0.9	0.8	1.2	0.7	1.7	0.7	1.8	0.7
	0.7	0.6	1.2	0.7	1.8	0.7	1.9	0.7
	0.4	0.3	0.4	0.2	0.6	0.2	0.7	0.3

1987 SIC revision at different times, the impact on estimates of employment and wages and salaries for the independent sector and other nonprofits was minimal. Further changes were made with the adoption of NAICS in 1999, which will have an impact on future estimates of nonprofit employment.

Sources: *U.S. Bureau of the Census,* Economic Census, *1997; U.S. Department of Labor, various years.*

FIGURE 2.5

Independent Sector: Employment by Gender, 1987 and 1998

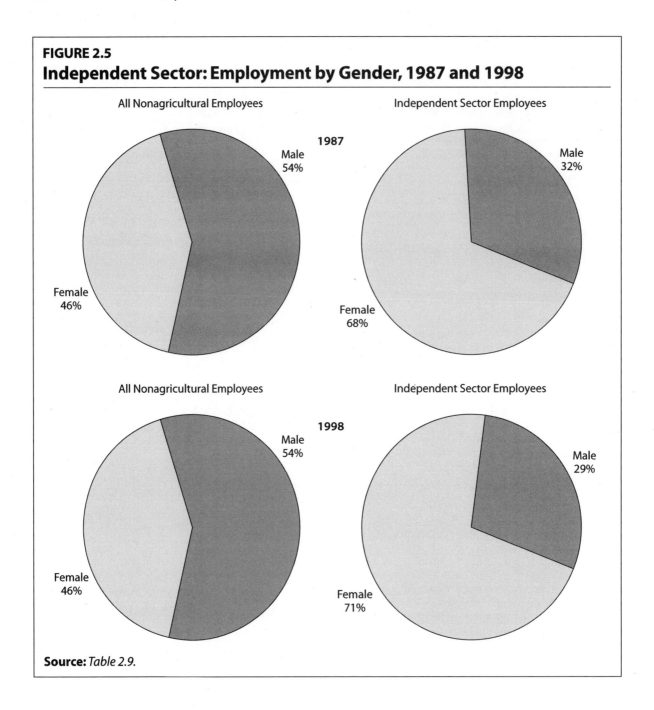

Source: *Table 2.9.*

the economy. The health services and social and legal services sub-sectors employed the highest share of African Americans (17 percent), whereas religious organizations employed the smallest share (8 percent; see Figure 2.6).

- In 1998, 7 percent of all employees in the independent sector were of Hispanic origin, compared with 10 percent in all sectors of the economy. Social and legal services had the highest rate of Hispanic employment among all subsectors. (See Table 2.10.)

TABLE 2.9

Independent Sector: Employee Demographics, Selected Characteristics and Years, 1987–1998

	All Nonagricultural Employees		Nonagricultural Employees, Excluding Independent Sector		Independent Sector Employees		
	Number (Thousands)	Percent	Number (Thousands)	Percent	Number (Thousands)	Percent	Percentage of Characteristic[b]
	(1)	(2)	(3)	(4)	(5)	(6)	(7)
1987							
Total	102,310	100.0	94,920	100.0	7,390	100.0	7.2
Male	55,411	54.2	53,060	55.9	2,351	31.8	4.2
Female	46,899	45.8	41,860	44.1	5,039	68.2	10.7
Total	16,714	16.3	15,306	16.1	1,408	19.1	8.4
African American	10,125	9.9	9,105	9.6	1,020	13.8	10.1
Hispanic[a]	6,589	6.4	6,201	6.5	388	5.3	5.9
1990							
Total	109,971	100.0	101,319	100.0	8,652	100.0	7.9
Male	58,944	53.6	56,236	55.5	2,708	31.3	4.6
Female	51,027	46.4	45,083	44.5	5,944	68.7	11.6
Total	19,795	18.0	18,180	17.9	1,615	18.7	8.2
African American	11,657	10.6	10,487	10.4	1,170	13.5	10.0
Hispanic[a]	8,138	7.4	7,693	7.6	445	5.1	5.5
1992							
Total	108,604	100.0	99,476	100.0	9,128	100.0	8.4
Male	58,972	54.3	56,114	56.4	2,858	31.3	4.8
Female	49,632	45.7	43,362	43.6	6,270	68.7	12.6
Total	19,223	17.7	17,495	17.6	1,728	18.9	9.0
African American	10,969	10.1	9,730	9.8	1,239	13.6	11.3
Hispanic[a]	8,254	7.6	7,765	7.8	489	5.4	5.9
1997							
Total	122,690	100.0	112,071	100.0	10,619	100.0	8.7
Male	65,639	53.5	62,528	55.8	3,111	29.3	4.7
Female	57,051	46.5	49,543	44.2	7,508	70.7	13.2
Total	25,029	20.4	22,832	20.4	2,197	20.7	8.8
African American	13,496	11.0	11,958	10.7	1,538	14.5	11.4
Hispanic[a]	11,533	9.4	10,874	9.7	659	6.2	5.7
1998							
Total	125,826	100.0	114,926	100.0	10,900	100.0	8.7
Male	67,317	53.5	64,124	55.8	3,193	29.3	4.7
Female	58,509	46.5	50,802	44.2	7,707	70.7	13.2
Total	26,297	20.9	23,981	20.9	2,316	21.2	8.8
African American	14,218	11.3	12,652	11.0	1,566	14.4	11.0
Hispanic[a]	12,079	9.6	11,329	9.9	750	6.9	6.2

[a] Persons of Hispanic origin may be of any race.
[b] Result of column 5 divided by column 1.

Sources: U.S. Department of Labor, various years; authors' estimates.

TABLE 2.10

Independent Sector: Employee Demographics by Subsector, Selected Characteristics, 1992, 1997, and 1998

SIC Code	Subsector	Number (Thousands)				Percent			
		All	Female	African American	Hispanic[a]	All	Female	African American	Hispanic[a]
1992									
80	Health services	4,250.2	3,320.8	705.4	246.5	100.0	78.1	16.6	5.8
82,873(892)[b]	Education and research	1,878.3	1,126.1	180.5	85.9	100.0	60.0	9.6	4.6
866	Religious organizations	960.3	431.2	68.2	42.3	100.0	44.9	7.1	4.4
81,83	Social and legal services	1,428.2	1,032.8	230.5	86.3	100.0	72.3	16.1	6.0
864	Civic, social, and fraternal organizations	420.9	264.7	37.0	15.6	100.0	62.9	8.8	3.7
483,792,84	Arts and culture	165.4	77.1	14.5	11.0	100.0	46.6	8.8	6.7
6732	Foundations	25.0	17.7	2.7	1.6	100.0	70.8	10.8	6.4
	Total	9,128.3	6,270.4	1,238.9	489.2	100.0	68.7	13.6	5.4
1997									
80	Health services	4,617.6	3,588.9	810.2	302.4	100.0	77.7	17.5	6.5
82,873(892)[b]	Education and research	2,294.9	1,422.6	243.7	142.6	100.0	62.0	10.6	6.2
866	Religious organizations	1,206.5	585.2	105.0	6.8	100.0	48.5	8.7	0.6
81,83	Social and legal services	1,825.3	1,483.8	309.6	163.6	100.0	81.3	17.0	9.0
864	Civic, social, and fraternal organizations	443.2	303.6	44.8	25.7	100.0	68.5	10.1	5.8
483,792,84	Arts and culture	199.4	101.0	21.2	15.8	100.0	50.7	10.6	7.9
6732	Foundations	32.0	22.7	3.6	2.0	100.0	70.9	11.3	6.3
	Total	10,618.9	7,507.8	1,538.1	658.9	100.0	70.7	14.5	6.2
1998									
80	Health services	4,681.0	3,614.9	811.0	319.0	100.0	77.2	17.3	6.8
82,873(892)[b]	Education and research	2,349.8	1,433.5	253.0	149.4	100.0	61.0	10.8	6.4
866	Religious organizations	1,266.4	643.3	101.3	69.7	100.0	50.8	8.0	5.5
81,83	Social and legal services	1,910.9	1,577.4	331.9	167.6	100.0	82.5	17.4	8.8
864	Civic, social, and fraternal organizations	455.2	311.8	46.0	26.4	100.0	68.5	10.1	5.8
483,792,84	Arts and culture	204.8	103.2	18.8	15.6	100.0	50.4	9.2	7.6
6732	Foundations	32.0	22.6	4.0	2.5	100.0	70.6	12.5	7.8
	Total	10,900.1	7,706.7	1,566.0	750.2	100.0	70.7	14.4	6.9

Note: SIC = Standard Industrial Classification.

[a] Persons of Hispanic origin may be of any race.

[b] Not elsewhere classified.

Sources: U.S. Bureau of the Census, Economic Census; U.S. Department of Labor, various years.

FIGURE 2.6

Independent Sector: Employment of Minorities by Subsector, 1998

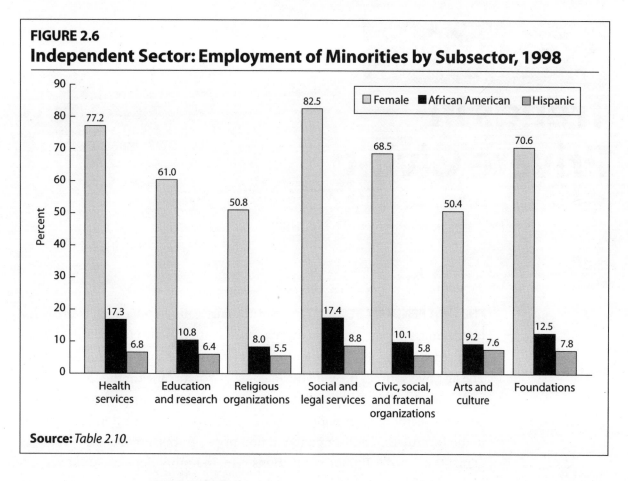

Legend: ☐ Female ■ African American ▨ Hispanic

Subsector	Female	African American	Hispanic
Health services	77.2	17.3	6.8
Education and research	61.0	10.8	6.4
Religious organizations	50.8	8.0	5.5
Social and legal services	82.5	17.4	8.8
Civic, social, and fraternal organizations	68.5	10.1	5.8
Arts and culture	50.4	9.2	7.6
Foundations	70.6	12.5	7.8

Source: *Table 2.10.*

References

American Hospital Association. *Hospital Statistics.* Chicago: Health Forum, 2000.

Hodgkinson, V. A., and Weitzman, M. S. *Nonprofit Almanac: Dimensions of the Independent Sector.* (Various editions.) San Francisco: Jossey-Bass, various years.

U.S. Bureau of the Census. *Economic Census.* Washington, D.C.: U.S. Government Printing Office, 1997.

U.S. Bureau of the Census. *Census of Service Industries.* (Various editions.) Washington, D.C.: U.S. Government Printing Office, various years.

U.S. Bureau of the Census. *Statistical Abstract of the United States.* (Various editions.) Washington, D.C.: U.S. Government Printing Office, various years.

U.S. Department of Commerce, Bureau of Economic Analysis. *Survey of Current Business.* (Various editions.) Washington, D.C.: U.S. Government Printing Office, various years.

U.S. Department of Education, National Center for Education Statistics. "Projection of Education Statistics to 2010." [http://nces.ed.gov/pubs2000/2000071.pdf]. Aug. 2000.

U.S. Department of Labor, Bureau of Labor Statistics. *Employment and Earnings.* (Various editions.) Washington, D.C.: U.S. Government Printing Office, various years.

Chapter 3

Trends in Private Giving

THE INDEPENDENT SECTOR has traditionally relied on various sources for its revenue stream. The three major sources are private contributions, government funding, and payments received for dues and program services. The last two sources provide the major share of income for the sector. However, private giving remains an important source of support for the independent sector as it provides flexibility, added quality, and independence in the formulation and implementation of programs. Smaller nonprofit organizations and religious institutions remain highly dependent on private giving of time and money to conduct their business. The level of private giving also acts as a barometer of public support for the activities of the independent sector. This chapter assesses overall trends in total private giving as well as the components that make up private giving—individual giving and volunteering, foundation giving, and corporate contributions. Reference will also be made to economic and tax policy changes that influence or affect private giving behavior. In brief, private giving trends indicate the following:

- Giving from all sources (individuals, foundations, and corporations) reached nearly $178 billion in 1998. Controlling for inflation, private giving rose by 47 percent from 1988 to 1998. AAFRC Trust for Philanthropy estimates indicated private giving would top $190 billion in 1999.

- Religious congregations and their activities continue to receive the largest share of total private giving.

- Gifts from individuals and their bequests have made up 85 percent of all private giving, reaching more than $150 billion in 1998.

- Between 1995 and 1998 gifts from individuals have increased by over $10 billion annually—a new giving record.

- Between 1992 and 1997 noncash contributions as well as cash contributions of persons who claimed charitable deductions on their tax returns increased almost equally, by approximately $18 billion.

- Tax incentives (such as the ability to claim a deduction for charitable contributions) influence the level of giving, as confirmed by data from both the IRS and INDEPENDENT SECTOR's surveys on giving and volunteering.

- In 1998, 56 percent of the adult American population volunteered, which constituted an estimated $226 billion in donated time—a record-setting level.

- Gifts from foundations, as reported by the Foundation Center, reached $19.5 billion in 1998. In inflation-adjusted dollars, foundation giving increased by 81 percent between 1990 and 1998.

Total Private Giving

Included in private giving are cash and in-kind gifts from living persons, personal bequests, foundations, and corporations. Historically, private tax-deductible contributions have assisted private nonprofit organizations in their current operations and programs as well as in a variety of other purposes as well. Private donations can be made for capital expenditures (such as buildings), for endowments, and for academic scholarships and fellowships. Contributions are also made to public institutions, such as schools, universities, hospitals, libraries, museums, and government units. The AAFRC Trust for Philanthropy provides annual estimates of private giving by source in its publication *Giving USA*. These figures, in combination with INDEPENDENT SECTOR's estimates for charitable donations by individuals, provide an overall estimate for total private giving in the United States.

- In 1998 total private giving from all sources reached nearly $178 billion. Data over ten years show that private giving more than doubled from 1988 ($87.8 billion) to 1998 ($177.8 billion). (See Table 3.1.)

- Based on *Giving USA* estimates, total private giving reached more than $190 billion in 1999.

- Table 3.1 shows total contributions from all private sources in relation to current operating expenditures in nonprofit organizations and to total national income. Although neither set of figures fully reflects the independent sector, the table does include most private contributions and the current operating expenditures associated with this sector. When these estimates are examined, some broad inferences can be made concerning the changing role of private

TABLE 3.1

Total Private Contributions as a Percentage of National Income and Nonprofit Current Operating Expenditures, 1964–1998

	Billions of Current Dollars			Private Giving as a Percentage of:	
Year	Total Private Giving	National Income	Nonprofit Current Operating Expenditures	National Income	Nonprofit Current Operating Expenditures
	(1)	(2)	(3)	(4)	(5)
1964	13.6	542.0	28.0	2.51	48.6
1965	14.7	589.5	30.6	2.49	48.0
1966	15.8	646.6	34.4	2.44	45.9
1967	17.0	681.5	38.4	2.49	44.3
1968	18.8	743.4	43.4	2.53	43.3
1969	20.6	802.4	50.0	2.57	41.2
1970	21.0	837.1	55.8	2.51	37.6
1971	23.4	903.5	62.0	2.59	37.7
1972	24.4	1,000.0	68.6	2.44	35.6
1973	25.5	1,127.0	76.4	2.26	33.4
1974	26.8	1,211.5	85.2	2.21	31.5
1975	28.5	1,301.8	94.6	2.19	30.1
1976	31.8	1,455.9	103.2	2.18	30.8
1977	35.1	1,635.4	112.8	2.15	31.1
1978	38.5	1,859.8	126.4	2.07	30.5
1979	43.0	2,075.0	141.8	2.07	30.3
1980	48.6	2,242.1	162.0	2.17	30.0
1981	55.3	2,496.1	182.8	2.22	30.3
1982	59.2	2,601.9	204.0	2.28	29.0
1983	63.2	2,795.4	225.8	2.26	28.0
1984	68.8	3,161.2	247.8	2.18	27.8
1985	71.7	3,379.2	267.2	2.12	26.8
1986	83.3	3,524.5	292.0	2.36	28.5
1987	82.9	3,802.0	331.2	2.18	25.0
1988	87.8	4,149.6	373.6	2.12	23.5
1989	94.6	4,390.6	411.4	2.15	23.0
1990	98.8	4,640.9	457.2	2.13	21.6
1991	103.4	4,755.5	496.8	2.17	20.8
1992	108.9	4,993.7	538.8	2.18	20.2
1993	115.9	5,251.1	572.6	2.21	20.2
1994	121.5	5,556.1	604.4	2.19	20.1
1995	129.1	5,876.2	636.8	2.20	20.3
1996	143.7	6,210.2	673.0	2.31	21.4
1997	162.0	6,634.9	708.2	2.44	22.9
1998	177.8	7,036.4	743.2	2.53	23.9

Sources: *Total private contribution estimates from 1964–1984 are from the AAFRC Trust for Philanthropy, Giving USA, various years. Subsequent estimates of private contributions were prepared by INDEPENDENT SECTOR. They combine INDEPENDENT SECTOR's estimates for gifts from individuals and those of the AAFRC Trust for Philanthropy, Giving USA, various years, for personal bequests and gifts by foundations and corporations. National income was derived from Council of Economic Advisers, 2000, table B-26. Current operating expenditures were calculated in Table 1.8 based on the gross domestic product of nonprofit institutions as reported in Council of Economic Advisers, 2000, table B-10.*

FIGURE 3.1

Private Contributions as a Percentage of Current Operating Expenditures, 1964–1998

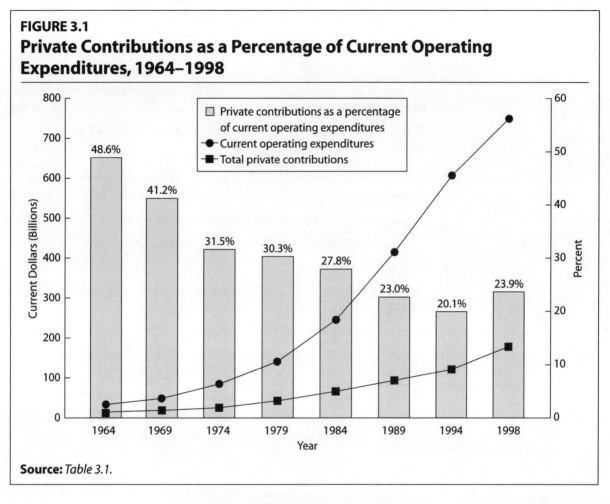

Source: *Table 3.1.*

contributions and their relationship to current operating expenses in the independent sector over time.

- Total private contributions as a percentage of current operating expenditures has steadily declined, from 49 percent in 1964 to a low of 20 percent in 1994, recovering to 24 percent by 1998 (see Figure 3.1).

- In the 1960s private contributions provided more than 40 percent of current expenditures of nonprofits but fell to one quarter in the 1990s (see Table 3.1). Increasing government support for health care, hospitals, education, and human services accounts for much of the change. Hospitals in particular have not relied on private contributions as an important source of revenue, depending more on fees from services as well as payments from government programs such as Medicare and Medicaid.

- As a percentage of national income, private giving peaked in 1971 at 2.6 percent, fell to a low of 2.1 percent in 1978–1979, then recovered to 2.5 percent in 1998 (see Table 3.1). The economic boom of the

1990s and the increased wealth ensuing from it have contributed to unprecedented levels of philanthropic giving.

- AAFRC estimates on the distribution of private contributions from all sources (individuals, foundations, and corporations), as well as INDEPENDENT SECTOR's surveys on giving and volunteering, show that religion consistently receives the largest share of total private giving among nine recipient areas. (See Table 3.2 and Figure 3.2.)

- AAFRC data indicate that although the amount of money donated to religious institutions has not dropped in absolute terms, religious organizations' share of total private contributions diminished from a high of 53 percent in 1995 to 44 percent in 1998 (see Table 3.2).

- Education receives the second largest share of private contributions ($24.6 billion in 1998), overtaking health since the mid-1980s and widening its lead since then. From 1997 to 1998, health, human services, environment, and public and societal benefit experienced substantial gains in their share of private contributions. From 1997 to 1998 the arts and culture subsector received about the same amount of dollars (between $10.5 billion and $10.6 billion), but its share of total private contributions declined. (Preliminary figures indicate that giving to the arts increased in 1999.)

FIGURE 3.2
Distribution of Private Contributions by Recipient Area, 1998

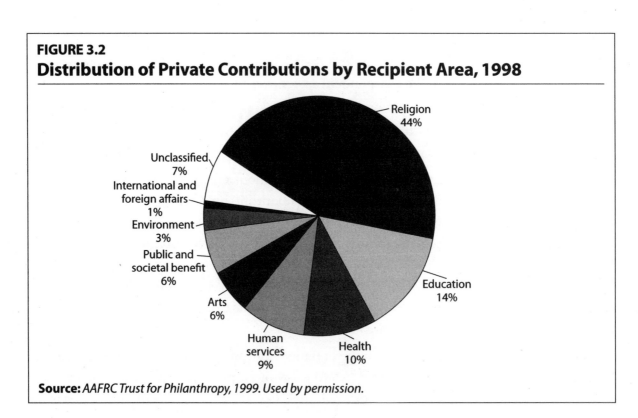

Source: *AAFRC Trust for Philanthropy, 1999. Used by permission.*

TABLE 3.2

Distribution of Private Contributions by Recipient Area: AAFRC Trust for Philanthropy Estimates, 1968–1998

Year	Total[a] (Billions of Dollars)	Total (Percent)	Religion (Percent)	Education (Percent)	Health (Percent)	Human Services (Percent)	Arts (Percent)	Public and Societal Benefit (Percent)	Environment (Percent)	International Affairs (Percent)	Unclassified (Percent)
1968	18.85	100.0	44.7	12.6	11.0	12.3	3.2	2.3			14.0
1969	20.66	100.0	43.7	12.3	11.2	13.1	3.5	2.7			13.6
1970	21.04	100.0	44.4	12.4	11.4	13.9	3.2	2.2			12.6
1971	23.44	100.0	43.0	11.7	11.1	12.8	4.3	2.9			14.1
1972	24.44	100.0	41.3	12.2	11.5	12.9	4.5	3.4			14.2
1973	25.59	100.0	41.1	12.1	12.1	12.0	4.9	2.4			15.3
1974	26.88	100.0	44.0	11.3	12.5	11.2	4.3	2.5			14.1
1975	28.56	100.0	44.9	9.9	12.6	10.3	4.3	2.8			15.2
1976	31.85	100.0	44.5	10.3	12.3	9.5	4.3	3.2			15.8
1977	35.21	100.0	48.2	10.3	11.6	10.1	6.6	3.5			9.7
1978	38.57	100.0	47.6	10.7	11.7	10.0	6.2	2.8			11.0
1979	43.11	100.0	46.8	10.5	11.5	10.4	6.3	2.9			11.6
1980	48.63	100.0	45.7	10.2	11.0	10.1	6.5	3.0			13.5
1981	55.28	100.0	45.3	10.4	10.5	10.2	6.6	3.2			13.7
1982	59.11	100.0	47.5	10.2	10.4	10.7	8.4	2.8			10.0
1983	63.21	100.0	50.4	10.5	10.6	11.3	6.7	3.0			7.6
1984	68.58	100.0	51.8	10.6	10.0	11.5	6.6	2.8			6.7
1985	71.69	100.0	53.3	11.4	10.8	11.9	7.1	3.1			2.5
1986	83.25	100.0	50.1	11.3	10.1	11.0	7.0	2.9			7.6
1987	82.21	100.0	52.9	12.0	11.2	12.0	7.7	3.5	2.4	0.9	(2.6)
1988	88.04	100.0	51.3	11.6	10.9	11.9	7.7	3.6	2.5	1.0	(0.6)
1989	98.43	100.0	48.5	11.1	10.1	11.6	7.6	3.9	1.9	1.0	4.2
1990	101.37	100.0	49.1	12.2	9.8	11.7	7.8	4.9	2.5	1.3	0.8
1991	105.01	100.0	47.6	12.8	9.2	10.6	8.4	4.7	2.6	1.4	2.6
1992	110.41	100.0	49.7	12.9	9.3	10.5	8.4	4.6	2.7	1.3	0.5
1993	116.54	100.0	48.3	13.2	9.3	10.7	8.2	4.7	2.6	1.4	1.7
1994	119.17	100.0	50.5	13.9	9.7	9.8	8.1	5.1	2.8	1.6	(1.6)
1995	124.31	100.0	53.3	14.2	10.1	9.4	8.0	5.7	3.0	1.4	(5.2)
1996	138.64	100.0	51.0	13.8	10.0	8.8	7.9	5.5	2.7	1.2	(0.9)
1997	157.69	100.0	46.1	14.1	8.9	8.0	6.7	5.3	2.6	1.2	7.0
1998	174.52	100.0	43.6	14.1	9.7	9.2	6.0	6.2	3.0	1.2	7.0

Note: *Giving to some categories prior to 1985 cannot be compared to giving since 1985 because of different statistical tabulation and analysis procedures. For the environment and international affairs categories, earlier years have not been estimated by AAFRC Trust for Philanthropy.*

[a] *Totals differ slightly from earlier tables, which use INDEPENDENT SECTOR's own estimates for individual giving compared to those of the AAFRC Trust for Philanthropy.*

Source: *AAFRC Trust for Philanthropy, 1999. Used by permission.*

Giving by Individuals

Historically, contributions by living individuals and charitable bequests have represented more than 85 percent of all private giving (see Figure 3.3). In 1998 charitable giving by individuals reached over $138 billion. Since 1995 personal giving has been increasing by well over $10 billion annually, a new philanthropic record. Personal bequests in 1998 added another $13.6 billion. (See Table 3.3.)

FIGURE 3.3

Sources of Private Contributions, 1980, 1990, and 1998

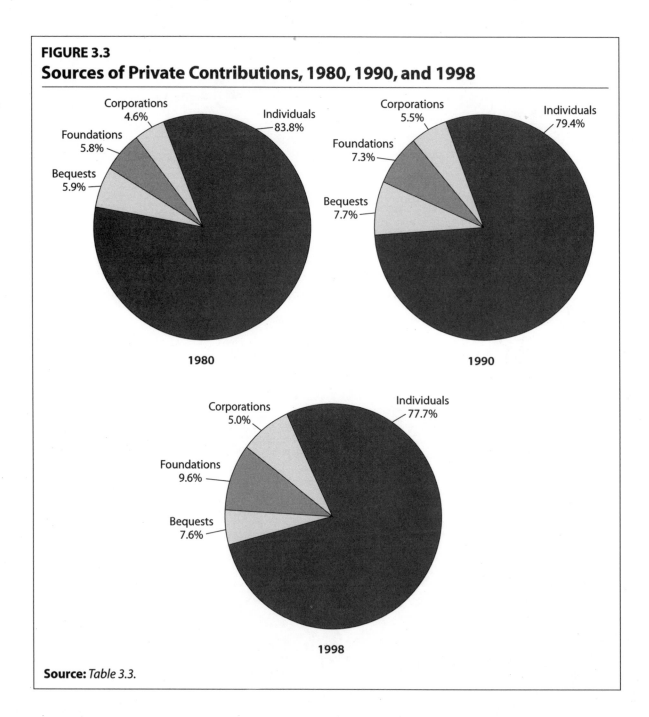

Source: *Table 3.3.*

TABLE 3.3

Total Private Contributions by Source, 1964–1998

Year	Total Private Giving Amount (Billions of Dollars)	Percent	Gifts by Individuals Amount (Billions of Dollars)	Percent	Personal Bequests Amount (Billions of Dollars)	Percent	Gifts by Foundations Amount (Billions of Dollars)	Percent	Gifts by Corporations Amount (Billions of Dollars)	Percent
1964	13.6	100.0	11.2	82.4	1.0	7.0	0.8	6.1	0.6	4.4
1965	14.7	100.0	11.8	80.3	1.0	6.9	1.1	7.7	0.7	4.8
1966	15.8	100.0	12.4	78.5	1.3	8.2	1.3	7.9	0.8	4.9
1967	17.0	100.0	13.4	78.8	1.4	8.2	1.4	8.2	0.8	4.7
1968	18.8	100.0	14.8	78.5	1.6	8.5	1.6	8.5	0.9	4.8
1969	20.6	100.0	15.9	77.3	2.0	9.7	1.8	8.7	0.9	4.5
1970	21.0	100.0	16.2	77.1	2.1	10.1	1.9	9.0	0.8	3.9
1971	23.4	100.0	17.6	75.4	3.0	12.8	2.0	8.3	0.9	3.6
1972	24.4	100.0	19.4	79.4	2.1	8.6	2.0	8.2	1.0	4.0
1973	25.5	100.0	20.5	80.5	2.0	7.8	2.0	7.8	1.1	4.2
1974	26.8	100.0	21.6	80.6	2.1	7.7	2.1	7.9	1.1	4.1
1975	28.5	100.0	23.5	82.6	2.2	7.8	1.7	5.8	1.2	4.0
1976	31.8	100.0	26.3	82.8	2.3	7.2	1.9	6.0	1.3	4.2
1977	35.1	100.0	29.6	84.2	2.1	6.0	2.0	5.7	1.5	4.4
1978	38.5	100.0	32.1	83.4	2.6	6.8	2.2	5.6	1.7	4.4
1979	43.0	100.0	36.6	85.1	2.2	5.2	2.2	5.2	2.1	4.8
1980	48.6	100.0	40.7	83.8	2.9	5.9	2.8	5.8	2.3	4.6
1981	55.3	100.0	46.0	83.2	3.6	6.5	3.1	5.6	2.6	4.8
1982	59.2	100.0	47.6	80.5	5.2	8.8	3.2	5.3	3.1	5.3
1983	63.2	100.0	52.1	82.4	3.9	6.1	3.6	5.7	3.7	5.8
1984	68.8	100.0	56.5	82.1	4.0	5.9	4.0	5.7	4.1	6.0
1985	71.7	100.0	57.4	80.1	4.8	6.7	4.9	6.8	4.6	6.5
1986	83.3	100.0	67.1	80.6	5.7	6.8	5.4	6.5	5.0	6.0
1987	82.9	100.0	65.2	78.7	6.6	7.9	5.9	7.1	5.2	6.3
1988	87.8	100.0	69.7	79.4	6.6	7.5	6.2	7.0	5.3	6.1
1989	94.6	100.0	75.6	79.9	7.0	7.4	6.6	6.9	5.5	5.8
1990	98.8	100.0	78.5	79.4	7.6	7.7	7.2	7.3	5.5	5.5
1991	103.4	100.0	82.6	79.9	7.8	7.5	7.7	7.5	5.3	5.1
1992	108.9	100.0	86.2	79.2	8.2	7.5	8.6	7.9	5.9	5.4
1993	115.9	100.0	91.4	78.8	8.5	7.4	9.5	8.2	6.5	5.6
1994	121.5	100.0	94.8	78.1	10.0	8.2	9.7	8.0	7.0	5.7
1995	129.1	100.0	100.5	77.8	10.7	8.3	10.6	8.2	7.3	5.7
1996	143.7	100.0	112.7	78.4	11.5	8.0	12.0	8.4	7.5	5.2
1997	162.0	100.0	127.3	78.6	12.6	7.8	13.9	8.6	8.2	5.1
1998[a]	177.8	100.0	138.2	77.7	13.6	7.6	17.1	9.6	8.9	5.0

Note: *Owing to rounding, percentage figures may not total 100.*

[a] *Preliminary estimates.*

Sources: *Estimates of gifts by individual persons for the years after 1985 are based on calculations made by INDEPENDENT SECTOR using factors related to charitable deductions claimed in 1985 and 1986 by both itemizers and nonitemizers. The tax code for these two years allowed nonitemizers to claim a deduction for their charitable contributions (50 percent of their contribution in 1985 and 100 percent in 1986). Estimates of gifts by individuals prior to 1985, as well as all years for personal bequests, gifts by foundations, and gifts by corporations, are derived from AAFRC Trust for Philanthropy, 1999.*

- Between 1964 and 1994 per capita individual giving in constant 1997 dollars rose steadily from $302 in 1964 to $394 in 1994, with the exception of 1986, when per capita giving peaked at $408 (see Table 3.4). The 1986 phenomenon was influenced by three factors. In 1986 the tax law allowed taxpayers who filed nonitemized returns to claim, in addition to their standard deductions, all of their charitable contributions. The 1986 tax reform also reduced a variety of tax rates, which provided incentives, particularly for wealthy taxpayers, to increase charitable contributions in 1986, when the cost of giving was lower than it would be in 1987. Finally, the stock market performed exceptionally well in 1986, creating new wealth.

- Since 1995, per capita giving has been increasing at an extraordinary rate, reaching $511 by 1998 (see Figure 3.4). As a result of a robust economy, fueled by a booming technology industry that was fast producing new multimillionaires, per capita giving in 1996 finally exceeded the record set in 1986.

- Between 1987 and 1997 estates worth $600,000 or more were subject to federal estate taxes. The tax code, however, allowed estates to

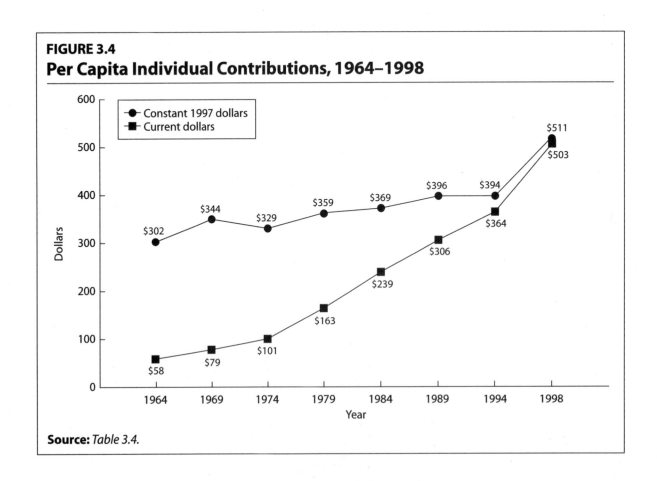

FIGURE 3.4
Per Capita Individual Contributions, 1964–1998

Source: *Table 3.4.*

TABLE 3.4

Total Per Capita Contributions and Individual Contributions as a Percentage of Personal Income, 1964–1998

Year	Private Giving (Billions of Dollars)			Per Capita Individual Giving[a]		Personal Income	
	Total Current Dollars	From Individuals	Total Population (Midyear, in Millions)	Current Dollars	Constant 1997 Dollars	Total	Individual Giving as a Percentage of Personal Income[b]
	(1)	(2)	(3)	(4)	(5)	(6)	(7)
1964	13.6	11.2	191.9	58	302	515.8	2.2
1965	14.7	11.8	194.3	61	309	557.4	2.1
1966	15.8	12.4	196.6	63	312	606.4	2.0
1967	17.0	13.4	198.8	67	324	650.4	2.1
1968	18.8	14.8	200.7	73	339	714.5	2.1
1969	20.6	15.9	202.7	79	344	780.8	2.0
1970	21.0	16.2	205.1	79	327	841.1	1.9
1971	23.4	17.6	207.7	85	337	905.1	1.9
1972	24.4	19.4	209.9	92	354	994.3	1.9
1973	25.5	20.5	211.9	97	350	1,113.4	1.8
1974	26.8	21.6	213.9	101	329	1,225.6	1.8
1975	28.5	23.5	216.0	109	325	1,331.7	1.8
1976	31.8	26.3	218.1	121	340	1,475.4	1.8
1977	35.1	29.6	220.3	134	355	1,637.1	1.8
1978	38.5	32.1	222.6	144	355	1,848.3	1.7
1979	43.0	36.6	225.1	163	359	2,081.5	1.8
1980	48.6	40.7	227.7	179	348	2,323.9	1.8
1981	55.3	46.0	230.0	200	353	2,599.4	1.8
1982	59.2	47.6	232.2	205	341	2,768.4	1.7
1983	63.2	52.1	234.3	222	358	2,946.9	1.8
1984	68.8	56.5	236.4	239	369	3,274.8	1.7
1985	71.7	57.4	238.5	241	359	3,515.0	1.6
1986	83.3	67.1	240.7	279	408	3,712.4	1.8
1987	82.9	65.2	242.9	268	379	3,962.5	1.6
1988	87.8	69.7	245.1	284	386	4,272.1	1.6
1989	94.6	75.6	247.4	306	396	4,599.8	1.6
1990	98.8	78.5	250.0	314	386	4,903.2	1.6
1991	103.4	82.6	252.7	327	385	5,085.4	1.6
1992	108.9	86.2	255.4	338	386	5,390.4	1.6
1993	115.9	91.4	258.1	354	393	5,610.0	1.6
1994	121.5	94.8	260.6	364	394	5,888.0	1.6
1995	129.1	100.5	263.1	382	402	6,200.9	1.6
1996	143.7	112.7	265.5	424	434	6,547.4	1.7
1997	162.0	127.3	268.0	475	475	6,951.1	1.8
1998[c]	177.8	138.2	270.6	511	503	7,358.9	1.9

[a] Private individual giving (column 2) divided by population (column 3).
[b] Private individual giving (column 2) divided by personal income (column 6).
[c] Preliminary estimates.

Sources: *See Table 3.3 for private giving data. Population and personal income data are derived from Council of Economic Advisers, 2000, tables B-27 and B-29.*

TABLE 3.5

Estate Tax Returns and Charitable Bequests of $600,000 or More, Selected Years, 1987–1997

	1987	1990	1992	1993	1994	1995	1996	1997
Number of returns	45,113	50,367	59,176	60,211	68,595	69,755	79,321	90,006
Gross estate (billions of current dollars)	66.6	87.1	98.9	103.7	117.0	117.7	137.4	162.3
Gross estate (billions of constant 1997 dollars)	94.1	107.0	113.1	115.2	126.7	124.0	140.6	162.3
Number of bequests	8,987	9,709	11,053	11,119	11,869	13,039	14,233	15,575
Percentage of total returns	19.9	19.3	18.7	18.5	17.3	18.7	17.9	17.3
Total bequests (billions of current dollars)	4.0	5.5	6.8	7.3	9.3	8.7	10.2	14.3
Total bequests (billions of constant 1997 dollars)	5.7	6.8	7.8	8.1	10.1	9.2	10.4	14.3
Percentage of gross estate	6.0	6.3	6.9	7.0	7.9	7.4	7.4	8.8

Note: *Constant 1997 dollars are based on the implicit price deflators for gross domestic product, as published in Council of Economic Advisers, 1999.*

Source: *Internal Revenue Service,* Statistics of Income Bulletin, *various years.*

reduce their tax liabilities through charitable bequests. From 1987 to 1997 the number of estate returns filed doubled, rising from 45,000 to 90,000, and increased in constant dollar value from $94 billion to $162 billion (see Table 3.5). For the same period total charitable bequests in constant 1997 dollars increased one and a half times, from $5.7 billion to $14.3 billion (see Figure 3.5).

- Charitable bequests represented 6.0 percent of the value of gross estates in 1987, rising to 8.8 percent in 1997 (see Table 3.5). Recently the estate tax has come under fire from critics who question its fairness and ability to generate charitable contributions. Its proponents, however, argue that it provides a powerful incentive for philanthropic giving, particularly among the wealthy, by allowing estates to deduct 100 percent of their charitable contributions.

Estimates of Individual Giving Based on IRS Records

- Table 3.6 summarizes INDEPENDENT SECTOR's estimates of total individual giving by tax filers, classified by itemizer and nonitemizer status (see the section on Chapter Three in Resource B for details on estimating individual giving from IRS records). The impact of the tax incentives created by the 1986 tax reform, in the form of increasing contributions for 1986, is clearly demonstrated in the table. In

FIGURE 3.5
Number and Amount of Charitable Bequests by Year Filed, 1987–1997

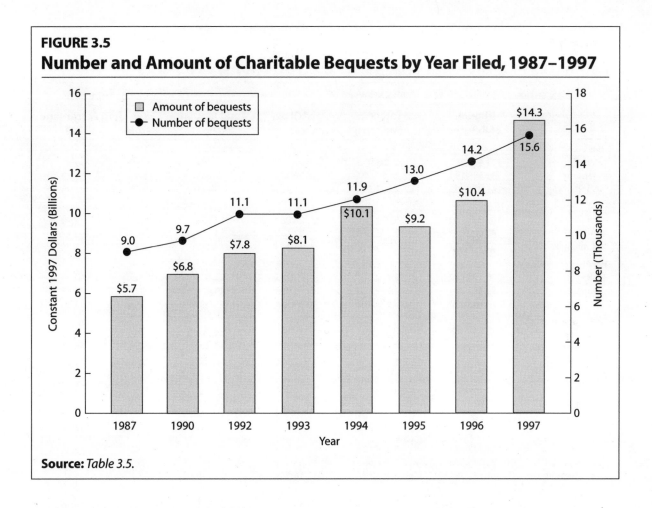

Source: *Table 3.5.*

1986 nonitemizers could deduct all charitable contributions. This was replaced in 1987 by the standard deduction provision, which included, among other items, charitable contributions. Charitable contributions as a percentage of adjusted gross income (AGI) increased markedly from 1985 to 1986 but declined temporarily in 1987 compared with 1986. Deductions for charitable contributions of itemizers as a percentage of their AGI in 1986 reached a record high of 3.12 percent, which was not surpassed until 1997. Estimates for nonitemizers peaked at 1.76 percent in 1986 and have since stayed below that level.

- Itemizers can also include in their charitable deductions noncash contributions (such as property, jewelry, works of art, and so on) at their current market value. In 1987 noncash contributions constituted 12.4 percent of total charitable contributions of itemizers. By 1997 this ratio had dramatically risen to 28.2 percent. (See Figure 3.6.)

TABLE 3.6

Estimates of Individual Charitable Contributions, 1985–1997

	All Returns			Charitable Contributions		
	Number of Returns	**Total AGI (Millions)**	**AGI per Return**	**Total Amount (Millions)**	**Per Return**	**As a Percentage of AGI**
1985						
All	101,660,287	2,305,952	22,683	57,394	565	2.49
Itemizer	39,848,184	1,582,587	39,715	47,963	1,204	3.03
Nonitemizer	61,812,103	723,365	11,703	9,431	153	1.30
1986						
All	103,045,170	2,481,681	24,083	67,094	651	2.70
Itemizer	40,667,008	1,725,714	42,435	53,816	1,323	3.12
Nonitemizer	62,378,162	755,967	12,119	13,278	213	1.76
1987						
All	106,996,270	2,772,824	25,915	65,164	609	2.35
Itemizer	35,627,790	1,799,048	50,496	49,624	1,393	2.76
Nonitemizer	71,368,480	973,776	13,644	15,540	218	1.60
1988						
All	109,708,280	3,083,020	28,102	69,734	636	2.26
Itemizer	31,902,985	1,887,494	59,164	50,949	1,597	2.70
Nonitemizer	77,805,295	1,195,526	15,366	18,785	241	1.57
1989						
All	112,135,673	3,256,359	29,039	75,588	674	2.32
Itemizer	31,972,317	1,971,222	61,654	55,459	1,735	2.81
Nonitemizer	80,163,356	1,285,137	16,031	20,129	251	1.57
1990						
All	113,717,138	3,405,428	29,946	78,500	690	2.31
Itemizer	32,174,940	2,046,651	63,610	57,242	1,779	2.80
Nonitemizer	81,542,198	1,358,777	16,663	21,258	261	1.56
1991						
All	114,730,123	3,464,524	30,197	82,561	720	2.38
Itemizer	32,489,918	2,056,805	63,306	60,574	1,864	2.95
Nonitemizer	82,240,205	1,407,719	17,117	21,987	267	1.56
1992						
All	113,604,503	3,629,129	31,945	86,177	759	2.37
Itemizer	32,540,614	2,183,969	67,115	63,843	1,962	2.92
Nonitemizer	81,063,889	1,445,160	17,827	22,334	276	1.55
1993						
All	114,601,819	3,723,340	32,489	91,431	798	2.46
Itemizer	32,821,464	2,241,087	68,281	68,354	2,083	3.05
Nonitemizer	81,780,355	1,482,253	18,125	23,077	282	1.56
1994						
All	115,943,131	3,907,518	33,702	94,831	818	2.43
Itemizer	33,017,754	2,342,834	70,957	70,545	2,137	3.01
Nonitemizer	82,925,377	1,564,684	18,869	24,286	293	1.55
1995						
All	118,218,327	4,189,354	35,437	100,463	850	2.40
Itemizer	34,007,717	2,542,781	74,771	74,991	2,205	2.95
Nonitemizer	84,210,610	1,646,573	19,553	25,472	302	1.55
1996						
All	120,351,208	4,535,975	37,689	112,666	936	2.48
Itemizer	35,414,589	2,812,927	79,428	86,159	2,433	3.06
Nonitemizer	84,936,619	1,723,048	20,286	26,507	312	1.54
1997						
All	122,421,991	4,969,950	40,597	127,301	1,040	2.56
Itemizer	36,624,595	3,130,184	85,647	99,192	2,708	3.17
Nonitemizer	85,797,396	1,839,766	21,443	28,109	328	1.53

Note: *AGI = adjusted gross income.*

Sources: *Internal Revenue Service,* Statistics of Income—Individual Income Tax Returns, *various years; authors' estimates.*

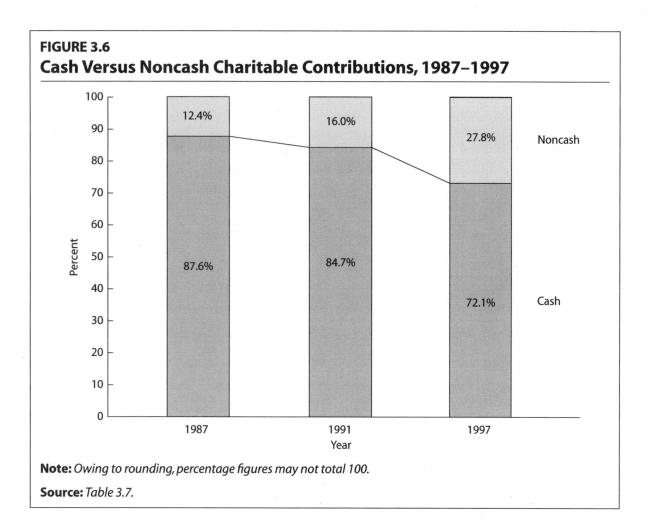

FIGURE 3.6
Cash Versus Noncash Charitable Contributions, 1987–1997

Note: *Owing to rounding, percentage figures may not total 100.*

Source: *Table 3.7.*

- Between 1992 and 1997 the $18.3 billion increase in noncash contributions nearly matched dollar for dollar the $18.8 billion increase in cash contributions (see Table 3.7).

- Based on IRS data, the average charitable contribution (in constant 1997 dollars) of tax filers who claimed deductions for charitable contributions increased dramatically between 1986 and 1998, from $2,138 to $3,163—an increase of 45 percent (see Table 3.8).

- The volatility of noncash contributions (or giving from wealth) is apparent from Table 3.9, which focuses on reported charitable contributions of filers with an AGI of $1 million or more. For the period 1985 to 1987, noncash contributions as a percentage of total contributions rose from 42.6 percent in 1985 to a high of 65.0 percent in 1986 (partly in anticipation of tax law changes), then declined to 28.3 percent in 1987. In contrast, for the period 1995 to 1997, this percentage steadily climbed from 35.8 percent in 1995 to a high of 62.5 percent in 1997.

TABLE 3.7

Distribution of Cash and Noncash Charitable Contributions of Itemizers, 1985–1998

Year	Total Charitable Contributions (Thousands of Dollars)	Percent	Cash Contributions (Thousands of Dollars)	Percent	Non-Cash Contributions (Thousands of Dollars)	Percent
1985	47,962,848	100	41,371,619	86.3	6,591,229	13.7
1986	53,815,978	100	43,168,816	80.2	10,647,169	19.8
1987	49,623,906	100	43,448,099	87.6	6,175,807	12.4
1988	50,949,273	100	42,834,342	84.1	6,711,616	13.2
1989	55,459,205	100	46,553,194	83.9	7,550,914	13.6
1990	57,242,767	100	48,485,664	84.7	7,494,016	13.1
1991	60,573,565	100	51,277,927	84.7	9,681,786	16.0
1992	63,843,281	100	53,647,642	84.0	9,632,779	15.1
1993	68,354,293	100	55,784,521	81.6	12,278,893	18.0
1994	70,544,542	100	56,229,759	79.7	14,739,299	20.9
1995	74,991,519	100	59,589,837	79.5	13,521,937	18.0
1996	86,159,305	100	65,658,168	76.2	21,298,819	24.7
1997	99,191,362	100	72,426,402	73.0	27,961,174	28.2
1998[a]	109,011,966	100	79,669,042	73.1	29,342,924	26.9

Note: *Owing to rounding, the sum of cash and noncash contributions may not equal total contributions.*

[a] *Preliminary estimates.*

Source: *Internal Revenue Service,* Statistics of Income—Individual Income Tax Returns, *Table 2.1, various years.*

Insights from the Giving and Volunteering Survey

Since 1987 INDEPENDENT SECTOR has been conducting periodic national surveys on giving and volunteering in the United States. Data from these surveys provide valuable insights into the charitable giving behavior of households but should not be used to derive aggregate estimates. A crucial reason for this is that the surveys do not adequately sample high-income households ($200,000 or more in total household income), which account for a large part of total giving. Consequently, any attempt to calculate aggregate giving on the basis of these surveys will yield estimates that fall short of those derived from IRS administrative data. In addition to providing behavioral data on the giving of money, the surveys also include information on the giving of time, that is, on volunteering.

Giving

- As data gathered from various years of INDEPENDENT SECTOR's giving and volunteering survey confirm, households that file itemized tax returns give considerably more than those that do not itemize (see Table 3.10). In 1998 alone the average household contribution

TABLE 3.8

Average Charitable Contribution of All Itemizers and Itemizers with Charitable Deductions, 1985–1998

| | | | | | Average Charitable Contribution | | | |
| | Number of Itemized Returns | | Total Charitable Deductions | | All Returns | | With Charitable Deductions | |
Year	All	With Charitable Deductions	Current Dollars (Millions)	Constant 1997 Dollars (Millions)[a]	Current Dollars (Millions)	Constant 1997 Dollars (Millions)	Current Dollars (Millions)	Constant 1997 Dollars (Millions)
1985	39,848,184	36,228,636	47,693	71,141	1,197	1,785	1,316	1,964
1986	40,667,008	36,857,590	53,816	78,809	1,323	1,938	1,460	2,138
1987	35,627,790	32,229,545	49,624	70,111	1,393	1,968	1,540	2,175
1988	31,902,985	29,110,570	50,949	69,124	1,597	2,167	1,750	2,375
1989	31,972,317	29,132,485	55,459	71,784	1,735	2,245	1,904	2,464
1990	32,174,938	29,230,264	57,243	70,295	1,779	2,185	1,958	2,405
1991	32,489,919	29,551,348	60,574	71,381	1,864	2,197	2,050	2,415
1992	32,540,614	29,603,407	63,843	73,035	1,962	2,244	2,157	2,467
1993	32,821,464	29,799,000	68,354	75,923	2,083	2,313	2,294	2,548
1994	33,017,754	29,848,727	70,544	76,399	2,137	2,314	2,363	2,560
1995	34,007,717	30,540,638	74,991	78,977	2,205	2,322	2,455	2,586
1996	35,414,589	31,591,984	86,159	88,136	2,433	2,489	2,727	2,790
1997	36,624,595	32,612,634	99,191	99,191	2,708	2,708	3,041	3,041
1998[b]	38,126,203	33,932,321	109,012	107,340	2,859	2,815	3,213	3,163

[a] *Based on the Consumer Price Indices as reported in Council of Economic Advisers, 2000.*
[b] *Preliminary estimates.*

Source: *Internal Revenue Service,* Statistics of Income—Individual Income Tax Returns, *various years.*

of respondents who itemized ($1,277) was over three times more than that of nonitemizers (see Figure 3.7).

- The survey results also indicate that the ability to claim charitable deductions has an impact on the level of charitable giving (see Table 3.10). Among all households, contributing households that itemized and claimed charitable deductions consistently gave the highest average contribution ($1,798) and the highest percentage of income in 1998 (see Figure 3.8 and Table 3.10).

- On average, contributing households that claimed charitable deductions on their tax returns gave 2.7 percent of their household income

TABLE 3.9

Cash and Noncash Charitable Contributions of Itemizers with AGI* of $1 Million or More, 1985–1987 and 1995–1998

Year	Number of Returns	Percentage of All Returns with Contribution Deductions	Total Contributions (Thousands of Dollars)	Cash (Thousands of Dollars)[a]	Cash as a Percentage of Total	Noncash (Thousands of Dollars)	Noncash as a Percentage of Total
1985	16,928	0.05	2,495,374	1,432,741	57.4	1,062,633	42.6
1986	31,334	0.09	6,621,193	2,318,634	35.0	4,302,559	65.0
1987	32,932	0.10	3,359,739	2,409,976	71.7	949,763	28.3
1995	78,447	0.25	8,845,408	5,677,245	64.2	3,168,163	35.8
1996	99,728	0.32	13,648,238	6,168,502	45.2	7,479,736	54.8
1997	128,684	0.39	18,618,418	6,977,075	37.5	11,641,343	62.5
1998	151,683	0.45	21,141,556	9,902,609	46.8	11,236,947	53.2

*AGI = adjusted gross income.

[a] Cash contributions have been adjusted to equal the difference between noncash and total contributions. The difference between published IRS data on cash contributions and those shown here are estimated to be carry-over amounts from previous years.

Source: Internal Revenue Service, Statistics of Income—Individual Income Tax Returns, various years.

FIGURE 3.7

Average Contributions of Itemizers and Nonitemizers, 1998

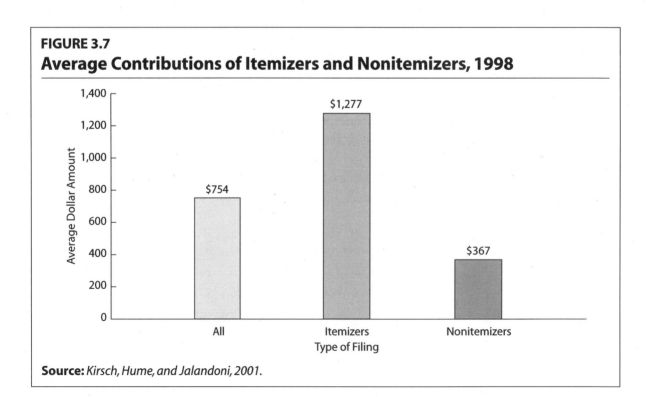

Source: Kirsch, Hume, and Jalandoni, 2001.

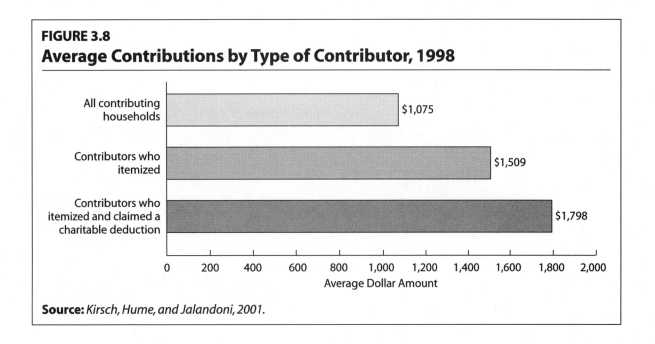

FIGURE 3.8

Average Contributions by Type of Contributor, 1998

Source: *Kirsch, Hume, and Jalandoni, 2001.*

to charity, compared with 0.9 percent for households that did not claim charitable deductions.

- In 1995 the major activity areas that had the largest share of household contributors were religion (48 percent), health (27 percent), human services (25 percent), youth development (21 percent), and education (20 percent; see Figure 3.9). Among independent sector organizations, most household contributors (95.7 percent) gave to religion-related activities (see Table 3.11).

Volunteering

- A major part of individual giving involves the giving of time to individuals and organizations without receiving monetary compensation for efforts expended. In 1998 an estimated 109.4 million American adults eighteen years of age and older (55.5 percent) volunteered an average of 3.5 hours per week. This was the highest level of volunteer participation ever recorded by INDEPENDENT SECTOR's giving and volunteering surveys in over ten years. (See Table 3.12.)

- In 1998 about 19.9 billion hours were spent in both formal volunteer activities with organizations (15.8 billion hours) and informal volunteer activities (4.1 billion hours). (Informal volunteer activities include helping friends and family or providing assistance on an ad hoc basis to organizations.) The total hours spent on formal volunteering represented an equivalent of 9.3 million full-time employees at an estimated value of $226 billion. (See Table 3.12.)

TABLE 3.10

Average Contributions by Itemizer Versus Nonitemizer Status, Selected Years, 1987–1998

	1987	1989	1991	1993	1995	1998
All respondents[a]						
Percentage of all respondents	100.0	100.0	100.0	100.0	100.0	100.0
Average household contribution	562	734	649	646	696	754
Average household income	34,498	35,972	36,797	37,493	41,484	45,428
Average percentage of household income given	1.5	2.0	1.7	1.7	1.7	1.7
Itemizers[b]						
Percentage of all respondents	49.5	41.2	2.3	37.1	38.2	40.5
Average household contribution	828	1,185	1,064	1,146	1,336	1,277
Average household income	42,503	47,105	50,936	49,556	56,274	61,782
Average percentage of household income given	1.8	2.6	2.1	2.2	2.4	2.1
Nonitemizers[c]						
Percentage of all respondents	50.4	58.8	57.7	62.9	61.8	59.5
Average household contribution	294	363	347	332	271	367
Average household income	26,626	28,228	26,385	29,481	30,481	33,775
Average percentage of household income given	0.9	1.2	1.3	1.2	0.9	1.1
Contributors only						
Percentage of all respondents	71.0	75.1	72.2	73.4	68.5	70.1
Average household contribution	790	978	899	880	1,017	1,075
Average household income	37,113	39,361	41,222	41,350	46,637	50,483
Average percentage of household income given	1.9	2.5	2.2	2.1	2.2	2.1
Itemizers[b]						
Percentage of all respondents	40.4	35.8	36.6	32.4	31.8	34.3
Average household contribution	1,014	1,458	1,230	1,313	1,607	1,509
Average household income	43,393	48,912	53,037	51,492	58,544	63,665
Average percentage of household income given	2.1	3.0	2.3	2.4	2.8	2.4
Nonitemizers[c]						
Percentage of all respondents	30.6	39.3	35.6	41.0	36.7	35.8
Average household contribution	483	543	563	509	465	619
Average household income	28,070	30,675	29,043	32,085	34,224	37,388
Average percentage of household income given	1.5	1.8	2.0	1.6	1.4	1.7

[a] Includes both contributors and noncontributors.

[b] Includes itemizers who did not intend to claim, or who were uncertain about claiming, a charitable deduction on their tax returns.

[c] Includes respondents who did not know about their itemizer status.

Source: Hodgkinson, Weitzman, and the Gallup Organization, Giving and Volunteering, various years.

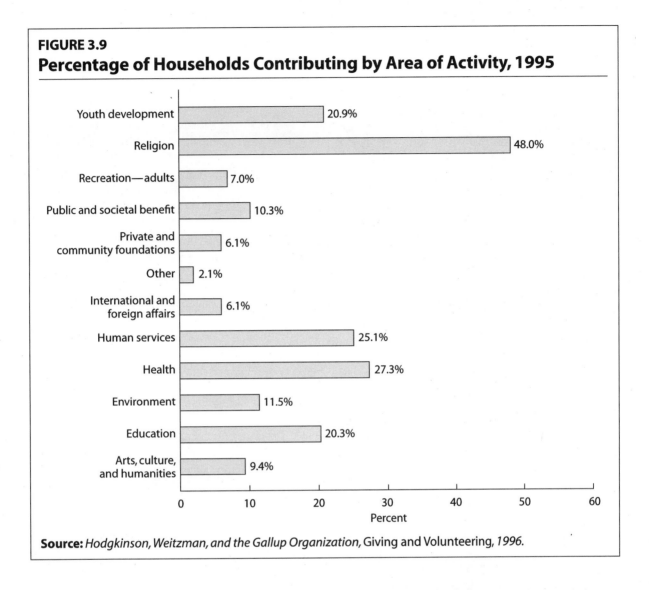

FIGURE 3.9
Percentage of Households Contributing by Area of Activity, 1995

Source: *Hodgkinson, Weitzman, and the Gallup Organization,* Giving and Volunteering, *1996.*

- Volunteers in 1998 worked mostly in the following major activity areas: informal volunteering, religion, youth development, education, and human services (see Figure 3.10). Although most of the activity areas experienced an increase in the percentage of volunteers, the areas of religion and health declined between 1995 and 1998 (see Table 3.13).

- Many people volunteer for more than one organization. In 1998 the average number of volunteer assignments per volunteer was 1.67, the highest level ever reached—a direct result of the increased percentage of the population volunteering that year.

The following demographic characteristics of volunteers can be observed based on the results of the 1998 survey on giving and volunteering (see Table 3.14):

TABLE 3.11

Distribution of Household Contributors by Type of Recipient Organization and Sector, Selected Years, 1987–1995

	All Households (Percent)[c]	Total, All Sectors (Percent)	Private Sector — Independent Sector				Government Sector			
			All (Percent)	Religious Institutions (Percent)	Other Charitable Organizations (Percent)	For-Profit Organizations (Percent)	All (Percent)	Federal (Percent)	State (Percent)	Local (Percent)
1995[a]										
Arts, culture, and humanities	9.4	100.0	67.1	3.6	63.5	9.4	23.5	1.1	6.6	15.8
Education	20.3	100.0	50.5	18.3	32.2	5.6	43.9	0.2	4.8	38.9
Environment	11.5	100.0	78.5	5.7	72.8	3.4	18.0	4.9	4.5	8.6
Health	27.3	100.0	86.4	12.4	74.0	6.9	6.7	1.0	1.8	3.9
Human services	25.1	100.0	86.2	14.2	72.0	2.4	11.5	0.8	3.7	7.0
International and foreign affairs	6.1	100.0	73.5	25.5	48.0	4.0	22.4	18.6	0.0	3.8
Other	2.1	100.0	71.8	20.5	51.3	22.0	6.2	0.0	0.0	6.2
Private and community foundations	6.1	100.0	72.0	9.8	62.2	6.9	21.1	5.5	1.7	13.9
Public and societal benefit	10.3	100.0	69.2	8.9	60.3	3.1	27.9	2.7	3.8	21.4
Recreation—adults	7.0	100.0	53.3	7.5	45.8	14.5	32.2	2.4	5.6	24.2
Religion	48.0	100.0	98.4	95.7	2.7	0.8	0.8	0.0	0.1	0.7
Youth development	20.9	100.0	75.8	16.0	59.8	3.7	20.5	0.8	0.5	19.2
Distribution of household contributors	n/a	100.0	80.0	33.5	46.5	4.4	15.8	1.7	2.4	11.7
Distribution of estimated contributions	n/a	100.0	89.6	62.7	26.9	2.9	7.4	0.6	2.4	4.4
1991[b]										
Distribution of household contributors	n/a	100.0	70.1	32.0	38.1	4.1	25.8	1.5	3.9	20.5
Distribution of estimated contributions	n/a	100.0	82.0	60.9	21.1	2.7	15.3	0.8	2.2	12.3
1989										
Distribution of household contributors	n/a	100.0	75.5	32.2	43.3	4.4	20.1	1.8	4.0	14.3
Distribution of estimated contributions	n/a	100.0	85.3	61.9	23.4	2.5	12.1	0.9	2.1	9.1
1987										
Distribution of household contributors	n/a	100.0	81.2	39.7	41.5	1.9	16.9	1.8	3.5	11.6
Distribution of estimated contributions	n/a	100.0	88.7	67.1	21.6	1.2	9.9	0.9	2.0	7.0

Note: *n/a* = not applicable. Owing to rounding, percentage figures may not total 100.

[a] *Data not available from 1999 survey.*

[b] *"Political organization" and "work-related organization" categories were added to the 1992 survey, which showed that 11.7 percent of household contributors and 7.1 percent of estimated contributions were in the area of "other nonprofits."*

[c] *There were 99.6 million households in the United States as of March 1996, 95.7 million households in March 1992, 93.3 million households in March 1990, and 91.1 million households in March 1988. Based on the Current Population Reports.*

Source: *Hodgkinson, Weitzman, and the Gallup Organization, Giving and Receiving, various years.*

TABLE 3.12

Volunteers: Number, Hours, and Dollar Value, Selected Years, 1987–1998

	1987	1989	1991	1993	1995	1998
Civilian noninstitutional population eighteen years and older (millions)[a]	176.7	180.9	184.4	187.1	190.5	197.1
Percentage of population volunteering	45.3	54.4	51.1	47.7	48.8	55.5
Total number of volunteers (millions)	80.0	98.4	94.2	89.2	93.0	109.4
Assigned hourly wages for volunteers[b]	10.06	10.82	11.56	12.13	12.84	14.30
Average weekly hours per volunteer	4.7	4.0	4.2	4.2	4.2	3.5
Average annual hours per volunteer	244.4	208.0	217.6	218.4	218.4	182.0
Annual hours volunteered (billions)	19.6	20.5	20.5	19.5	20.3	19.9
Annual hours volunteered, excluding informal volunteering (billions)[c]	14.9	15.7	15.2	15.0	15.7	15.8
Full-time equivalent employment, excluding informal volunteering, at 1,700 hours per year per employee (millions)	8.8	9.2	9.0	8.8	9.2	9.3
Total assigned dollar value of volunteer time, excluding informal volunteering (billions of dollars)	149.9	169.9	175.7	182.0	201.6	225.9

[a] *Population as of March of the following year as reported by the U.S. Bureau of the Census in its* Statistical Abstract of the United States.

[b] *Based on the average hourly wage for nonagricultural workers in 1987, 1989, 1991, 1993, 1995, and 1998, as published in Council of Economic Advisers, 1999, and increased by 12 percent to estimate fringe benefits.*

[c] *Informal volunteering includes helping neighbors or organizations on an ad hoc basis (for example, baby-sitting for free or helping in school fairs).* Formal volunteering *involves regular work for an organization.*

Source: *Saxon-Harrold and others, 1999.*

- Females (61 percent) tend to volunteer more than males (49 percent).

- Adults between the ages of thirty-five and fifty-four represented the highest percentage of the population volunteering.

- Adults in household income brackets of $40,000 or more were more likely to volunteer than those with lower incomes (see Figure 3.11).

- College graduates, people who worked part-time, and married persons were more likely to volunteer than other respondents (see Table 3.14).

- The independent sector is the primary recipient of formal volunteering. In 1998, 70 percent of volunteer time was spent in the independent sector, 16 percent in the government sector, 10 percent in the for-profit sector, and 3 percent in other nonprofits (see Table 3.15).

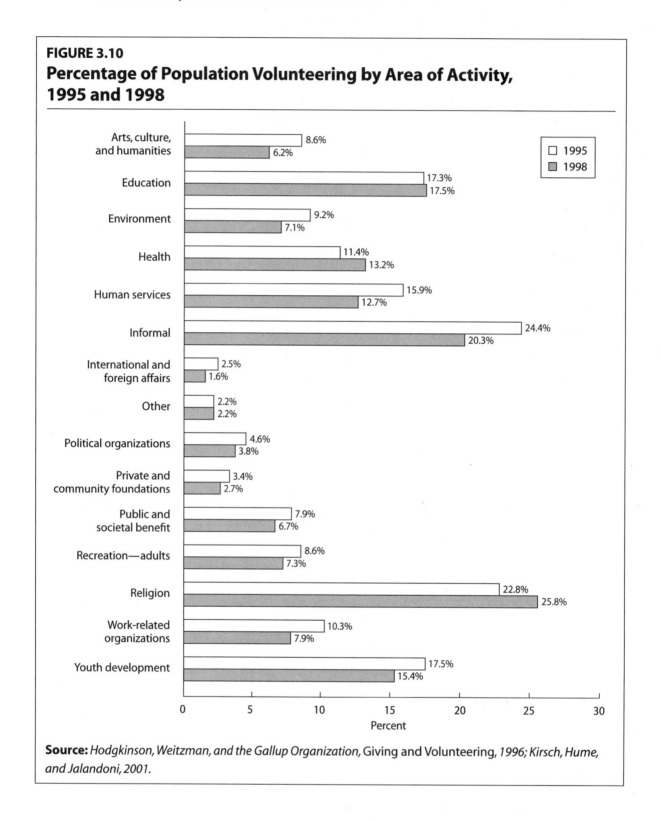

FIGURE 3.10

Percentage of Population Volunteering by Area of Activity, 1995 and 1998

Source: *Hodgkinson, Weitzman, and the Gallup Organization,* Giving and Volunteering, *1996; Kirsch, Hume, and Jalandoni, 2001.*

- Religious institutions benefited from 36 percent of all volunteer hours expended in 1998. Nearly 23 percent of the population volunteered for activities related to religion, the highest level among all activity areas studied. (See Table 3.15.)

TABLE 3.13

Percentage of Population Eighteen Years and Older Volunteering by Area of Activity, Selected Years, 1987–1998

	1987[a]	1989	1991	1993	1995	1998
Volunteers as a percentage of the population eighteen years and older	45.3	54.4	51.1	47.7	48.8	55.5
Area of volunteer activity						
Informal volunteering	18.8	25.7	23.4	17.2	20.3	24.4
Arts, culture, and humanities	4.3	7.3	6.2	4.4	6.2	8.6
Education	15.5	16.3	15.4	15.7	17.5	17.3
Environment	—	6.3	8.6	6.2	7.1	9.2
Health	—	11.9	12.9	10.8	13.2	11.4
Human services	—	14.0	12.1	9.8	12.7	15.9
International and foreign affairs	1.6	1.6	2.3	1.3	1.6	2.5
Other	—	2.5	2.7	2.5	2.2	2.2
Political organizations	4.8	4.9	4.7	3.7	3.8	4.6
Private and community foundations	—	2.3	2.3	2.2	2.7	3.4
Public and societal benefit	—	7.7	6.4	5.4	6.7	7.9
Recreation—adults	—	8.5	6.7	5.4	7.3	8.6
Religion	20.5	28.6	26.8	24.1	25.8	22.8
Work-related organizations	5.1	8.7	7.1	6.9	7.9	10.3
Youth development	—	15.8	14.7	11.7	15.4	17.5
Total	70.6	162.1	152.3	127.3	150.4	166.6

Note: *Respondents could report volunteering in more than one area. Owing to multiple responses, totals do not equal 100 percent. For 1987, information on some categories is not available because these categories were included as part of other categories in the survey.*

[a] *Many areas for 1987 are not comparable for later years.*

Source: *Hodgkinson, Weitzman, and the Gallup Organization,* Giving and Volunteering, *various years; Kirsch, Hume, and Jalandoni, 2001.*

Giving by Foundations

Foundations are classified into four groups: independent, operating, corporate, and community. They are defined as follows:

- Independent foundations are private, nonoperating, grant-making foundations (such as the Ford Foundation) and include family foundations (such as the Lilly Endowment or Annenberg Foundation). They are by far the largest group in terms of number, asset size, and grants made.

- Operating foundations are private foundations that use their resources primarily to conduct research or to provide direct services. (The J. Paul Getty Trust, which operates the Getty Museum in California, is an example.) Grants used by these foundations directly

TABLE 3.14

Percentage of Population Eighteen Years and Older Volunteering, Selected Characteristics and Years, 1988–1999

	March 1988		March 1990		March 1992		March 1994		May 1996		March 1999	
	Previous 12 Months	Previous Month	Previous 12 Months	Previous Month	Previous 12 Months	Previous Month	Previous 12 Months	Previous Month	Previous 12 Months	Previous Month	Previous 12 Months	Previous Month
Total	45	39	54	43	51	39	48	39	49	40	56	39
Gender												
Male	44	37	52	41	49	35	44	36	45	36	49	33
Female	47	41	56	45	53	42	51	42	52	44	62	44
Race												
White	48	41	57	45	53	40	51	41	52	43	59	41
Other than white[a]			37	29	41	29	28	25	36	26	45	34
African American	28	24	38	29	43	31	29	25	35	27	47	36
Hispanic[b]	27	23	36	30	38	29	32	28	40	32	46	29
Age												
18–24	42	35	43	32	48	29	45	33	38	26	46	29
25–34	45	38	62	49	53	41	46	38	51	42	55	41
35–44	54	48	64	52	61	48	55	47	55	46	67	49
45–54	48	41	56	44	56	42	54	43	55	47	63	45
55–64	47	40	51	41	49	37	47	39	48	41	50	34
65–74	40	33	47	30	42	32	43	36	45	36	47	33
75 or older	29	25	32	27	27	20	36	26	34	29	43	25
Income												
Under $10,000	23	20	30	22	32	21	34	25	35	25	42	21
$10,000–$19,999	40	34	42	32	38	29	37	28	34	27	42	28
$20,000–$29,999	50	43	56	44	51	37	53	41	45	35	44	28
$30,000–$39,999	51	43	64	48	56	42	56	52	46	37	54	38
$40,000–$49,999	44	38	67	57	67	51	55	47	53	44	68	52
$50,000–$74,999	57	52	63	50	61	48	61	54	60	50	65	50
$75,000–$99,999	50	43	62	52	63	53	58	45	65	57	64	50
$100,000 or more	62	53	74	58	74	54	68	53	69	59	71	47

Category										
Religion										
Catholic[c]	39	33	51	39	51	37	40	34	49	38
Protestant[c]	47	40	57	43	53	41	51	42	49	41
Other[c]	55	49	59	45	57	45	58	47	58	47
None[c]	29	22	41	28	37	23	35	22	40	32
Marital Status										
Married	50	43	59	47	56	44	52	44	56	47
Single	40	33	44	34	48	32	41	31	40	29
Divorced, separated, or widowed	34	29	47	37	36	24	40	32	41	33
Employment status										
Employed	49	43	60	47	59	45	52	44	52	43
Full-time employed	48	41	57	45	58	43	50	43	50	42
Part-time employed	54	48	42	60	61	50	61	47	58	49
Not employed	38	33	45	34	43	33	41	32	46	36
Retired	35	32	39	28	34	26	41	33	40	32
Education										
High school or less	34	29	42	32	38	27	37	28	36	28
Technical, trade school, or some college	56	49	66	46	62	45	53	43	54	44
College	64	54	74	59	77	60	67	61	71	61

Note: *The years shown are the years when the interviews were held.*

[a] *Not available for 1988. This category was not included in the survey.*

[b] *Persons of Hispanic origin may be of any race.*

[c] *Not available for 1999. This category was not included in the survey.*

Sources: *Hodgkinson, Weitzman, and the Gallup Organization, Giving and Receiving, 1996; Kirsch, Hume, and Jalandoni, 2001.*

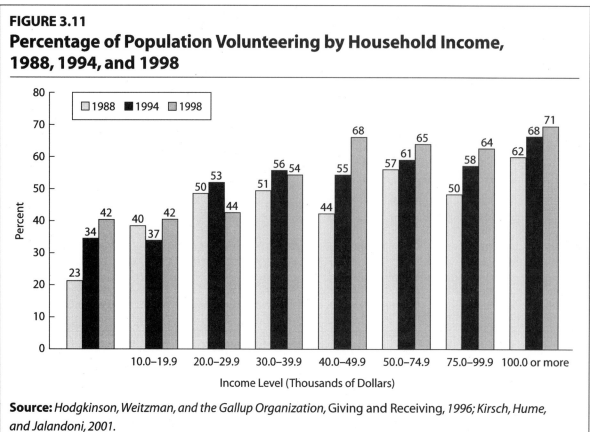

FIGURE 3.11

Percentage of Population Volunteering by Household Income, 1988, 1994, and 1998

Source: *Hodgkinson, Weitzman, and the Gallup Organization,* Giving and Receiving, *1996; Kirsch, Hume, and Jalandoni, 2001.*

support their programs. Both independent and operating foundations rely heavily on income endowed by an individual or a family.

- Corporate foundations are private foundations that maintain close ties with their parent companies, which are usually their primary funding sources. (Wal-Mart Foundation is an example.)

- Community foundations rely on contributions from a wide pool of donors; they are generally small in size and direct most of their grants to organizations in their local communities.

The Foundation Center's *Foundation Yearbook* provides detailed facts and figures on various aspects of foundation growth and giving. According to the Foundation Center's revised estimates, in 1998 giving by foundations reached $19.5 billion and accounted for close to 10 percent of all private giving. In contrast, giving by foundations only made up 5.8 percent of all private giving in 1980.

- The Foundation Center reports that there were 46,832 active foundations in the United States in 1998 (see Figure 3.12). This represents a 6.1 percent increase from 1997 and a 44.5 percent increase from 1990.

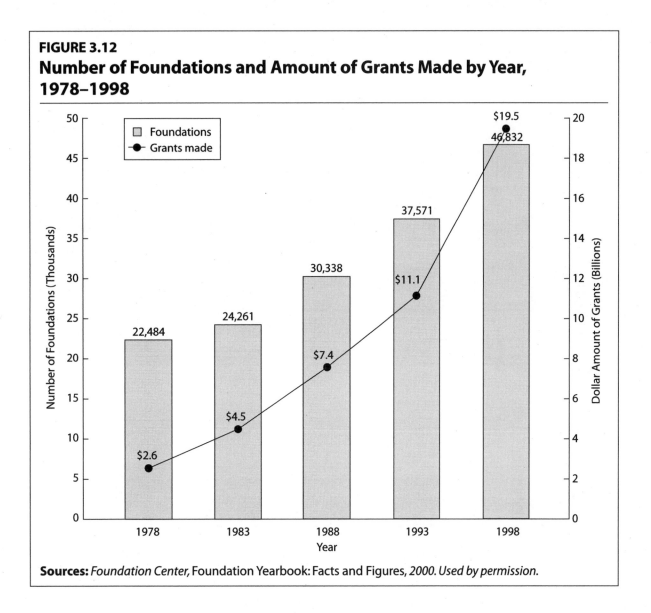

FIGURE 3.12

Number of Foundations and Amount of Grants Made by Year, 1978–1998

Sources: *Foundation Center,* Foundation Yearbook: Facts and Figures, *2000. Used by permission.*

- In 1998 total estimated foundation assets reached $385.1 billion, an increase of 16.7 percent from the previous year and a 170.0 percent (117.0 percent in inflation-adjusted dollars) increase from 1990. Between 1994 and 1998 foundation assets nearly doubled from $195.8 billion to $385.1 billion. (See Table 3.16.)

- Foundation giving totaled $19.5 billion in 1998, up 22 percent from 1997; the preliminary estimate for 1999 is $22.8 billion. Between 1990 and 1998 foundation grants increased by 124 percent (or 81 percent in constant 1997 dollars), closely mirroring the increase in foundation asset size. (See Table 3.16.)

- In 1998, 89.2 percent of all active foundations were independent foundations, 5.6 percent were operating foundations, 4.3 percent

TABLE 3.15

Distribution of Adult Volunteers by Area of Activity and Sector, Selected Years, 1988–1998

	Percentage of Population[a] (Percent)	All Sectors (Percent)	Nonprofit Sector — Independent Sector				Business Sector		Government Sector		
			All (Percent)	Religious Institutions (Percent)	Other Charitable Organizations (Percent)	Other Nonprofit Organizations (Percent)	For-Profit Organizations (Percent)	All (Percent)	Federal (Percent)	State (Percent)	Local (Percent)
Past Twelve Months from March 1999											
Arts, culture, and humanities	8.6	100.0	67.6	13.4	54.2	0.0	18.6	13.7	0.0	4.4	9.3
Education	17.3	100.0	50.7	22.8	27.9	0.0	5.9	43.4	0.0	3.0	40.4
Environment	9.2	100.0	73.5	10.0	63.5	0.0	7.6	18.2	3.2	2.8	12.2
Health	11.4	100.0	69.4	18.6	50.8	0.0	15.7	14.5	1.8	2.1	10.6
Human services	15.9	100.0	74.4	23.1	51.3	0.0	6.4	18.9	1.6	4.9	12.4
International and foreign affairs	2.5	100.0	70.0	28.4	41.6	0.0	10.8	15.9	8.9	4.4	2.6
Other	2.2	100.0	58.6	12.6	46.0	0.0	10.2	30.7	0.9	8.2	21.6
Political organizations	4.6	100.0	9.1	9.1	0.0	55.0	5.3	29.8	3.8	8.2	17.8
Private and community foundations	3.4	100.0	63.9	17.8	46.1	0.0	18.9	16.8	1.0	2.3	13.5
Public and societal benefit	7.9	100.0	70.1	10.0	60.1	0.0	5.0	24.9	0.0	1.3	23.6
Recreation—adults	8.6	100.0	63.9	21.2	42.7	0.0	10.4	25.5	1.2	0.4	23.9
Religion	22.8	100.0	94.2	87.9	6.3	0.0	2.8	3.0	0.6	0.8	1.6
Work-related organizations	10.3	100.0	7.7	7.7	0.0	41.9	34.4	15.7	1.7	3.4	10.6
Youth development	17.5	100.0	72.7	26.8	45.9	0.0	5.6	21.6	0.4	0.4	20.8
Types of organizations in which volunteers reported working	n/a	100.0	65.2	29.5	35.7	4.8	9.8	20.2	1.5	2.6	16.1
Distribution of volunteer hours	n/a	100.0	70.4	36.3	34.1	3.0	10.2	16.4	1.2	1.3	13.9
Assigned dollar value	n/a	225.9	159.0	82.0	77.0	6.8	23.0	37.0	2.7	2.9	31.4
Past Twelve Months from March 1996											
Types of organizations in which volunteers reported working	n/a	100.0	69.2	32.4	36.8	4.0	6.8	20.0	1.7	3.0	15.3
Distribution of volunteer hours	n/a	100.0	74.7	37.8	36.9	2.8	5.6	17.2	0.6	2.3	14.3
Assigned dollar value	n/a	201.5	150.5	76.2	74.4	5.6	11.3	34.7	1.2	4.6	28.8

Past Twelve Months from March 1992

Types of organizations in which volunteers reported working	n/a	100.1	62.1	28.9	33.2	3.9	7.5	26.6	2.3	2.8	21.5
Distribution of volunteer hours	n/a	100.0	65.9	33.5	32.4	2.2	6.5	25.3	1.7	2.5	21.1
Assigned dollar value	n/a	176.4	116.2	59.1	57.2	3.9	11.5	44.6	3.0	4.4	37.2

Past Twelve Months from March 1990

Types of organizations in which volunteers reported working	n/a	100.0	61.1	28.2	32.9	4.8	6.3	27.7	1.7	4.8	21.2
Distribution of volunteer hours	n/a	100.0	65.1	34.4	30.7	3.2	5.5	26.2	1.2	4.3	20.7
Assigned dollar value	n/a	167.8	109.3	57.8	51.5	5.4	9.3	43.9	2.0	7.1	34.7

Past Twelve Months from March 1988

Types of organizations in which volunteers reported working	n/a	100.0	62.4	26.9	35.5	4.1	4.6	28.9	2.5	4.5	21.9
Distribution of volunteer hours	n/a	100.0	72.0	45.3	26.6	1.7	3.6	22.7	1.4	3.3	18.1
Assigned dollar value	n/a	149.8	107.8	67.9	39.9	2.5	5.4	4.0	2.0	4.9	27.1

Note: Owing to rounding or nonresponse, percentage figures may not total 100.

[a] The civilian noninstitutional population of the United States eighteen years of age and older was approximately 197.7 million in March 1998, 190.5 million in March 1996, 184.4 million in March 1992, 180.9 million in March 1990, and 176.7 million in March 1988.

Sources: Hodgkinson, Weitzman, and the Gallup Organization, Giving and Receiving, 1996; Kirsch, Hume, and Jalandoni, 2001.

TABLE 3.16

Foundation Giving: Grants Made, Gifts Received, and Assets, 1975–1998

Year	Grant-Making Foundations		Grants Made[a]		Gifts Received		Assets[b]	
	Number	1975 = 100	Amount (Billions of Dollars)	1975 = 100	Amount (Billions of Dollars)	1978 = 100	Amount (Billions of Dollars)	1975 = 100
1975	21,887	100.0	1.94	100.0			30.13	100.0
1976	21,447	98.0	2.23	114.9			34.78	115.4
1977	22,152	101.2	2.35	121.1			35.37	117.4
1978	22,484	102.7	2.55	131.4	1.61	100.0	37.27	123.7
1979	22,535	103.0	2.85	146.9	2.21	137.3	41.59	138.0
1980	22,088	100.9	3.43	176.8	1.98	123.0	48.17	159.9
1981	21,967	100.4	3.79	195.4	2.39	148.4	47.57	157.9
1982	23,770	108.6	4.49	231.4	4.00	248.4	58.67	194.7
1983	24,261	110.8	4.48	230.9	2.71	168.3	67.87	225.3
1984	24,859	113.6	5.04	259.8	3.36	208.7	74.05	245.8
1985	25,639	117.1	6.03	310.8	4.73	293.8	102.06	338.7
1986								
1987	27,661	126.4	6.66	343.3	4.96	308.1	115.44	383.1
1988	30,338	138.7	7.42	382.5	5.16	320.5	122.08	405.2
1989	31,990	146.2	7.91	407.7	5.52	342.9	137.54	456.5
1990	32,401	148.1	8.68	447.4	4.97	308.7	142.48	472.9
1991	33,356	152.5	9.21	474.7	5.47	339.8	162.91	540.7
1992	35,765	163.4	10.21	526.3	6.18	383.9	176.82	586.9
1993	37,571	171.7	11.11	572.7	7.76	482.0	189.21	628.0
1994	38,807	177.4	11.29	582.0	8.08	501.9	195.79	649.8
1995	40,140	183.5	12.26	632.0	10.26	637.3	226.74	752.5
1996	41,588	190.0	13.84	713.4	16.02	995.0	267.58	888.1
1997	44,146	201.8	15.99	824.2	15.83	983.2	329.91	1,095.0
1998	46,832	214.0	19.46	1,003.1	22.57	1,401.9	385.05	1,278.0

[a] Grants made *include grants, scholarships, employee matching gifts, and other amounts separated as "grants and contributions paid during the year" on Form 990-PF.*

[b] *Figures represent the market value of assets.*

Source: *Foundation Center,* Foundation Yearbook: Facts and Figures, *2000. Used by permission.*

were corporate foundations, and less than 1 percent were community foundations (see Figure 3.13 and Table 3.17).

- Independent foundations held 84.9 percent of total assets in 1998, followed by community foundations (with 6.0 percent), operating foundations (with 5.7 percent), and corporate foundations (with 3.4 percent; see Figure 3.13 and Table 3.17).

- In 1998 independent foundations accounted for 76.8 percent of all grants; corporate foundations, 12.6 percent; community foundations, 7.5 percent; and operating foundations, 3.2 percent (see Figure 3.13 and Table 3.17).

FIGURE 3.13

Distribution of Foundation Types by Number, Assets, and Grants Made, 1998

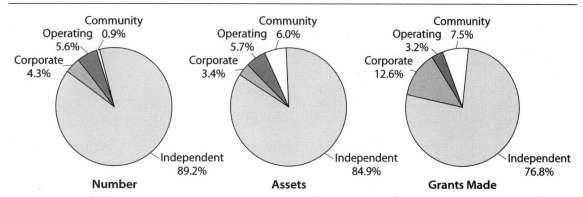

Sources: *Foundation Center,* Foundation Giving: Yearbook, *various years; Foundation Center,* Foundation Growth, *2000. Used by permission.*

- Data also indicate that a very small number of foundations (190 in 1998) held 52 percent of total foundation assets (close to $200 billion) and distributed 37 percent of total grants (see Table 3.18).

- The years between 1990 and 1998 saw the greatest increase in the number of large foundations (those with assets of $1 million or more) established. On average, 433 large foundations were founded annually between 1980 and 1989. From 1990 through 1998, 5,421 large foundations were created, for an average of 602 each year. A majority of these new foundations were independent foundations. (See Table 3.19.)

- Over 80 percent of the total amount given out by foundations in 1998 was directed to five major areas: education (24.4 percent), health (16.5 percent), human services (15.0 percent), arts and culture (14.8 percent), and public and societal benefit (11.8 percent). Human services and education received the largest number of grants. In recent years this pattern has remained fairly consistent. (See Table 3.20.)

Giving by Corporations

Corporate contributions constitute the third major source of funds for private giving. These contributions are made either directly by the company or separately through incorporated company-sponsored foundations. Corporations may also provide cash or in-kind contributions that often do not

TABLE 3.17

Foundation Giving: Number, Assets, Gifts Received, and Grants Made by Type of Foundation, 1994–1998

	Foundations		Grants Made[a]		Gifts Received		Assets[b]	
	Number	Percent	Amount (Millions)	Percent	Amount (Millions)	Percent	Amount (Millions)	Percent
1994								
Independent	34,319	88.4	8,840	78.3	4,861	60.1	167,230	85.4
Corporate	1,951	5.0	1,626	14.4	1,746	21.6	7,256	3.7
Operating	2,134	5.5	172	1.5	464	5.7	11,235	5.7
Community	403	1.0	653	5.8	1,011	12.5	10,071	5.2
Total	38,807	100.0	11,291	100.0	8,082	100.0	195,792	100.0
1995								
Independent	35,602	88.7	9,419	76.8	5,490	53.5	191,700	84.5
Corporate	1,946	4.8	1,699	13.9	1,772	17.3	8,687	3.8
Operating	2,179	5.4	339	2.8	1,657	16.2	13,965	6.2
Community	413	1.0	806	6.6	1,341	13.1	12,383	5.5
Total	40,140	100.0	12,262	100.0	10,260	100.0	226,735	100.0
1996								
Independent	36,885	88.7	10,714	77.4	11,375	71.0	226,574	84.7
Corporate	1,969	4.7	1,836	13.3	2,150	13.4	9,459	3.5
Operating	2,323	5.6	334	2.4	665	4.1	15,690	5.9
Community	411	1.0	951	6.9	1,830	11.4	15,858	5.9
Total	41,588	100.0	13,836	100.0	16,019	100.0	267,582	100.0
1997								
Independent	39,248	88.9	12,375	77.4	11,013	69.6	282,618	85.7
Corporate	2,029	4.6	2,066	12.9	1,872	11.8	10,887	3.3
Operating	2,466	5.6	351	2.2	724	4.6	16,705	5.1
Community	403	0.9	1,192	7.4	2,224	14.0	19,700	6.0
Total	44,146	100.0	15,985	100.0	15,833	100.0	329,910	100.0
1998								
Independent	41,751	89.2	14,934	76.8	16,270	72.1	326,949	84.9
Corporate	2,022	4.3	2,446	12.6	2,654	11.8	13,109	3.4
Operating	2,622	5.6	619	3.2	1,067	4.7	22,039	5.7
Community	437	0.9	1,458	7.5	2,582	11.4	22,955	6.0
Total	46,832	100.0	19,457	100.0	22,573	100.0	385,052	100.0

Note: *Owing to rounding, the sum of individual items may not equal column totals.*

[a] Grants made *include grants, scholarships, and employee matching gifts. They do not include program-related investments (such as loans, loan guarantees, equity investments, and other investments made by foundations to organizations to forward their charitable purposes), set-asides, or program expenses.*
[b] *Figures represent the market value of assets.*

Sources: *Foundation Center,* Foundation Giving: Yearbook, *various years; Foundation Center,* Foundation Growth, *2000. Used by permission.*

get reported as charitable contributions. Figures for corporate foundation giving are compiled by the Foundation Center, and additional information is gathered through surveys conducted by The Conference Board and the Chronicle of Philanthropy, which reports on contributions of some of the largest U.S. corporations. Total corporate giving estimates prepared by AAFRC Trust for Philanthropy are based on itemized corporate deductions reported to the IRS, factoring in gifts to corporate foundations.

TABLE 3.18

Foundation Giving: Grants by Foundation Asset Size, 1996–1998

	Foundations		Grants Made[a]		Assets[b]	
	Number	**Percent**	**Amount (Thousands)**	**Percent**	**Amount (Thousands)**	**Percent**
1996						
$250 million or more	135	0.3	5,158,351	37.3	135,509,743	50.6
$50 million–$249.9 million	510	1.2	2,459,875	17.8	52,230,368	19.5
$10 million–$49.9 million	1,985	4.8	2,571,899	18.6	41,271,415	15.4
$1 million–$9.9 million	10,152	24.4	2,367,921	17.1	31,451,229	11.8
Under $1 million	28,806	69.3	1,277,965	9.2	7,119,215	2.7
Total	41,588	100.0	13,836,010	100.0	267,581,971	100.0
1997						
$250 million or more	165	0.4	5,743,315	35.9	170,727,622	51.7
$50 million–$249.9 million	612	1.4	2,999,328	18.8	62,674,836	19.0
$10 million–$49.9 million	2,439	5.5	3,130,555	19.6	51,458,983	15.6
$1 million–$9.9 million	11,879	26.9	2,692,226	16.8	37,479,379	11.4
Under $1 million	29,051	65.8	1,420,007	8.9	7,569,477	2.3
Total	44,146	100.0	15,985,431	100.0	329,910,297	100.0
1998						
$250 million or more	190	0.4	7,278,648	37.4	199,760,919	51.9
$50 million–$249.9 million	721	1.5	3,773,342	19.4	74,212,287	19.3
$10 million–$49.9 million	2,820	6.0	3,612,298	18.6	59,492,925	15.5
$1 million–$9.9 million	13,853	29.6	3,183,919	16.4	43,602,991	11.3
Under $1 million	29,248	62.5	1,608,627	8.3	7,982,576	2.1
Total	46,832	100.0	19,456,832	100.0	385,051,697	100.0

Note: *Owing to rounding, the sum of individual items may not equal column totals.*

[a] Grants made *include grants, scholarships, and employee matching gifts. They do not include program-related investments (such as loans, loan guarantees, equity investments, and other investments made by foundations to organizations to forward their charitable purposes), set-asides, or program expenses.*
[b] *Figures represent the market value of assets.*

Sources: *Foundation Center,* Foundation Giving: Yearbook, *1998, 1999; Foundation Center,* Foundation Yearbook: Facts and Figures, *2000. Used by permission.*

- AAFRC Trust for Philanthropy estimated that total corporate giving (both by corporations and their foundations) in 1998 reached $8.9 billion (see Table 3.3). (Nonmonetary forms of support, which may include advertising, marketing, or public relations assistance, are excluded from this amount.)

- According to Foundation Center data, corporate foundation giving increased from $1.6 billion in 1994 to over $2.4 billion in 1998, even as the number of corporate foundations remained fairly stable at about 2,000. This represents a 50 percent increase over a four-year period (Foundation Center, *Foundation Giving: Yearbook,* various years; Foundation Center, *Foundation Growth,* 2000).

- Corporate giving as a percentage of corporate pretax income has hovered at about 1 percent in recent years according to data compiled by both AAFRC and The Conference Board (see Table 3.21).

TABLE 3.19

Number of Larger Foundations Created by Year, Through 1998

Decade Created	All		Independent		Corporate		Community		Operating	
	Num-ber	Annual Average	Num-ber	Annual Average	Num-ber	Annual Average	Num-ber	Annual Average	Num-ber	Annual Average
Before 1900	103		87		0		0		16	
1900–1909	26	3	22	2	0		0		4	
1910–1919	81	8	58	6	1		16	2	6	1
1920–1929	166	17	136	14	3		19	2	8	1
1930–1939	217	22	197	20	8	1	3		9	1
1940–1949	854	85	748	75	62	6	23	2	21	2
1950–1959	2,121	212	1,751	175	309	31	31	3	30	3
1960–1969	2,069	207	1,811	181	168	17	45	5	45	5
1970–1979	1,269	127	1,066	107	104	10	67	7	32	3
1980–1989	4,332	433	3,795	380	312	31	104	10	121	12
1990–1998[a]	5,421	602	4,912	546	238	26	75	8	196	22
Data not available	514		470		13		9		22	
Total	17,173		15,053		1,218		392		510	

Note: *Data included are for foundations with at least $1 million in assets or making grants of $100,000 or more in 1997–1998. Annual averages are not available for some years. Owing to rounding, the sum of individual items may not equal column totals.*

[a] *Data are incomplete for the period 1994–1998.*

Source: *Foundation Center,* Foundation Yearbook: Facts and Figures, *2000. Used by permission.*

TABLE 3.20

Foundation Giving: Number and Value of Grants by NTEE Major Categories, 1995–1998

	Number of Grants		Dollar Value of Grants		Average Dollar Value of Grants
	Number	Percent	Amount (Thousands)	Percent	
1995					
Arts and culture	10,730	14.5	758,686	12.0	71
Education	15,340	20.8	1,583,603	25.1	103
Environment and animals	4,068	5.5	314,155	5.0	77
Health	9,393	12.7	1,095,533	17.3	117
Human services	17,146	23.2	1,040,427	16.5	61
International and foreign affairs	2,197	3.0	220,119	3.5	100
Public and societal benefit	8,984	12.2	731,836	11.6	81
Science and social science	3,550	4.8	438,141	6.9	123
Religion	2,228	3.0	125,633	2.0	56
Other	127	0.2	9,740	0.2	77
Total	73,763	100.0	6,317,874	100.0	86
1996					
Arts and culture	11,137	14.2	899,932	12.4	81
Education	16,358	20.9	1,852,445	25.4	113
Environment and animals	4,404	5.6	393,676	5.4	89
Health	10,420	13.3	1,179,670	16.2	113
Human services	18,036	23.0	1,261,853	17.3	70
International and foreign affairs	2,468	3.2	235,439	3.2	95
Public and societal benefit	9,509	12.1	847,226	11.6	89
Science and social science	3,555	4.5	440,292	6.0	124
Religion	2,317	3.0	160,433	2.2	69
Other	92	0.1	8,200	0.1	89
Total	78,296	100.0	7,279,164	100.0	93
1997					
Arts and culture	12,424	14.4	1,012,847	12.7	82
Education	18,285	21.2	1,901,764	23.8	104
Environment and animals	4,992	5.8	414,258	5.2	83
Health	11,366	13.2	1,324,413	16.6	117
Human services	19,630	22.8	1,226,661	15.3	62
International and foreign affairs	2,720	3.2	300,363	3.8	110
Public and societal benefit	10,176	11.8	970,110	12.1	95
Science and social science	4,043	4.7	626,865	7.8	155
Religion	2,454	2.8	158,074	2.0	64
Other	113	0.1	9,302	0.1	82
Total	86,203	100.0	7,994,658	99.4	93
1998					
Arts and culture	14,105	14.5	1,439,157	14.8	102
Education	20,080	20.7	2,366,631	24.4	118
Environment and animals	5,871	6.0	539,774	5.6	92
Health	11,816	12.2	1,602,137	16.5	136
Human services	22,923	23.6	1,455,932	15.0	64
International and foreign affairs	2,918	3.0	313,485	3.2	107
Public and societal benefit	12,076	12.4	1,149,085	11.8	95
Science and social science	4,139	4.2	612,723	6.3	148
Religion	3,153	3.2	220,536	2.3	70
Other	139	0.1	11,933	0.1	86
Total	97,220	100.0	9,711,395	100.0	100

Note: *Owing to rounding, the sum of individual items may not equal column totals.*

Source: *Foundation Center,* Foundation Giving Trends, *2000. Used by permission.*

TABLE 3.21

Median Corporate Contributions as a Percentage of U.S. Pretax Income, by Industry, 1997–1998

			Contributions	
	Number of Reporting Companies	Total U.S. Pretax Income (Thousands)	Amount (Thousands)	As a Percentage of Pretax Income
1997				
Chemicals and allied products	10	340,000	2,863	0.8
Computers and office equipment	6	1,257,500	23,247	1.8
Food, beverage, and tobacco	7	387,700	26,706	6.9
Paper and allied products	6	166,130	2,751	1.7
Petroleum, gas, and mining	11	1,108,000	6,058	0.5
Other manufacturing[a]	38	395,537	8,777	2.2
Total manufacturing	78	409,850	6,019	1.5
Banking	12	444,142	5,808	1.3
Insurance	22	181,860	950	0.5
Retail and wholesale trade	5	308,000	6,067	2.0
Utilities	18	468,093	2,866	0.6
Other services[b]	12	770,750	5,748	0.7
Total nonmanufacturing	69	300,000	2,311	0.8
Total all companies	147	335,000	3,483	1.0
1998				
Chemicals and allied products	5	614,100	4,453	0.7
Computers and office equipment	4	676,000	26,067	3.9
Petroleum, gas, and mining	5	728,000	24,448	3.4
Other manufacturing[b]	23	485,100	11,094	2.3
Total manufacturing	37	533,800	12,189	2.3
Banking	7	919,000	10,788	1.2
Insurance	17	230,000	1,271	0.6
Utilities	9	369,752	2,123	0.6
Other services[b]	8	594,900	9,698	1.6
Total nonmanufacturing	41	352,900	2,435	0.7
Total all companies	78	485,550	4,192	0.9

Note: *Figures in this table were derived from a sample of U.S. corporations weighted toward larger companies. Figures are median numbers, and totals are not sums of industry numbers. Companies with income losses are excluded from this table.*

[a] *Includes aerospace and defense; architecture; electrical equipment; furniture; footwear; industrial and commercial equipment; metals; nontire rubber products; pharmaceuticals; printing, publishing, and media; scientific, photographic, and control equipment; soaps and cosmetics; transportation equipment; diversified manufacturing; food, beverage, and tobacco; and paper and allied products.*
[b] *Includes construction; finance; health care; package delivery; rail transportation; service management; telecommunications; and retail and wholesale trade.*

Source: *The Conference Board, 1997, 1998. Used by permission.*

References

AAFRC Trust for Philanthropy. *Giving USA.* (Various editions.) New York: AAFRC Trust for Philanthropy, various years.

The Conference Board. *Annual Survey of Corporate Contributions.* (Various editions.) New York: The Conference Board, various years.

Council of Economic Advisers, Office of the President. *Economic Report of the President.* Washington, D.C.: U.S. Government Printing Office, various years.

Foundation Center. *Foundation Growth and Giving Estimates: 1999 Preview.* New York: Foundation Center, 2000.

Foundation Center. *Foundation Giving Trends: Update on Funding Priorities.* New York: Foundation Center, 2000.

Foundation Center. *Foundation Giving: Yearbook of Facts and Figures on Private, Corporate and Community Foundations.* (Various editions.) New York: Foundation Center, various years.

Foundation Center. *Foundation Yearbook: Facts and Figures on Private and Community Foundations.* New York: Foundation Center, 2000.

Hodgkinson, V. A., Weitzman, M. S., and the Gallup Organization. *Giving and Volunteering in the United States.* (Various editions.) Washington, D.C.: INDEPENDENT SECTOR, various years.

Hodgkinson, V. A., and Weitzman, M. S. *Nonprofit Almanac: Dimensions of the Independent Sector.* (Various editions.) San Francisco: Jossey-Bass, various years.

Internal Revenue Service. *Statistics of Income Bulletin.* (Various editions.) Washington, D.C.: U.S. Government Printing Office, various years.

Internal Revenue Service. *Statistics of Income—Individual Income Tax Returns.* (Various editions.) Washington, D.C.: U.S. Government Printing Office, various years.

Kirsch, A. D., Hume, K., and Jalandoni, N. T. *Giving and Volunteering in the United States: Findings from a National Survey.* (1999 edition.) Washington, D.C.: INDEPENDENT SECTOR, 2001.

Saxon-Harrold, S.K.E., and others. *Giving and Volunteering in the United States, 1999—Executive Summary.* Washington, D.C.: INDEPENDENT SECTOR, 1999.

U.S. Bureau of the Census. *Statistical Abstract of the United States.* (119th ed.) Washington, D.C.: U.S. Government Printing Office, 1999.

Chapter 4

The Financial Trends and Condition of the Independent Sector

THIS CHAPTER REVIEWS the financial condition of the independent sector and its major subsectors. Estimates in this chapter cover 501(c)(3) public charities, religious organizations, and private foundations and 501(c)(4) organizations. As in previous editions of the *Nonprofit Almanac*, these estimates were developed from a variety of public and private sources, including U.S. Bureau of the Census (various years), U.S. Department of Labor (various years), U.S. Department of Commerce (various years), American Hospital Association (various years), and U.S. Department of Education (various years). In an effort to assemble a reasonable and consistent portrait of the sector from these various sources, a circular schematic that frames the independent sector's activities, outputs, expenditures, and other elements has been used as a guide (see Figure B.2 in Resource B). The estimates outlined in Chapter Four differ from those presented in Chapter Five, which are based solely on figures reported by 501(c)(3) organizations to the IRS on Form 990. Data in Chapter Five were processed by the National Center for Charitable Statistics in conjunction with INDEPENDENT SECTOR. Owing to the difference in data sources, and also because 501(c)(3) organizations are but one component of the independent sector, numbers and percentages will differ between the two chapters. Overall, the distribution patterns of sources and disposition of revenue are similar between the two chapters, confirming the prevailing financial trends of the independent sector and its subsectors.

In brief, the key financial trends in the independent sector are the following:

- Total annual revenue for the independent sector in 1997 was estimated at $665 billion. Nearly 90 percent of all funds came from three main sources: private payments in the form of dues and fees for services (38 percent); government grants and contracts (31 percent);

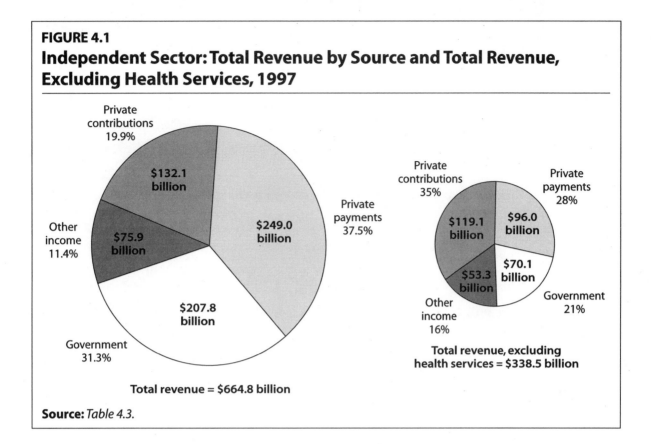

FIGURE 4.1

Independent Sector: Total Revenue by Source and Total Revenue, Excluding Health Services, 1997

Private contributions 19.9%

$132.1 billion

Other income 11.4%

$75.9 billion

Private payments 37.5%

$249.0 billion

$207.8 billion

Government 31.3%

Total revenue = $664.8 billion

Private contributions 35%

$119.1 billion

Private payments 28%

$96.0 billion

$53.3 billion

$70.1 billion

Other income 16%

Government 21%

Total revenue, excluding health services = $338.5 billion

Source: *Table 4.3.*

and private contributions (20 percent). The remainder (11 percent) came from other sources, including income from assets and investments. (See Figure 4.1.)

- There are wide variations in funding trends among the subsectors, with individual subsectors more heavily dependent on one source of income than others. Religion and the arts are more reliant on private charitable contributions than the other subsectors are, whereas social and legal services are heavily dependent on funding from government sources. Education obtains over half of its total revenue from private payments received for dues and services.

- The health services subsector continues to receive the largest share of total revenue (49 percent), with estimated total funds of $326 billion. In constant 1997 dollars this represented a 9 percent increase from its 1992 revenue of $299 billion.

- Although the education and research subsector had the second largest share of total revenue in 1997 ($119 billion), its share decreased considerably from 25 percent in 1977 to 18 percent in 1997.

- Social and legal services had revenue of $76.9 billion in 1997. Its share of total revenue of the entire independent sector grew from 9 percent in 1977 to 12 percent in 1997.

- Total revenue for religious organizations in 1997 was $76.3 billion, with 95 percent of it coming from private contributions.

- Revenue of the arts and culture subsector nearly doubled from $8.2 billion in 1992 to $15.4 billion in 1997. Private contributions generally make up 40 percent or more of its annual revenue. It had 2.3 percent of the independent sector's total revenue.

Trends in Total Revenue for the Independent Sector

The independent sector, which is composed largely of 501(c)(3) public charities and 501(c)(4) organizations, is unique in that it relies on a variety of revenue streams to finance its operations rather than on any single major source, as do the business (for-profit) and government sectors. Business entities depend largely on the sale of goods and services to customers to cover their operating costs, and government relies primarily on taxes to meet its obligations. The independent sector generates revenue from payments received for dues and for services it provides; from government payments and private contributions from individuals, corporations, and foundations; and from income generated by its assets and investments.

Tables 4.1–4.5 summarize the major trends in revenue from various sources and in the distribution of funds for the independent sector and its subsectors for the period 1977 to 1997.

- In 1997 total annual revenue for the independent sector was estimated at $665 billion (see Table 4.1). The major sources of funds for the independent sector in 1997 were private payments in the form of dues, fees, and charges (38 percent); government payments in the form of grants or contracts (31 percent); and private contributions from all sources (20 percent). Together these three sources of funds represented 89 percent of total annual funds. Other forms of revenue accounted for 11 percent of total annual funds. During the twenty years since 1977, the share of funds received from the government rose and private payments inched up, but estimates indicate that private payments are back to 1977 levels. (See Figure 4.2.)

- Between 1987 and 1992 total revenue for the sector experienced a remarkable annual growth rate of 7.2 percent. For the following five-year period covering 1992 to 1997, the annual rate of change in total revenue declined to 2.7 percent. (See Figure 4.3.)

- This change is partly explained by changes in government policy and funding to the sector. Figures indicate that the annual rate of change in payments received from government sources was correspondingly high between 1987 and 1992 (9.6 percent), largely caused by the expansion of coverage in Medicare and Medicaid payments in health services. However, between 1992 and 1997 the rate of change slowed to 2.6 percent, accompanying changes in policy and restrictions introduced on Medicare and Medicaid payments. (See Figure 4.3.)

- Changes in the annual rate of private payments received from dues and fees for services also dropped from 6.2 percent between 1987 and 1992 to 1.8 percent between 1992 and 1997 (see Figure 4.3). Increased competition from for-profit firms offering services traditionally provided by nonprofit organizations (such as hospitals, health clinics, and child day-care centers) may account for much of this change.

- Economic conditions and tax policy changes have influenced variations in the annual rate of change for private contributions. A strong economy, low inflation rate, and changes in tax laws in 1981 contributed to the high rate of change of 6.4 percent for private contributions between 1982 and 1987. Changes to tax laws in 1981 allowed nonitemizers to deduct percentages of their charitable contributions until 1986, when they could deduct the entire amount. This encouraged tax filers to bunch their charitable deductions in 1986 in order to take advantage of the opportunity to maximize their deductions. This provision was eliminated for 1987, contributing partly to a slower rate of change for private contributions (2.6 percent) between 1987 and 1992. Another factor contributing to the slowdown was the ensuing economic recession of the early 1990s. The annual rate of change for private contributions improved to 4.3 percent between 1992 and 1997, fueled by a strong economy and major gains in the stock market, which boosted individual and foundation giving. The booming technology industry produced a new set of multimillionaire philanthropists.

- The distribution of total revenue among the different subsectors varies widely. In 1997 the health services subsector had the largest share of annual revenue (49.0 percent), followed by the education and research subsector (18.0 percent). Together these two subsectors had 67.0 percent of total revenue in the independent sector. The social and legal services subsector received 11.5 percent of total revenue, and the religious organizations subsector had 11.5 percent.

TABLE 4.1

Independent Sector: Revenue and Current Operating Expenditures, Selected Years, 1977–1997

Year	Total Revenue[a]		Private Contributions		Private Payments		Government Sector		Other Income		Current Operating Expenditures	Wages and Salaries[a]	
	Amount (Billions of Dollars)	Percent	Amount (Billions of Dollars)	Percent	Amount (Billions of Dollars)	Percent	Amount (Billions of Dollars)	Percent	Amount (Billions of Dollars)	Percent	Amount (Billions of Dollars)	Amount (Billions of Dollars)	Percentage of Current Operating Expenditures
Including health services													
1977	111.1	100.0	29.2	26.3	41.7	37.5	29.5	26.6	10.7	9.6	91.1	46.7	51.3
1982	211.9	100.0	46.2	21.8	82.1	38.7	59.5	28.1	24.1	11.4	172.3	80.7	46.8
1987	316.7	100.0	72.6	22.9	129.2	40.8	88.5	27.9	26.4	8.4	272.7	116.0	42.5
1992	508.5	100.0	93.7	18.4	198.7	39.1	159.4	31.3	56.8	11.2	435.8	184.2	42.3
1997	664.8	100.0	132.1	19.9	249	37.5	207.8	31.3	75.9	11.4	551.6	244.1	44.3
Excluding health services													
1977	59.8	100.0	25.2	42.1	16.5	27.6	12.9	21.6	5.2	8.7	47.8	23.7	49.6
1982	107.1	100.0	40.0	37.3	30.6	28.6	23.0	21.5	13.5	12.6	83.7	36.3	43.4
1987	165.5	100.0	64.5	39.0	50.9	30.8	33.7	20.4	16.4	9.9	135.5	54.5	40.2
1992	247.2	100.0	84.4	34.1	72.5	29.3	53.0	21.4	37.4	15.1	198.2	77.8	39.3
1997	338.5	100.0	119.1	35.2	96	28.4	70.1	20.7	53.3	15.7	254.3	110.1	43.3

[a] Does not include the assigned value of volunteers. The difference between total revenue and total current operating expenditures is accounted for by grants, payments to affiliates, and excess and deficit for the year.

Sources: Detailed sources for revenue figures are listed in Table 4.2. Wages and salaries are based on U.S. Bureau of the Census, various years; U.S. Department of Labor, various years.

FIGURE 4.2

Independent Sector: Total Revenue by Source, 1977–1997

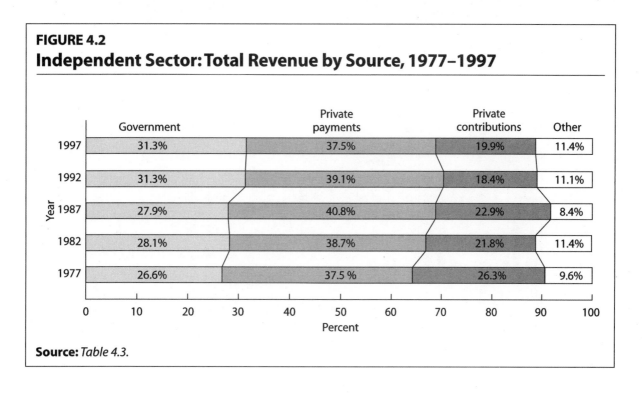

Source: *Table 4.3.*

FIGURE 4.3

Independent Sector: Annual Rates of Change for Selected Financial Items, 1977–1997

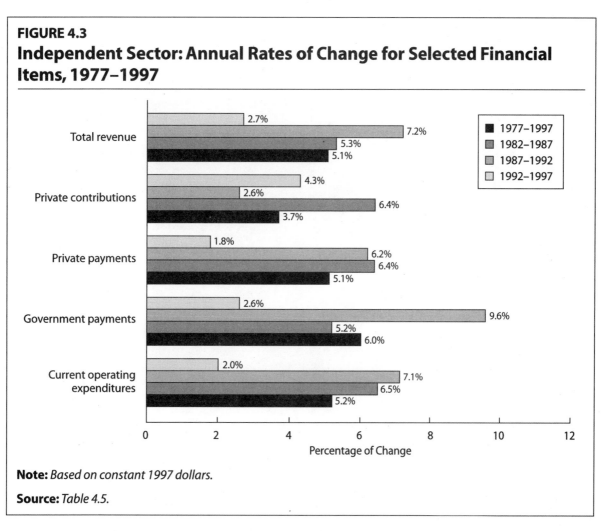

Note: *Based on constant 1997 dollars.*

Source: *Table 4.5.*

TABLE 4.2

Independent Sector: Sources of Revenue and Distribution of Funds by Subsector, Selected Years, 1977–1997

	Total Revenue[a] (Billions)	Private Contributions Subtotal (Billions)	Source of Revenue Payments Private Sector (Billions)	Government Sector (Billions)	Subtotal (Billions)	Other Receipts Endowment, Investment Income, and Other (Billions)	Church (Billions)	Subtotal (Billions)	Distribution of Funds Current Operating Expenditures[b] (Billions)	Construction, Capital Improvements, and Other (Billions)
	(1)	(2)	(3)	(4)	(5)	(6)	(7)	(8)	(9)	(10)
1977										
Health services	51.3	4.0	25.2	16.6	41.8	2.1	3.4	5.5	43.3	8.0
Education and research	27.4	2.4	14.5	5.0	19.5	3.8	1.7	5.5	23.7	3.7
Religious organizations[c]	13.6	17.0	—	—	0.0	1.9	(5.3)	(3.4)	9.6	4.0
Social and legal services	10.3	3.3	1.0	5.6	6.6	0.3	0.1	0.4	8.5	1.8
Civic, social, and fraternal organizations	4.2	1.2	0.5	2.1	2.6	0.3	0.1	0.4	4.0	0.2
Arts and culture	1.7	0.7	0.5	0.2	0.7	0.3	—	0.3	1.5	0.2
Foundations[d]	2.6	(1.9)	2.5	—	2.5	2.0	—	2.0	0.5	2.1
Total revenue	111.1	29.2	41.7	29.5	71.2	10.7	0.0	10.7	91.1	20.0
Percentage	100.0	26.3	37.5	26.6	64.1	9.6	0.0	9.6	82.0	18.0
1982										
Health services	104.8	6.2	51.5	36.5	88.0	5.0	5.6	10.6	88.6	16.2
Education and research	47.7	4.0	25.3	8.1	33.4	7.3	3.0	10.3	40.5	7.2
Religious organizations[c]	22.4	28.1	—	—	0.0	3.2	(8.9)	(5.7)	16.0	6.4
Social and legal services	20.4	5.1	3.1	11.2	14.3	0.8	0.2	1.0	16.9	3.5
Civic, social, and fraternal organizations	5.8	1.7	0.8	2.9	3.7	0.3	0.1	0.4	5.6	0.2
Arts and culture	4.8	1.9	1.4	0.8	2.2	0.7	—	0.7	3.3	1.5
Foundations[d]	6.0	(3.0)	2.2	—	2.2	6.8	—	6.8	1.4	4.6
Total revenue	211.9	46.2	82.1	59.5	141.6	24.1	0.0	24.1	172.3	39.6
Percentage	100.0	21.8	38.7	28.1	66.8	10.8	0.0	11.4	81.3	17.7
1987										
Health services	151.2	8.1	78.3	54.8	133.1	4.5	5.5	10.0	137.2	14.0
Education and research	70.0	9.1	38.7	12.8	51.5	5.9	3.5	9.4	62.3	7.7
Religious organizations[c]	41.9	43.6	3.1	—	3.1	4.7	(9.5)	(4.8)	29.9	12.0
Social and legal services	32.2	8.0	6.1	15.5	21.6	2.3	0.3	2.6	27.5	4.7
Civic, social, and fraternal organizations	9.4	3.1	1.2	4.5	5.7	0.5	0.1	0.6	8.6	0.8

	Column 1	Column 2	Column 3	Column 4	Column 5	Column 6	Column 7	Column 8	Column 9	Column 10
Arts and culture	6.0	2.4	1.8	0.9	2.7	0.8	0.1	0.9	5.2	0.8
Foundations[d]	6.0	(5.5)	3.8	—	3.8	7.7	—	7.7	2.0	4.0
Total revenue	316.7	72.6	129.2	88.5	217.7	26.4	0.0	26.4	272.7	44.0
Percentage	100.0	22.9	40.8	27.9	68.7	8.1	0.0	8.3	86.1	13.5
1992										
Health services	261.3	9.3	126.2	106.4	232.6	14.4	5.0	19.4	237.6	23.7
Education and research	94.5	12.0	53.8	18.9	72.7	7.3	2.5	9.8	84.5	10.0
Religious organizations[c]	58.3	55.1	3.9	3.9	7.3	(8.0)	(0.7)	41.1	17.2	
Social and legal services	55.9	11.2	9.8	28.0	37.8	6.6	0.3	6.9	48.3	7.6
Civic, social, and fraternal organizations	14.7	4.6	3.0	4.9	7.9	2.1	0.1	2.2	13.6	1.1
Arts and culture	8.2	3.3	2.0	1.2	3.2	1.6	0.1	1.7	7.7	0.5
Foundations[d]	15.7	(8.9)	7.1	—	7.1	17.4	0.1	17.5	3.0	12.6
Total revenue	508.6	93.7	198.7	159.4	358.1	56.7	0.1	56.8	435.8	72.7
Percentage	100.0	18.4	39.1	31.3	70.4	10.5	0.0	11.2	85.7	13.4
1997										
Health services	326.3	13.0	153.0	137.7	290.7	17.5	5.1	22.6	297.3	29.0
Education and research	119.0	16.0	66.7	23.1	89.8	10.5	2.7	13.2	101.1	22.9
Religious organizations[c]	76.3	72.8	6.8	6.8	5.1	(8.4)	(3.3)	53.6	22.7	
Social and legal services	76.9	15.1	14.5	40.1	54.6	6.8	0.4	7.2	66.2	10.7
Civic, social, and fraternal organizations	17.9	6.3	3.7	5.4	9.1	2.4	0.1	2.5	16.3	1.6
Arts and culture	15.4	6.7	4.3	1.5	5.8	2.8	0.1	2.9	12.0	3.4
Foundations[d]	33.0	(13.6)	15.8	—	15.8	30.8	0.0	30.8	5.1	27.9
Total revenue	664.8	132.1	249.0	207.8	456.8	75.9	0.0	75.9	551.6	118.2
Percentage	100.0	19.9	37.5	31.3	68.7	11.4	0.0	11.4	82.2	17.8

Note: Figures are not given when less than $50 million or when not applicable to a subsector. All figures are in current dollars. Owing to rounding, percentage figures may not total 100.

[a] Column 2 + column 5 + column 8; or column 9 + column 10.

[b] Specific estimates for wages and salaries, the major components of current operating expenditures, are shown in Table 2.8.

[c] Religious organizations both receive contributions and provide them to other organizations in the independent sector. To present net estimates for the independent sector and to estimate the sacerdotal activities of religious organizations, adjustments are made in the receipts for the religious organizations that show the estimated amount of money subtracted for use on nonsacerdotal activities.

[d] Foundation giving to the various subsectors of the independent sector is included in column 2. Foundations essentially are tax-exempt financial institutions engaged in receiving, investing, and distributing funds to organizations in the independent sector, to government institutions (such as public universities), and to individuals. In order to avoid counting both the receipt and the distribution of foundation funds in the overall assessment of total revenue for the independent sector, the net contributions of foundations to the independent sector are estimated by adding foundation giving to endowment and subtracting the grants of foundations to the independent sector from the total receipts of foundations.

— = Less than $50 million or no entry made because it does not apply to subsector.

Sources: Based on a distillation of information from various sources as detailed in Hodgkinson and Weitzman, Nonprofit Almanac, 1989, Table 8.1, pp. 177–179; authors' estimates.

TABLE 4.3

Independent Sector: Sources of Revenue and Distribution of Funds by Subsector, Selected Years, 1977–1997

| | Private Contributions | Payments | | | Other Receipts | | | | Total Revenue[a] | Distribution of Funds | | |
	Subtotal (Percent)	Private Sector (Percent)	Government Sector (Percent)	Subtotal (Percent)	Endowment and Investment Income (Percent)	Church (Percent)	Other (Percent)	Subtotal (Percent)	(Percent)	Current Operating Expenditures[b] (Percent)	Construction and Capital Improvements (Percent)	Other, Including Change in Fund Holdings[c] (Percent)
	(1)	(2)	(3)	(4)	(5)	(6)	(7)	(8)	(9)	(10)	(11)	(12)
1977												
Health services	7.8	49.1	32.4	81.5	1.2	6.6	2.9	10.7	100.0	84.4	8.6	7.0
Education and research	8.8	52.9	18.2	71.2	5.5	6.2	8.4	20.1	100.0	86.5	7.7	5.8
Religious organizations[d]	125.0	—	—	—	44.0	(40.0)	9.6	(25.0)	100.0	70.6	3.7	25.7
Social and legal services	32.0	9.7	54.4	64.1	1.9	1.0	1.0	3.9	100.0	82.5	2.9	14.6
Civic, social, and fraternal organizations	28.6	11.9	50.0	61.9	2.4	2.4	4.8	9.5	100.0	95.2	2.4	2.4
Arts and culture	41.2	29.4	11.8	41.8	5.9	—	11.8	17.6	100.0	88.2	5.9	5.9
Foundations[e]	(73.0)	96.2	—	96.2	76.9	—	—	76.9	100.0	19.2	—	80.8
Total revenue	26.3	37.5	26.6	64.1	4.6	0.0	5.0	9.6	100.0	82.0	6.8	11.3
1982												
Health services	5.9	49.1	34.8	84.0	1.1	5.3	3.6	10.1	100.0	84.5	7.3	8.1
Education and research	8.4	53.0	17.0	70.0	5.9	6.3	9.4	21.6	100.0	84.9	8.0	7.1
Religious organizations[d]	125.4	—	—	—	4.4	(39.4)	9.7	(25.4)	100.0	71.4	3.6	25.0
Social and legal services	25.0	15.2	54.9	70.1	2.5	1.0	1.5	4.9	100.0	82.3	2.9	14.2
Civic, social, and fraternal organizations	29.3	13.8	50.0	63.8	1.7	1.7	3.4	6.8	100.0	96.6	1.7	1.7
Arts and culture	39.6	29.2	16.7	45.8	6.3	—	8.3	14.6	100.0	68.8	2.1	29.7
Foundations[e]	(50.0)	36.7	—	36.7	113.3	—	—	113.3	100.0	23.3	—	76.7
Total revenue	21.8	38.7	28.1	66.8	6.0	0.0	5.4	11.4	100.0	81.3	6.2	12.5
1987												
Health services	5.4	51.8	36.2	88.0	1.1	3.6	1.9	6.6	100.0	90.7	5.2	4.0
Education and research	13.0	55.3	18.3	73.6	5.7	5.0	2.7	13.4	100.0	89.0	7.0	4.0
Religious organizations[d]	104.1	7.4	—	7.4	2.1	(22.7)	9.1	(11.5)	100.0	71.4	11.5	17.2
Social and legal services	24.8	18.9	48.1	67.1	3.7	0.9	3.4	8.1	100.0	85.4	1.9	12.7

Civic, social, and fraternal organizations	33.0	12.8	47.9	60.6	1.1	4.3	6.4	100.0	91.5	1.1	7.4
Arts and culture	40.0	30.0	15.0	45.0	1.7	6.7	15.0	100.0	86.7	1.7	11.6
Foundations[e]	(91.7)	63.3	—	63.3	—	—	128.3	100.0	33.3	—	66.7
Total revenue	22.9	40.8	27.9	68.7	0.0	3.3	8.4	100.0	86.1	5.9	8.2
1992											
Health services	3.6	48.3	40.7	89.0	1.9	3.0	7.4	100.0	90.9	5.1	4.0
Education and research	12.7	57.0	20.0	77.0	2.6	2.4	10.3	100.0	89.4	6.8	3.8
Religious organizations[d]	94.5	6.7	—	6.7	(13.7)	10.3	(1.2)	100.0	70.5	10.3	19.2
Social and legal services	20.0	17.5	50.0	67.6	0.5	9.1	12.3	100.0	86.4	1.8	11.8
Civic, social, and fraternal organizations	31.3	20.4	33.3	53.7	0.7	12.2	15.0	100.0	92.5	1.4	6.1
Arts and culture	40.2	24.4	14.7	39.1	1.2	9.8	20.7	100.0	93.9	1.2	4.9
Foundations[e]	(57.0)	45.5	—	45.5	0.5	60.9	111.5	100.0	19.2	1.3	79.5
Total revenue	18.4	39.1	31.3	70.4	0.0	6.6	11.1	100.0	85.7	5.3	9.0
1997											
Health services	4.0	46.9	42.2	89.1	1.6	2.8	6.9	100.0	91.1	4.8	4.1
Education and research	13.4	56.1	19.4	75.5	2.3	2.9	11.1	100.0	84.9	7.6	11.6
Religious organizations[d]	95.4	8.9	—	8.9	(11.0)	3.7	(4.3)	100.0	70.2	10.6	19.1
Social and legal services	19.6	18.9	52.1	71.0	0.5	6.4	9.4	100.0	86.1	1.3	12.6
Civic, social, and fraternal organizations	35.2	20.7	30.2	50.8	0.6	7.3	14.0	100.0	91.1	1.1	7.8
Arts and culture	43.5	27.9	9.7	37.7	0.6	11.7	18.8	100.0	77.9	1.9	20.1
Foundations[e]	(41.2)	47.9	—	47.9	0.0	60.9	93.3	100.0	15.5	0.6	83.9
Total revenue	19.9	37.5	31.3	68.7	0.0	6.5	11.4	100.0	82.2	5.2	12.6

Note: *Figures are not given when less than $50 million or when not applicable to a subsector.*

[a] Column 1 + column 4 + column 8; or column 10 + column 11 + column 12.

[b] Specific estimates for wages and salaries, the major components of current operating expenditures, are shown in Table 2.8.

[c] This is a residual item representing the difference between total funds and the sum of current operating expenditures and capital construction and improvements.

[d] Religious organizations both receive contributions and provide them to other organizations in the independent sector.

[e] Foundation contributions to the various subsectors of the independent sector are included in the rows in column 1, which is why these contributions show up as a negative estimate for foundations. Foundation giving to the various subsectors of the independent sector is included in column 2. Foundations essentially are tax-exempt financial institutions engaged in receiving, investing, and distributing funds to organizations in the independent sector, to government institutions (such as public universities), and to individuals. In order to avoid counting both the receipt and the distribution of foundation funds in the overall assessment of total revenue for the independent sector, the net contributions of foundations to the independent sector are estimated by adding foundation giving to endowment and subtracting the grants of foundations to the independent sector from the total receipts of foundations.

—— = Less than $50 million or no entry made because it does not apply to subsector.

Source: *Table 4.2.*

TABLE 4.4

Independent Sector: Financial Characteristics by Subsector, Selected Measures and Years, 1977–1997

	Current Dollars							
	Total (Billions)	**Total, Excluding Health Services (Billions)**	**Health Services (Billions)**	**Education and Research (Billions)**	**Religious Organizations (Billions)**	**Social and Legal Services (Billions)**	**Civic, Social, and Fraternal Organizations (Billions)**	**Arts and Culture (Billions)**
1977								
Total revenue	111.1	59.8	51.3	27.4	13.6	10.3	4.2	1.7
Private contributions	29.2	25.2	4.0	2.4	17.0	3.3	1.2	0.7
Private sector payments	41.7	16.5	25.2	14.5	—	1.0	0.5	0.5
Government sector payments	29.5	12.9	16.6	5.0	—	5.6	2.1	0.2
Current operating expenditures	91.1	47.8	43.3	23.7	9.6	8.5	4.0	1.5
1982								
Total revenue	211.9	107.1	104.8	47.7	22.4	20.4	5.8	4.8
Private contributions	46.2	40.0	6.2	4.0	28.1	5.1	1.7	1.9
Private sector payments	82.1	30.6	51.5	25.3	—	3.1	0.8	1.4
Government sector payments	59.5	23.1	36.5	8.1	—	11.2	2.9	0.8
Current operating expenditures	172.3	83.7	88.6	40.5	16.0	16.9	5.6	3.3
1987								
Total revenue	316.7	165.5	151.2	70.0	41.9	32.2	9.4	6.0
Private contributions	72.6	64.5	8.1	9.1	43.6	8.0	3.1	2.4
Private sector payments	129.2	50.9	78.3	38.7	3.1	6.1	1.2	1.8
Government sector payments	88.5	33.7	54.8	12.8	—	15.5	4.5	0.9
Current operating expenditures	272.7	135.5	137.2	62.3	29.9	27.5	8.6	5.2
1992								
Total revenue	508.6	247.3	261.3	94.5	58.3	55.9	14.7	5.2
Private contributions	93.7	84.4	9.3	12.0	55.1	11.2	4.6	3.3
Private sector payments	198.7	72.5	126.2	53.8	3.9	9.8	3.0	3.3
Government sector payments	159.4	53.0	106.4	18.9	—	28.0	4.9	1.2
Current operating expenditures	435.8	198.2	237.6	84.5	41.1	48.3	13.6	7.7
1997								
Total revenue	664.8	338.5	326.3	119.0	76.3	76.9	17.9	15.4
Private contributions	132.1	119.1	13.0	16.0	72.8	15.1	6.3	6.7
Private sector payments	249.0	96.0	153.0	66.7	6.8	14.5	3.7	4.3
Government sector payments	207.8	70.1	137.7	23.1	—	40.1	5.4	1.5
Current operating expenditures	551.6	254.3	297.3	96.1	53.6	66.2	16.3	12.0

Note: *Revenue and current operating expenditures do not include the assigned value of volunteers. The difference between total revenue and total current operating expenditures is accounted for by grants and benefits, payments to affiliates, and the excess or deficit for the year. Constant 1997 dollars are computed using the gross domestic product implicit price deflator.*
— = Less than $50 million or no entry made because it does not apply to subsector.

Sources: *Hodgkinson and Weitzman,* Nonprofit Almanac, *various years; authors' estimates.*

	Constant 1997 Dollars						
Total (Billions)	Total, Excluding Health Services (Billions)	Health Services (Billions)	Education and Research (Billions)	Religious Organizations (Billions)	Social and Legal Services (Billions)	Civic, Social, and Fraternal Organizations (Billions)	Arts and Culture (Billions)
244.4	131.6	112.9	60.3	29.9	22.7	9.2	3.7
64.2	55.4	8.8	5.3	37.4	7.3	2.6	1.5
91.7	36.3	55.4	31.9	—	2.2	1.1	1.1
64.9	28.4	36.5	11.0	—	12.3	4.6	0.4
200.4	105.2	95.3	52.1	21.1	18.7	8.8	3.3
317.9	160.7	157.2	71.6	33.6	30.6	8.7	7.2
69.3	60.0	9.3	6.0	42.2	7.7	2.6	2.9
123.2	45.9	77.3	38.0	—	4.7	1.2	2.1
89.3	34.7	54.8	12.2	—	16.8	4.4	1.2
258.5	125.6	132.9	60.8	24.0	25.4	8.4	5.0
411.7	215.2	196.6	91.0	54.5	41.9	12.2	7.8
94.4	83.9	10.5	11.8	56.7	10.4	4.0	3.1
168.0	66.2	101.8	50.3	4.0	7.9	1.6	2.3
115.1	43.8	71.2	16.6	—	20.2	5.9	1.2
354.5	176.2	178.4	81.0	38.9	35.8	11.2	6.8
581.8	282.9	298.9	108.1	66.7	63.9	16.8	9.4
107.2	96.5	10.6	13.7	63.0	12.8	5.3	3.8
227.3	82.9	144.4	61.5	4.5	11.2	3.4	2.3
182.3	60.6	121.7	21.6	—	32.0	5.6	1.4
498.5	226.7	271.8	96.7	47.0	55.3	15.6	8.8
664.8	338.5	326.3	119.0	76.3	76.9	17.9	15.4
132.1	119.1	13.0	16.0	72.8	15.1	6.3	6.7
249.0	96.0	153.0	66.7	6.8	14.5	3.7	4.3
207.8	70.1	137.7	23.1	—	40.1	5.4	1.5
551.6	254.3	297.3	101.1	53.6	66.2	16.3	12.0

TABLE 4.5

Independent Sector: Annual Rates of Change for Selected Financial Items, 1977–1997

| Beginning Year: | 1977 | 1977 | 1977 | 1977 | 1982 | 1982 | 1982 | 1987 | 1987 | 1992 |
| Ending Year: | 1982 | 1987 | 1992 | 1997 | 1987 | 1992 | 1997 | 1992 | 1997 | 1997 |
Number of Years:	5	10	15	20	5	10	15	5	10	5
Independent sector										
Total revenues	5.4	5.4	6.0	5.1	5.3	6.2	5.0	7.2	4.9	2.7
Private contributions	1.5	3.9	3.5	3.7	6.4	4.5	4.4	2.6	3.4	4.3
Private payments	6.1	6.2	6.2	5.1	6.4	6.3	4.8	6.2	4.0	1.8
Government payments	6.6	5.9	7.1	6.0	5.2	7.4	5.8	9.6	6.1	2.6
Total current operating expenditures	5.2	5.9	6.3	5.2	6.5	6.8	5.2	7.1	4.5	2.0
Independent sector, excluding health services										
Total revenue	4.1	5.0	5.2	4.9	6.0	5.8	5.1	5.6	4.7	3.7
Private contributions	1.6	4.2	3.8	3.9	6.9	4.9	4.7	2.9	3.6	4.3
Private payments	4.8	6.2	5.7	5.0	7.6	6.1	5.0	4.6	3.8	3.0
Government payments	4.1	4.4	5.2	4.6	4.8	5.8	4.8	6.7	4.8	2.9
Total current operating expenditures	3.6	5.3	5.3	4.4	7.0	6.1	4.8	5.2	3.5	2.3
Health services										
Total revenue	6.9	5.7	6.7	5.4	4.6	6.6	5.0	8.7	5.1	1.8
Private contributions	1.1	1.8	1.3	2.0	2.5	1.4	2.3	0.2	2.1	4.1
Private payments	6.9	6.3	6.6	5.2	5.7	6.5	4.7	7.2	4.2	1.2
Government payments	8.4	6.9	8.4	6.9	5.4	8.3	6.3	11.3	6.8	2.5
Total current operating expenditures	6.9	6.5	7.2	5.9	6.1	7.4	5.5	8.8	5.2	1.8
Education and research										
Total revenue	3.5	4.2	4.0	3.5	4.9	4.2	3.4	3.5	2.7	1.9
Private contributions	2.6	8.4	6.6	5.7	14.5	8.6	6.8	3.0	3.1	3.1
Private payments	3.5	4.7	4.5	3.8	5.8	5.0	3.8	4.1	2.9	1.6
Government payments	2.0	4.2	4.6	3.8	6.5	5.9	4.4	5.4	3.3	1.3
Total current operating expenditures	3.1	4.5	4.2	3.1	5.9	4.8	3.5	3.6	1.7	0.9

Religious organizations										
Total revenue	2.3	8.4	5.5	4.8	10.1	7.1	5.6	(0.0)	1.3	2.7
Private contributions	2.4	4.2	3.5	3.4	6.1	4.1	3.7	2.1	2.5	2.9
Total current operating expenditures	2.6	6.3	5.5	4.8	10.1	7.0	5.5	3.9	3.3	2.7
Social and legal services										
Total revenue	6.2	6.3	7.2	6.3	6.5	7.6	6.3	8.8	6.3	3.8
Private contributions	1.1	3.7	3.9	3.7	6.3	5.3	4.6	4.3	3.8	3.3
Private payments	16.1	13.7	11.5	9.9	11.3	9.2	7.9	7.2	6.2	5.3
Government payments	6.4	5.0	6.6	6.1	3.7	6.7	6.0	9.7	7.1	4.6
Total current operating expenditures	6.3	6.7	7.5	6.5	7.1	8.1	6.6	9.1	6.4	3.7
Civic, social, and fraternal organizations										
Total revenue	(1.2)	2.8	4.1	3.4	7.0	6.8	4.9	6.6	3.9	1.3
Private contributions	(0.7)	4.3	4.7	4.4	9.0	7.5	6.2	5.5	4.6	3.7
Private payments	1.8	3.6	7.9	6.3	5.4	11.1	7.8	17.1	9.0	1.5
Government payments	(1.2)	2.4	1.3	0.8	6.1	2.6	1.5	(0.9)	(0.8)	(0.7)
Total current operating expenditures	(0.9)	2.4	3.9	3.1	5.9	6.4	4.5	6.8	3.8	0.9
Arts and culture										
Total revenue	14.0	7.6	6.3	7.3	1.6	2.7	5.2	3.8	7.0	10.4
Private contributions	13.1	7.3	6.2	7.6	1.3	2.9	5.9	3.9	7.9	12.2
Private payments	13.8	7.8	5.0	7.1	1.8	0.9	4.9	(0.4)	6.3	13.5
Government payments	22.2	10.3	7.9	6.3	0.0	1.4	1.5	3.2	2.5	1.8
Total current operating expenditures	8.4	7.4	6.8	6.7	6.3	5.9	6.1	5.4	5.9	6.4

Note: *All figures are based on constant 1997 dollars.*

Source: *Table 4.4.*

The arts and culture subsector; civic, social, and fraternal organizations; and foundations shared 10.0 percent of total independent sector revenue. (See Figure 4.4.)

- In 1997 total current operating expenditures in the independent sector were $551.6 billion. Current operating expenditures were 83 percent of total revenue in 1997. Wages and salaries as a proportion of current operating expenditures declined from 51 percent in 1977 to 42 percent in 1992, reversing slightly upward to 44 percent by 1997. (See Table 4.1.)

Financial Trends in Health Services

- The health services subsector includes hospitals, nursing and personal care facilities, and other allied health services. The health services subsector continues to dominate the independent sector in revenue size, with estimated total revenue of $326 billion in 1997. It has consistently held the largest share of total independent sector revenue since 1977. (See Table 4.2.)

- In constant 1997 dollars the annual rate of change in total revenue for the health services subsector between 1987 and 1992 was at a high of 8.7 percent. For the following five-year period covering 1992 to 1997, however, the annual rate declined to 1.8 percent, the lowest rate experienced by any subsector. (See Figure 4.5.)

- The decline in the annual rate of total revenue for this subsector from 1992 to 1997 mirrored the significant decline in the rates of change for private and government payments. (See Figure 4.5.)

- The total current operating expenditures for the subsector in 1997 was estimated at $297 billion (see Table 4.2). Current operating expenditures were 91 percent of the subsector's total revenue (see Table 4.3). The annual rate of change from 1987 to 1992 in constant 1997 dollars was pegged at 8.7 percent, which then declined to 1.8 percent between 1992 and 1997 (see Table 4.5).

- The composition of revenue for the health services subsector has been shifting over the past twenty years, with government payments providing a bigger share and private contributions and payments declining. In 1997, 47 percent of funds came from private payments, 42 percent from government payments (including Medi-

FIGURE 4.4

Independent Sector: Distribution of Total Revenue by Subsector, 1977, 1987, and 1997

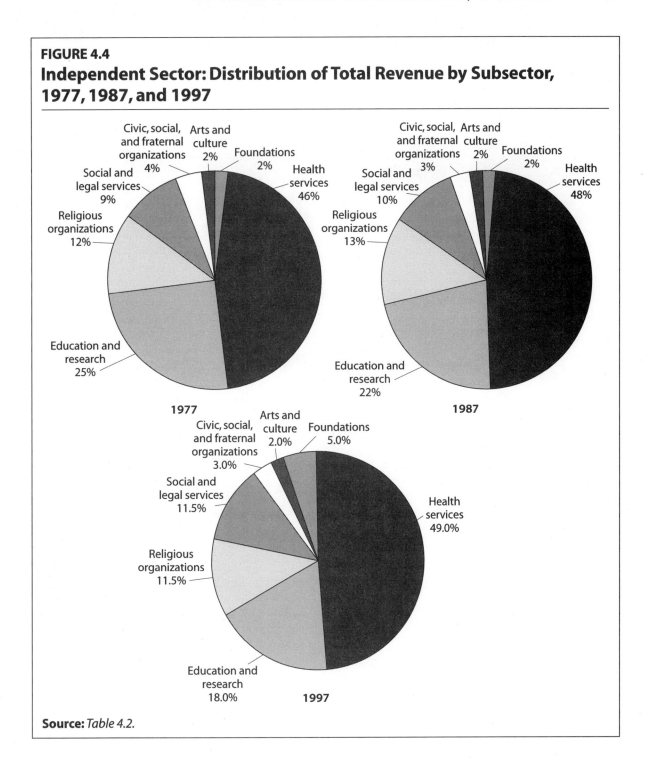

Source: *Table 4.2.*

care and Medicaid), 7 percent from other receipts, and 4 percent from private contributions. In 1977 the distribution of major sources of funds for the subsector was 49 percent from private payments, 32 percent from government payments, 11 percent from other receipts, and 8 percent from private contributions. (See Figure 4.6.)

FIGURE 4.5

Health Services Subsector: Annual Rates of Change for Selected Financial Items, 1977–1997

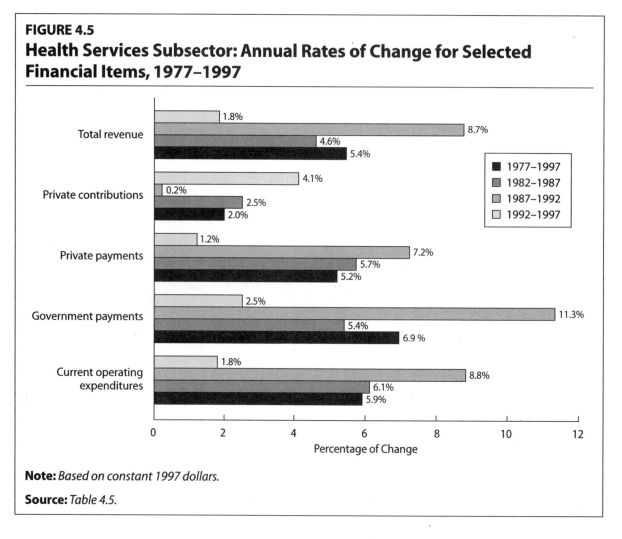

Note: *Based on constant 1997 dollars.*

Source: *Table 4.5.*

FIGURE 4.6

Health Services Subsector: Total Revenue by Source, 1977–1997

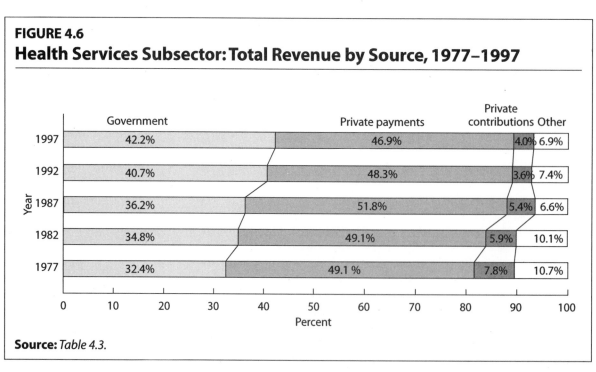

Source: *Table 4.3.*

Financial Trends in Education and Research Organizations

- In 1997 total revenue in the education and research subsector was $119 billion (see Table 4.2). Trends show that the annual rate of change for revenue in this subsector has been declining. Between 1982 and 1987 the annual rate of change for revenue was 4.9 percent. By 1992 to 1997 the rate had dropped to 1.9 percent. (See Figure 4.7.)

- Private nonprofit elementary and secondary schools; colleges and universities; libraries; educational services; and other educational, scientific, and research organizations constitute the education and research subsector. The education and research subsector's share of total independent sector revenue has been decreasing from a high of 25 percent in 1977, to 22 percent in 1987, and to 18 percent in 1997. This may be partly due to the slower growth in government payments directed to nonprofit educational institutions, particularly in

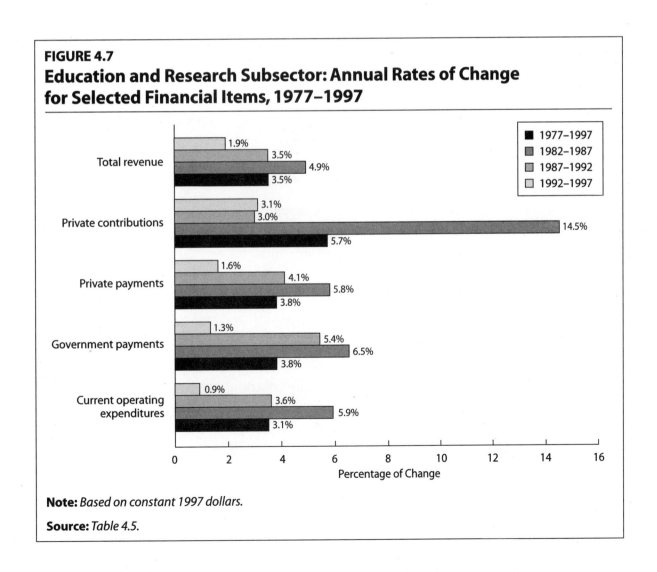

FIGURE 4.7

Education and Research Subsector: Annual Rates of Change for Selected Financial Items, 1977–1997

Note: *Based on constant 1997 dollars.*

Source: *Table 4.5.*

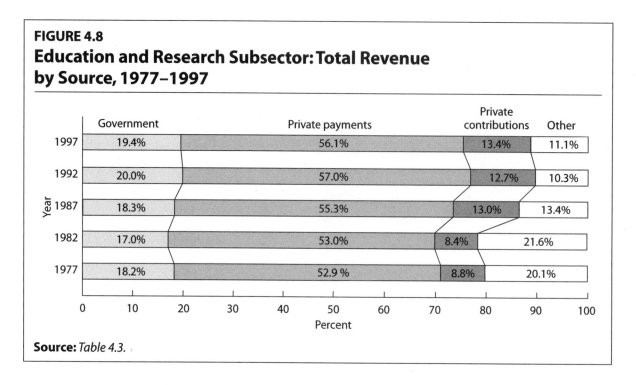

FIGURE 4.8
Education and Research Subsector: Total Revenue by Source, 1977–1997

Source: *Table 4.3.*

the field of higher education, where government support is mostly directed to public colleges and universities.

- Total current operating expenditures in the education and research subsector for 1997 were $101.1 billion (see Table 4.2). As with total revenue, the annual rate of change for operating expenses in constant 1997 dollars has been declining (see Figure 4.7). As a proportion of total revenue, expenditures declined from 87 percent in 1977 to 85 percent in 1997. (See Table 4.3.)

- The major sources of revenue for the education and research subsector in 1997 were private payments (56 percent), government payments (19 percent), private contributions (13 percent), and other receipts (11 percent). In 1977 the major sources of revenue were private payments (53 percent), government payments (18 percent), private contributions (9 percent), and other receipts (20 percent). (See Figure 4.8.)

- The education and research subsector substantially increased its share of funds from private contributions between 1977 and 1997, with amounts increasing threefold (in constant 1997 dollars) from $5.3 billion in 1977 to $16.0 billion in 1997 (see Table 4.4).

Financial Trends in Religious Organizations

Religious organizations are not required to report their financial activities to the government; as such, there is little information on their finances and services on a national scale. The last of two national surveys of the finances and activities of congregations conducted by INDEPENDENT SECTOR was in 1992. Estimates in this publication use changes in annual financial church data available from the Southern Baptist Convention (various years; see Resource B for details), along with information on private contributions derived from INDEPENDENT SECTOR's surveys on giving and volunteering.

- In 1997 total revenue in the religious organizations subsector was estimated at $76.3 billion (see Table 4.2). In constant 1997 dollars the annual change in total revenue between 1977 and 1997 was 4.8 percent (see Table 4.5).

- As indicated in Figure 4.9, total revenue in this subsector grew at an annual rate of 10.1 percent between 1982 and 1987, was stagnant between 1987 and 1992, and recovered to a rate of 2.7 percent between 1992 and 1997. Because this sector is highly dependent on private contributions, the rate of change in revenue was greatly affected by fluctuations in private contributions.

FIGURE 4.9

Religious Organizations Subsector: Annual Rates of Change for Selected Financial Items, 1977–1997

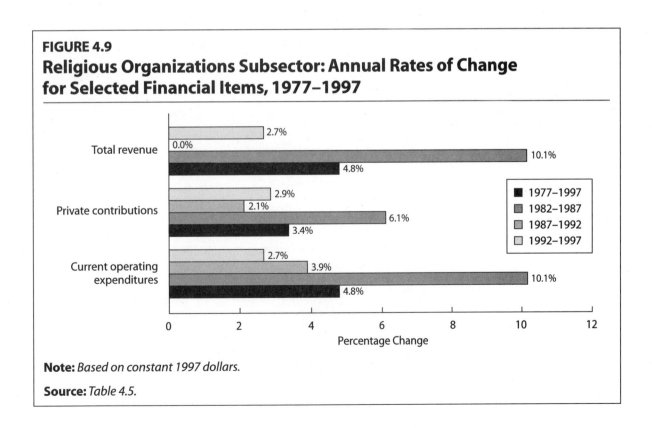

Note: *Based on constant 1997 dollars.*

Source: *Table 4.5.*

- Private contributions are the major source of funds for this subsector. In 1997 private contributions amounting to $73 billion accounted for 95 percent of the total revenue in religious institutions (see Tables 4.2 and 4.3). The highest annual rate of change for private contributions to religious organizations was between 1982 and 1987 (6.1 percent). Between 1992 and 1997 the rate declined to 2.9 percent. (See Figure 4.9.)

- In 1997 current operating expenditures for the religion subsector were $54 billion (see Table 4.2), or 70 percent of total revenue (see Table 4.3). Current operating expenditures grew at an annual rate of 10.1 percent between 1982 and 1987 but declined to a rate of 2.7 percent between 1992 and 1997 (see Table 4.5 and Figure 4.9).

Financial Trends in Social and Legal Services

- The social and legal services subsector includes legal assistance and several areas of social services (individual and family services, job training, child day care, residential care, and an array of other services). This group includes federated fundraising organizations (such as United Ways), community action and development groups, social change organizations, youth groups, senior citizens' organizations, and international relief and development organizations.

- In 1997 total revenue in the social and legal services subsector reached $76.9 billion (see Table 4.2). In constant 1997 dollars this represented an annual rate of increase of 6.3 percent between 1977 and 1997 (see Table 4.5). This was the second highest rate of change among all the subsectors, the highest (7.3 percent) being in arts and culture.

- The period of highest growth occurred between 1987 and 1992, when the annual rate of increase in total revenue for this subsector was at 8.8 percent. This was primarily a result of the increased annual rate of change in government funds directed to this subsector, which was at a high of 9.7 percent. Between 1992 and 1997 government funding slowed to a rate of 4.6 percent. Coupled with reduced growth rates in private payments and contributions, the rate of change in total revenue was reduced to 3.8 percent. (See Figure 4.10.)

- In 1997 the current operating expenditures for this subsector were $66 billion (see Table 4.2), or 86 percent of total revenue (see

FIGURE 4.10
Social and Legal Services Subsector: Annual Rates of Change for Selected Financial Items, 1977–1997

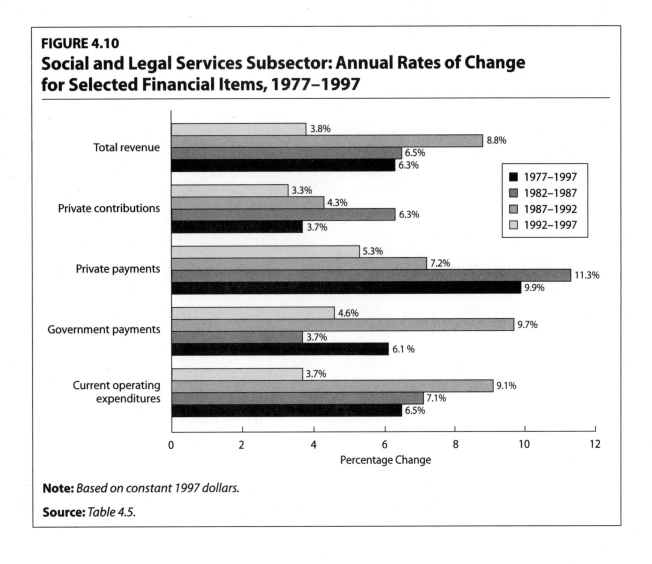

Legend:
- 1977–1997
- 1982–1987
- 1987–1992
- 1992–1997

Total revenue
- 3.8%
- 8.8%
- 6.5%
- 6.3%

Private contributions
- 3.3%
- 4.3%
- 6.3%
- 3.7%

Private payments
- 5.3%
- 7.2%
- 11.3%
- 9.9%

Government payments
- 4.6%
- 9.7%
- 3.7%
- 6.1%

Current operating expenditures
- 3.7%
- 9.1%
- 7.1%
- 6.5%

Percentage Change

Note: *Based on constant 1997 dollars.*

Source: *Table 4.5.*

Table 4.3). From 1982 to 1987, and again from 1987 to 1992, the rate of change for current operating expenditures in the social and legal services subsector outpaced total revenue. This improved slightly between 1992 and 1997, when the rate of change of operating expenditures (3.7 percent) was on par with that of total revenue (3.8 percent). (See Figure 4.10.)

- The major sources of funding in the social and legal services subsector in 1997 were government payments (52 percent), private contributions (20 percent), private sector payments (19 percent), and other receipts (9 percent; see Figure 4.11). Among all the subsectors, this subsector is the most reliant on support from government grants and payments, but the share of private payments received by this subsector has doubled—from 9.7 percent in 1977 to 18.9 percent in 1997.

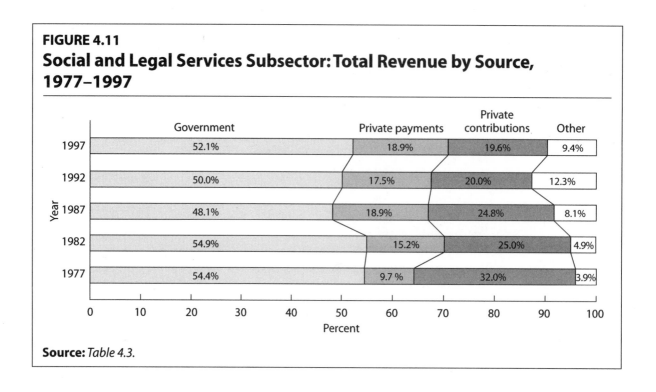

FIGURE 4.11
Social and Legal Services Subsector: Total Revenue by Source, 1977–1997

Source: *Table 4.3.*

Financial Trends in Arts and Cultural Organizations

- The arts and culture subsector is one of the smaller subsectors, representing just over 2 percent of the total annual funds of the independent sector in 1997. Included in this subsector are such activities and organizations as radio and television broadcasting, performing arts, producers, orchestras, entertainers, museums, and botanical gardens and zoological parks.

- Between 1992 and 1997 total revenue in the arts and culture subsector increased from $8.2 billion to $15.4 billion (see Table 4.2). Unlike other subsectors, which experienced a decline in the annual rate of change for total revenue between 1992 and 1997, arts and culture grew at a rate of 10.4 percent during that period (see Figure 4.12). This increase was largely triggered by the growth in funds received from both private contributions and private payments for this period. The economic boom of the early to mid-1990s saw an increased flow of funds to the arts.

- In 1997 the major sources of funding for the arts and culture subsector were private contributions (44 percent), private payments (28 percent), government payments (10 percent), and other receipts (19 percent). Private contributions have been providing an increasing share of total revenue for the arts and culture subsector since 1987, while the government's share has been diminishing (see Figure 4.13).

FIGURE 4.12

Arts and Culture Subsector: Annual Rates of Change for Selected Financial Items, 1977–1997

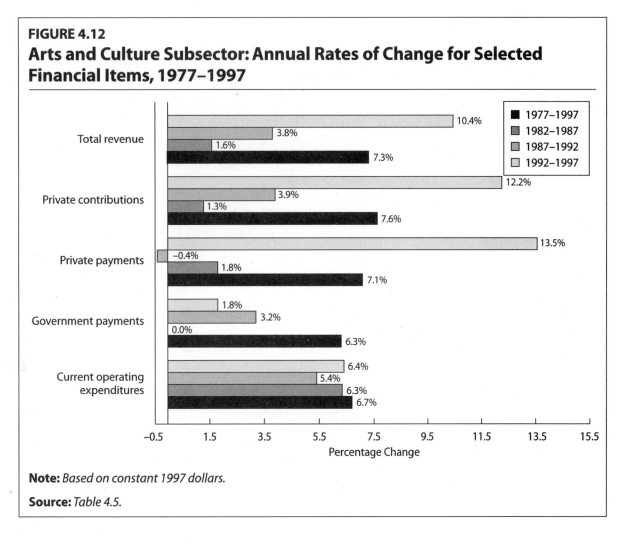

Note: *Based on constant 1997 dollars.*

Source: *Table 4.5.*

FIGURE 4.13

Arts and Culture Subsector: Total Revenue by Source, 1977–1997

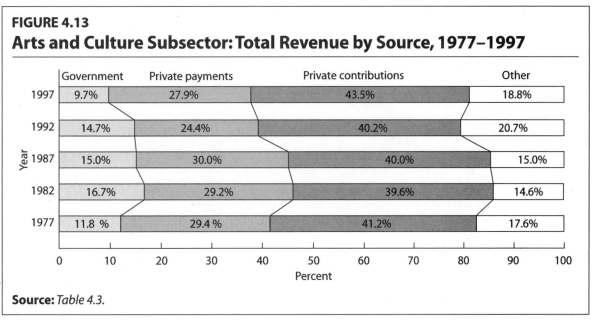

Source: *Table 4.3.*

Financial Trends in Other Subsectors

- In 1997 the civic, social, and fraternal organizations subsector, with $17.9 billion in total revenue, represented slightly less than 3 percent of total annual revenue in the independent sector (see Table 4.2). This subsector includes membership organizations such as alumni associations, scout organizations, citizens' associations, fraternities, veterans' associations, youth associations, and consumer education and public advocacy groups.

- In the civic, social, and fraternal organizations subsector in 1997, 35 percent of revenue came from private contributions, 30 percent from government, 21 percent from private payments, and 14 percent from other sources (see Figure 4.14). Total revenue in this subsector had the lowest annual rate of increase among all subsectors (1.3 percent) between 1992 and 1997 (see Table 4.5 and Figure 4.15).

- Foundations had estimated total revenue of $33 billion in 1997. The financial resources of foundations grew significantly in the late 1990s (Foundation Center, 2000, p. 1); (see Chapter Three of this book for further details on their financial activities). Foundations draw their revenue from a combination of new gifts and endowment income, although some make distributions from their assets.

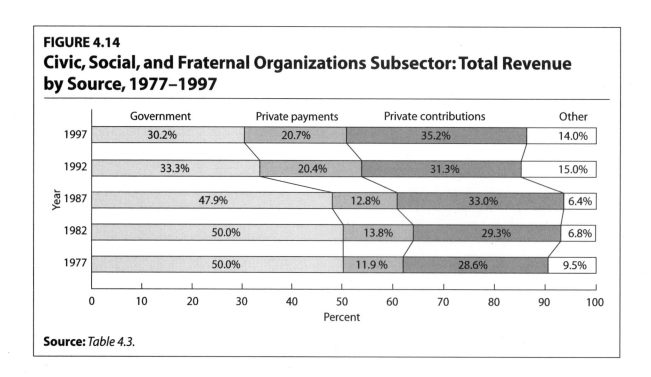

FIGURE 4.14

Civic, Social, and Fraternal Organizations Subsector: Total Revenue by Source, 1977–1997

Year	Government	Private payments	Private contributions	Other
1997	30.2%	20.7%	35.2%	14.0%
1992	33.3%	20.4%	31.3%	15.0%
1987	47.9%	12.8%	33.0%	6.4%
1982	50.0%	13.8%	29.3%	6.8%
1977	50.0%	11.9%	28.6%	9.5%

Source: Table 4.3.

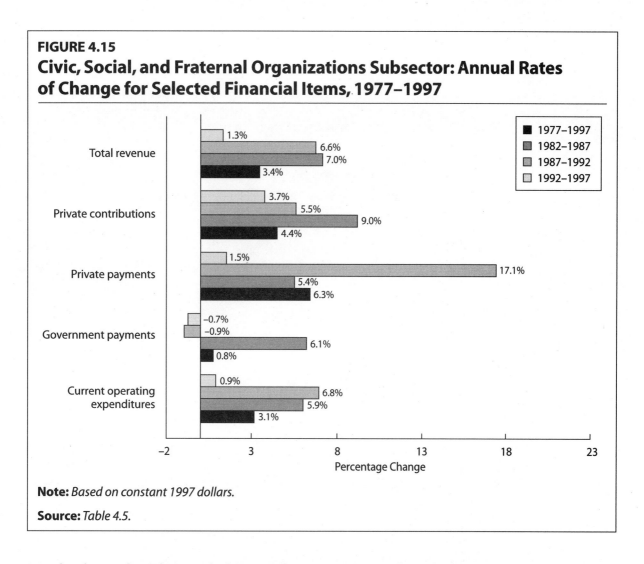

FIGURE 4.15

Civic, Social, and Fraternal Organizations Subsector: Annual Rates of Change for Selected Financial Items, 1977–1997

Legend:
- 1977–1997
- 1982–1987
- 1987–1992
- 1992–1997

Total revenue: 1.3%, 6.6%, 7.0%, 3.4%

Private contributions: 3.7%, 5.5%, 9.0%, 4.4%

Private payments: 1.5%, 17.1%, 5.4%, 6.3%

Government payments: −0.7%, −0.9%, 6.1%, 0.8%

Current operating expenditures: 0.9%, 6.8%, 5.9%, 3.1%

Percentage Change

Note: *Based on constant 1997 dollars.*

Source: *Table 4.5.*

Variations in Financial Trends Among Subsectors

Variations in the sources of revenue among the subsectors are evident from the preceding data and discussion. The following is a summary of variations in financial trends among the subsectors:

- The health services subsector is unique in that it derives a very small portion of its revenue (4 percent in 1997) from private contributions (see Table 4.3), compared with 35 percent for all other subsectors combined (see Table 4.1). This subsector is vulnerable to changes in private and government payments because these two sources account for 90 percent of its revenue. This is largely due to the fact that hospitals make up a large part of this subsector and receive fees for their services from private and government sources.

- The education and research subsector, which includes schools, colleges, and universities, relies on private payments for dues and services as a major source of income. Private payments made up 56.1 percent of total revenue in this subsector in 1997 (see Figure 4.8).

- Religious organizations have received little or no funding from private payments or the government; they depend largely on private contributions for most of their income.

- In 1997 the other subsectors that received the largest share of their funds from private contributions were arts and culture (44 percent) and civic, social, and fraternal organizations (35 percent; see Table 4.3).

- Government funding is the main source of income for the social and legal services subsector. Government funding accounted for 52 percent of the subsector's total revenue in 1997. (See Figure 4.11.)

- The proportion of funds received by source varies from one subsector to another. A decline in the amount of funding available from one major source may adversely affect one subsector more than another. The social and legal services subsector, for example, can be strongly affected by changes in government funding of programs related to human services, whereas religious organizations and the arts and culture subsector would be most affected by swings in private contributions. Independent sector organizations face a major challenge in striking a balance among the funding options available to them in order to create stability in their revenue sources.

References

American Hospital Association. *Hospital Statistics.* (Various editions.) Chicago: Health Forum, various years.

Foundation Center. *Foundation Giving Trends: Update on Giving Trends.* New York: Foundation Center, 2000.

Hodgkinson, V. A., and Weitzman, M. S. *Nonprofit Almanac: Dimensions of the Independent Sector.* (Various editions.) San Francisco: Jossey-Bass, various years.

Southern Baptist Convention. *Summary of Churches by State Convention.* (Various editions.) Nashville, Tenn.: Strategic Information and Planning Section, Sunday School Board, various years.

U.S. Bureau of the Census. *Economic Census.* (Various editions.) Washington, D.C.: U.S. Government Printing Office, various years.

U.S. Department of Commerce, Bureau of Economic Analysis. *Survey of Current Business.* (Various editions.) Washington, D.C.: U.S. Government Printing Office, various years.

U.S. Department of Education, National Center for Education Statistics. *Digest of Educational Statistics.* (Various editions.) Washington, D.C.: U.S. Government Printing Office, various years.

U.S. Department of Labor, Bureau of Labor Statistics. *Employment and Earnings.* (Various editions.) Washington, D.C.: U.S. Government Printing Office, various years.

Part Two

A Detailed Look at Reporting Public Charities

PART TWO presents an analysis performed primarily by the National Center for Charitable Statistics (NCCS) at the Urban Institute on the detailed financial information regarding public charities recognized by the IRS as tax exempt under section 501(c)(3) of the Internal Revenue Code. The data presented in the following chapter are based on information these organizations reported to the IRS, as contained in four different data files:

- *IRS Business Master File of Tax-Exempt Organizations (for 1992–1998).* This file includes basic descriptive information on all nonprofit organizations that have obtained *recognition of tax-exempt status* from the IRS. With the major exception of religious congregations and organizations with less than $5,000 in annual gross receipts, most nonprofits must obtain this recognition.

- *IRS Return Transaction File (for 1992–1998).* This file contains most of the revenue items, plus a number of other variables, for all organizations filing IRS Form 990 or 990-EZ.

- *IRS Statistics of Income (SOI) Exempt Organizations Sample File (for 1987–1997).* This file includes most financial variables on Form 990 for all large 501(c)(3) organizations (those with more than $10 million in assets for 1987 and 1992 and more than $30 million for 1997) plus a random sample of approximately four thousand smaller organizations stratified and weighted by asset level. The data are checked for consistency by the IRS and are considered highly reliable for research purposes. The total number of records is about thirteen thousand.

- *GuideStar-NCCS National Nonprofit Database (for 1998).* This database provides detailed information on more than five hundred variables for public charities that file IRS Form 990 (about 75 percent of all filers) and organizations that file IRS Form 990-EZ (the remaining 25 percent). Variables are manually entered from the forms, schedules, and attachments. If financial entries fail arithmetic checks, the data are rechecked for conformity to the original documents.

The estimates presented in Chapter Four differ from those in Chapter Five because the sources of data are different. Chapter Four presents financial trends for the independent sector, defined as organizations exempt from taxes under sections 501(c)(3), including congregations, and 501(c)(4) of the Internal Revenue Code. Data used in the tables are estimated based on the SOI file, modified by using a variety of public and private data sources, such as the Bureau of the Census, the Bureau of Labor Statistics, the Bureau of Economic Analysis, and the American Hospital Association, to better reflect the broader definition of the independent sector. The latest data available from these sources are for 1997.

Chapter Five, however, presents data only on organizations exempt from taxes under section 501(c)(3), excluding most congregations, and includes the more detailed financial information now available from the new GuideStar-NCCS National Nonprofit Database. Rather than relying on the SOI sample, Chapter Five summarizes data from all organizations that file IRS Form 990, and the information presented in the chapter reflects what has been reported, without major modification. A number of steps, detailed in Resource B and on the NCCS Web site (http://www.nccs.urban.org), were taken to check for errors in financial data.

A second major difference between the two chapters is the method used to divide the independent sector into subsectors. For purposes of discussion and analysis, Chapter Four divides the sector into health services; education and research; religious organizations; social and legal services; arts and culture; civic, social, and fraternal organizations; and foundations. These divisions are used because of the additional sources of data incorporated for the analysis. Chapter Five uses the National Taxonomy of Exempt Entities—Core Codes (NTEE-CC), a classification system in wide use in the nonprofit sector that groups organizations into ten major categories by their primary purpose, with further subdivision into more detailed groups. The tables presented in Chapter Five use the NTEE major categories and groups.

The same definitions for organizations that were identified as out-of-scope, or excluded from analysis, were used in both Chapters Four and Five. Out-of-scope organizations include mutual benefit organizations, foreign organizations, private foundations filing the wrong form, organizations with missing geographical identifiers, government-related organizations, and fundraising foundations controlled by public universities (see Resource B for further details).

Chapter 5

The Distribution and Finances of Public Charities

THIS CHAPTER REVIEWS the size, scope, and financial conditions of organizations exempt from taxation under section 501(c)(3) of the Internal Revenue Code, also known as "public charities." These charities are by far the largest component of the independent sector and have long played key roles in the United States. They include health, human services, arts and culture, education, research, and advocacy organizations. They range in size from the smallest homeless shelters to the largest hospitals and universities in the country. Their common characteristic is that they are registered as tax-exempt organizations under section 501(c)(3) and can receive tax-deductible contributions from individuals and corporations because they serve broad public purposes as defined by the IRS. Although private foundations (generally organizations established or endowed by a single corporation, individual, or family to support other charitable activities) are also exempt from taxes under the same section, they have been excluded from this analysis. Detailed information about private foundations is included in Chapter Three.

For the first time, more detailed financial information on 501(c)(3) organizations from the GuideStar-NCCS National Nonprofit Organization Database is presented. The database contains the information submitted by nonprofit organizations that file Form 990, the annual information return required by the IRS from organizations with over $25,000 in gross receipts each year. (Information for religious congregations is not included, because they are not required to register with the IRS or to file a Form 990, although some do.) The numbers and percentages detailed in this chapter for the organizations filing Form 990 may vary from those reported in Chapter Four because the organizations included and the sources of data are different. These differences are detailed in the introduction to Part Two.

The total number of all public charities exempt under section 501(c)(3) approached 1 million (984,330) in 1998 (see Table 5.1). This includes an estimate of 353,000 congregations in the United States that are not required to register, about 64,000 private foundations, and 567,000 public charities. This total does not include the innumerable small organizations with less than $5,000 in gross receipts, as these charities are not required to register with the IRS. Even the number registered, however, is quite different from the number filing Form 990. Registration and filing requirements are discussed in this chapter.

The information presented in this chapter focuses on the public charities that file Form 990, a group of about 224,000 entities in 1998. These organizations receive tax-deductible contributions and serve the public good. A detailed analysis of the numbers, activities, and finances of this group of charities gives an excellent indication of the contribution and role of this important segment of the U.S. economy.

In brief, key findings about reporting public charities (those that filed Form 990) include the following:

- The total number of reporting public charities grew from 161,125 in 1992 to 224,272 in 1998, an increase of 39 percent and an annual average growth rate of almost 6 percent.

- These are typically small organizations, with almost 98,000 (or 43 percent) reporting expenses of less than $100,000 in 1998 and almost 165,000 (or 73 percent) with expenses of less than $500,000. Fewer than 8,000 (or 4 percent of all reporting public charities) reported annual expenses of over $10 million in 1998.

- The reporting public charities are primarily human services (35 percent), education (16 percent), and health organizations (15 percent) or are in the arts, culture, and humanities subsector (11 percent).

- Total annual revenue reached nearly $693 billion in 1998, an increase of nearly 47 percent from 1992 (31 percent in constant dollars after adjustment for inflation). As reported on Forms 990, about 20.5 percent (or $142 billion) came from public support, defined as private contributions (12.5 percent) and government grants (8.0 percent). The largest proportion of revenue came from fees for services and goods (68.0 percent). The remaining revenue came from investments (7.7 percent) and other sources, including dues, rental income, and income from special events (3.8 percent).

- The public charities classified as health organizations received 57 percent of total revenue in 1998, with total funds reported of $392.5 billion. This actually decreased from a 61 percent share in

TABLE 5.1

Number of Charitable Organizations, Circa 1992, 1997, and 1998

	1992 Number	1992 Percent	1997 Number	1997 Percent	1998 Number	1998 Percent
501(c)(3) charities						
Total	781,024	100.0	952,232	100.0	984,330	100.0
Public charities registered with the IRS (excluding congregations)	383,968	49.2	541,604	56.9	567,237	57.6
Total congregations[a]	351,000	44.9	353,000	37.1	354,000	35.9
Congregations registered with the IRS	79,000	10.1	80,000	8.4	81,000	8.2
Congregations not registered with the IRS[b]	272,000	34.89	273,000	28.7	272,000	27.6
Private foundations	46,056	5.6	57,628	6.1	64,093	6.5
501(c)(3) charities registered with the IRS						
Total 501(c)(3) charitable organizations[c]	546,100		692,524		733,790	
Inactive 501(c)(3) charitable organizations	37,076		13,292		21,460	
Active 501(c)(3) charitable organizations[d]	509,024	100.0	679,232	100.0	712,330	100.0
Total public charities[e]	462,968	91.0	621,604	91.5	648,237	91.0
Out-of-scope organizations[f]	3,491	0.7	2,672	0.4	3,087	0.4
Mutual benefit organizations	558	0.1	678	0.1	652	0.1
Nonreporting organizations or organizations with less than $25,000 in gross receipts[g]	298,352	58.6	403,694	59.4	420,878	59.1
Total reporting public charities[h]	161,125	31.7	215,238	31.7	224,272	31.5
Reporting public charities—operating	144,606	28.4	191,774	28.2	199,724	28.0
Reporting public charities—supporting	16,519	3.2	23,464	3.5	24,548	3.4
Total private foundations[i]	46,056	9.0	57,628	8.5	64,093	9.0
Total reporting private foundations without financial data[h]	1,703	0.3	1,371	0.2	553	0.1
Total reporting private foundations with financial data	44,353	8.7	56,257	8.3	63,540	8.9
Reporting private foundations with financial data—grant-making[j]	37,194	7.3	46,192	6.8	51,997	7.3
Reporting private foundations with financial data—zero-grants[k]	7,159	1.4	10,065	1.5	11,543	1.6

[a] Christian, Jewish, and Muslim estimates only.

[b] Organizations are not required to register for a number of statutory reasons, including having less than $5,000 in gross receipts or being a religious congregation, denomination, or an integrated auxiliary of a congregation.

[c] Totals as reported in Internal Revenue Service, Annual Report, various years; and Internal Revenue Service, Data Book, various years.

[d] Total active 501(c)(3) organizations in the IRS Business Master Files (Exempt Organizations), 1993, 1998, 1999 (including registered congregations). See Resource B for details.

[e] Public charities are calculated by subtracting the number of private foundations from the estimated number of 501(c)(3) organizations.

[f] Foreign and government-associated organizations, organizations without state identifiers, and organizations individually excluded.

[g] Nonreporting organizations are calculated by subtracting the number of private foundations and reporting organizations from the total number of active 501(c)(3) organizations.

[h] Returns of organizations that are required to file and report positive dollar amounts for public support, total expenses, or total assets and are not defined as mutual benefit organizations.

[i] Refer to Resource B on reasons for the difference in definition and count with that reported by the Foundation Center.

[j] Includes operating foundations that give grants.

[k] Includes operating foundations and others that made no grants during the reported year.

Sources: Internal Revenue Service, Annual Report, various years; Internal Revenue Service, Data Book, various years; IRS Business Master Files (Exempt Organizations), 1993, 1998, 1999; IRS Return Transaction File, 1993, 1998, 1999 (returns received in those calendar years), as classified according to the National Taxonomy of Exempt Entities—Core Codes and adjusted by the National Center for Charitable Statistics. See Resource B for details.

1992. Fees for goods and services were the source of almost 86 percent of revenue in this subsector in 1998.

- Education organization revenue increased to nearly $129 billion in 1998, from $82.4 billion in 1992 (an increase of 56 percent in current dollars and 40 percent in constant dollars). The proportion of total revenue of reporting public charities increased slightly, from 17.5 percent in 1992 to 18.5 percent in 1998. Almost 54 percent of the subsector's revenue in 1998 came from fees for goods and services.

- Revenue for human services charities increased 71.5 percent (55.5 percent in constant dollars) from $53.5 billion in 1992 to $91.7 billion in 1998, and their proportion of total revenue also increased from 11 percent in 1992 to 13 percent in 1998. Almost 50 percent of revenue came from fees for goods and services, an additional 18 percent from private contributions, and 23 percent from government grants.

- Revenue of the arts, culture, and humanities subsector grew from $11.6 billion in 1992 to $19.4 billion in 1998, an increase of 67 percent (51 percent in constant dollars). The proportion of total revenue was 2.8 percent, a slight increase from the proportion in 1992. Fees from goods and services are a smaller proportion of revenue for this subsector (30 percent) than for others, with private contributions representing a higher proportion (almost 40 percent).

- The number of organizations in the environment and animal organizations category grew by almost 65 percent, from 4,530 in 1992 to 7,458 in 1998, a rate of increase that was much higher than in other subsectors; revenue grew by 85 percent, from $3.4 billion in 1992 to $6.3 billion in 1998. Almost half the revenue came from private contributions, and only 23 percent from fees for goods and services. The proportion of total revenue for all public charities from the environment and animals subsector, however, remained at less than 1 percent.

- Expenses for reporting public charities grew from $440.9 billion in 1992 to over $621.2 billion in 1998, an increase of almost 41 percent in current dollars (25 percent in constant dollars). For the sector, current operating expenses represented about 92 percent of total expenses in 1998. Paid personnel costs were reported as almost half of current operating expenses.

- There are wide variations in growth and sources of revenue and increases and allocation of expenses among the various types of reporting public charities. Although health and education organizations represent large proportions of the independent sector, their growth rates have been lower than in other subsectors, and they are heavily reliant on fees for goods and services as sources of income. Human services charities are the biggest proportion of these organizations but represent an increasing proportion of revenue in the independent sector; they are reliant on private contributions and government grants. Arts, culture, and humanities organizations receive even higher proportions of their revenue from private contributions, as do organizations in the environment and animals category.

- Assets for all reporting charities grew from $662 billion in 1992 to $1.2 trillion in 1998, a huge increase of almost 83 percent (67 percent in constant dollars). Health organizations held over 44 percent of total assets, with education adding another 29 percent. The subsector with the largest number of organizations—human services—held only 11 percent of total assets.

- Net assets (assets minus liabilities) of all reporting public charities increased by 100 percent (84 percent in constant dollars) from nearly $396 billion in 1992 to $791 billion in 1998. The health subsector grew at a slower pace (82 percent) but, with $298 billion in net assets in 1998, still held 38 percent of the total in the sector. Education organizations held 33 percent of total net assets, whereas human services organizations accounted for only 9 percent.

What Are Reporting Public Charities?

The information presented in this chapter focuses primarily on *reporting public charities,* or organizations that filed Form 990 with the IRS and were required to do so. In general, only organizations that receive more than $25,000 in gross receipts are required to file. Table 5.2 outlines the registration and filing requirements.

In 1998 there were nearly 1 million charitable organizations exempt from federal taxes under section 501(c)(3) of the Internal Revenue Code. These organizations are defined by the IRS as serving broad public purposes, including educational, religious, scientific, and literary activities. Relief of poverty and other public benefit actions also qualify under the definition. Approximately 57 percent of these organizations can be classified as public charities, 7 percent as private foundations, and the remaining 36 percent as religious congregations (see Figure 5.1). However, there are many organizations that are not included in this count.

TABLE 5.2

Registration and Filing Requirements for 501(c)(3) Organizations

	One-Time Registration for Tax Exemption	Annual Reporting to IRS on Form 990
"Nonreligious" public charities		
Less than $5,000 in annual gross receipts	Optional	Optional
$5,000–$24,999 in annual gross receipts	Required	Optional
$25,000 or more in annual gross receipts	Required	Required
Religious public charities		
Congregations, religious primary and secondary schools, denominations, and "integrated auxiliaries"	Optional	Optional
Religiously affiliated hospitals, universities, human service organizations, and others	Required to follow nonreligious public charity regulations	Required to follow nonreligious public charity regulations
Private foundations	Required regardless of size	Required regardless of size

Typically, congregations, most religious primary and secondary schools, and other religious organizations are not required to apply for tax-exempt status with the IRS, so most do not register. The estimated number of congregations in the United States was 354,000 in 1998 (see Table 1.3 in Chapter One). Only 81,000 of these had registered with the IRS (see Table 5.1).

Also missing from the data set are smaller organizations that receive less than $5,000 in gross receipts, such as many neighborhood or volunteer associations, and that are *not* required to apply for tax-exempt status. Studies indicate that if these smaller organizations (plus others that are not registered for various reasons) were included, the number of charities in the United States would increase by between 20 and 100 percent or more (Haycock, 1992; Smith, 1995; Gronbjerg, 1994).

Although there were nearly 734,000 registered public charities in 1998, over 20,000 of these were inactive. An *inactive* organization is defined as one that either reports itself as inactive or has had no contact with the IRS in several years. Of the active organizations, 91 percent were public charities, serving broad public purposes and entitled to receive tax-deductible contributions from individuals. The remaining 9 percent of the organizations were private foundations, most of which fund the activities of public charities (see Table 5.1). (These private foundations are discussed in detail in Chapter Three.)

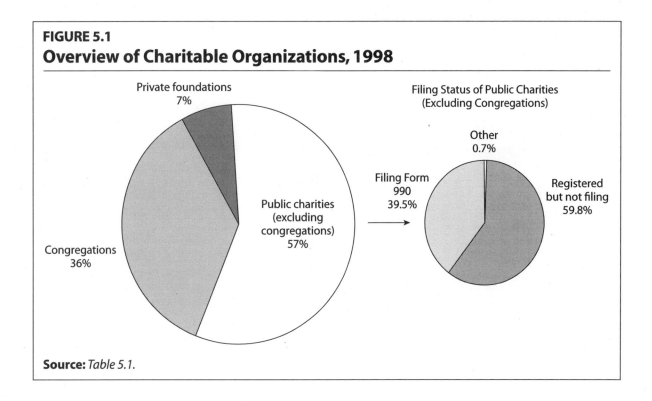

FIGURE 5.1
Overview of Charitable Organizations, 1998

Private foundations
7%

Congregations
36%

Public charities
(excluding
congregations)
57%

Filing Status of Public Charities
(Excluding Congregations)

Filing Form
990
39.5%

Other
0.7%

Registered
but not filing
59.8%

Source: *Table 5.1.*

The reporting public charities that are discussed in this chapter (that is, those filing Form 990 in 1998) numbered 224,272 in 1998 and represent 40 percent of the public charities (excluding congregations) that registered with the IRS (see Figure 5.1). Again, private foundations are not included among those filing Form 990.

Reporting Public Charities by Size and Age

Public charities range in size from small community groups to universities with billions of dollars in assets. The majority of these organizations were founded after 1985. Most of the largest are hospitals or higher education institutions. Overall, the largest organizations accounted for about three-fourths of total expenses and assets of all public charities and over half of *public support* (that is, private contributions from individuals, foundations, corporations, and other public charities, as well as government grants, but excluding government contracts and program service revenue).

- Among all reporting public charities, 73 percent reported expenses of less than $500,000 in 1998. Less than 18 percent reported expenses greater than $1 million, and less than 4 percent (about 8,000) reported expenses of $10 million or more. (See Figure 5.2.)

- Half of all reporting public charities (113,861) were founded after 1984, and over half of these newer organizations (60,178) were created after 1992 (see Table 5.3 and Figure 5.3).

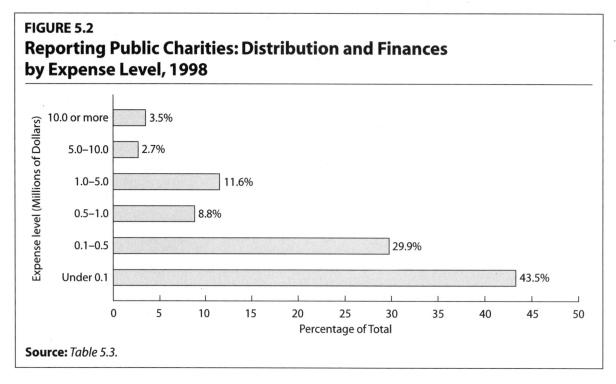

FIGURE 5.2
Reporting Public Charities: Distribution and Finances by Expense Level, 1998

Source: *Table 5.3.*

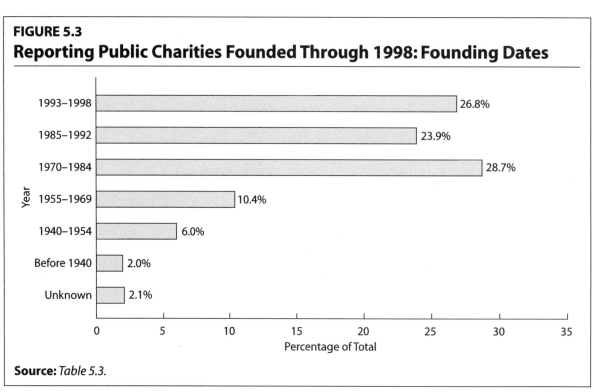

FIGURE 5.3
Reporting Public Charities Founded Through 1998: Founding Dates

Source: *Table 5.3.*

TABLE 5.3

Reporting Public Charities Founded Through 1998: Founding Date by Total Expenses

	Total	Before 1940	1940–1954	1955–1969	1970–1984	1985–1992	1993–1998	Unknown
Total								
Number of organizations	224,272	4,575	13,431	23,330	64,455	53,683	60,178	4,620
Percentage of total by year	100.0	100.0	100.0	100.0	100.0	100.0	100.0	100.0
Percentage of total by expense level	100.0	2.0	6.0	10.4	28.7	23.9	26.8	2.1
$ 0–$99,999								
Number of organizations	97,527	1,621	3,385	8,558	23,569	24,417	33,595	2,382
Percentage of total by year	43.5	35.4	25.2	36.7	36.6	45.5	55.8	51.6
Percentage of total by expense level	100.0	1.7	3.5	8.8	24.2	25.0	34.4	2.4
$ 100,000–$499,999								
Number of organizations	67,055	849	2,896	5,732	20,462	17,932	17,944	1,240
Percentage of total by year	29.9	18.6	21.6	24.6	31.7	33.4	29.8	26.8
Percentage of total by expense level	100.0	1.3	4.3	8.5	30.5	26.7	26.8	1.8
$ 500,000–$999,999								
Number of organizations	19,707	313	1,393	2,216	7,232	4,556	3,636	361
Percentage of total by year	8.8	6.8	10.4	9.5	11.2	8.5	6.0	7.8
Percentage of total by expense level	100.0	1.6	7.1	11.2	36.7	23.1	18.5	1.8
$ 1,000,000–$4,999,999								
Number of organizations	26,046	619	2,758	4,257	9,486	4,880	3,603	443
Percentage of total by year	11.6	13.5	20.5	18.2	14.7	9.1	6.0	9.6
Percentage of total by expense level	100.0	2.4	10.6	16.3	36.4	18.7	13.8	1.7
$ 5,000,000–$9,999,999								
Number of organizations	5,977	295	970	1,186	1,843	920	662	101
Percentage of total by year	2.7	6.4	7.2	5.1	2.9	1.7	1.1	2.2
Percentage of total by expense level	100.0	4.9	16.2	19.8	30.8	15.4	11.1	1.7
$ 10,000,000 or more								
Number of organizations	7,960	878	2,029	1,381	1,863	978	738	93
Percentage of total by year	3.5	19.2	15.1	5.9	2.9	1.8	1.2	2.0
Percentage of total by expense level	100.0	11.0	25.5	17.3	23.4	12.3	9.3	1.2

Note: *Reporting public charities include only organizations that both reported (filed IRS Form 990) and were required to report include religious congregations and organizations with less than $25,000 in gross receipts. Owing to rounding, percentage figures may not total 100.*

Sources: *IRS Business Master Files (Exempt Organizations), 1999; IRS Return Transaction File, 1999 (returns received in that calendar year), as classified according to the National Taxonomy of Exempt Entities—Core Codes and adjusted by the National Center for Charitable Statistics. See Resource B for details.*

- Not surprisingly, the larger organizations tend to be older. Only 22 percent of organizations with $10 million or more in expenses were created after 1984, compared with almost 60 percent of organizations with less than $100,000 in expenses (see Table 5.3).

Reporting Public Charities by Type and Age

The National Taxonomy of Exempt Entities (NTEE) is the standard classification system used to categorize the vast range of nonprofit organizations. It classifies organizations into twenty-six different groups in ten major categories. (See Resource A for a summary of the NTEE classification system.) Table 5.4 shows the founding dates of reporting public charities by NTEE major group.

Reporting nonprofit organizations are also divided into *operating public charities,* those that engage in a variety of activities serving the public good under the IRS definition, and *supporting public charities,* those that primarily distribute funds to the operating public charities. A local United Way is an example of a supporting organization. This differentiation helps avoid double-counting of revenue and expenses. For example, amounts that supporting charities transfer in the form of grants and allocations to operating charities are included as revenue for the operating charities, so the dollars could be counted twice in totals of all organizations in the independent sector unless they are counted separately.

- The most common categories of reporting public charities are human services (35 percent); education (16 percent); health (15 percent); and arts, culture, and humanities (11 percent; see Figure 5.4).

- About 11 percent of all public charities are supporting organizations that primarily distribute funds to operating public charities.

Finances of Reporting Public Charities, 1998

In 1998 reporting public charities (those filing Form 990, excluding private foundations) had total revenue of nearly $693 billion (see Table 5.5). Program service revenue, which includes, for example, college tuition payments, hospital patient revenue (from both government and private sources), and income sources such as ticket sales, accounted for 68 percent of total revenue (see Figure 5.5).

Public support, which includes individual contributions as well as government, corporate, and private foundation grants, constituted 20.5 percent of total revenue. Government grants included in public support represented

TABLE 5.4

Reporting Public Charities Founded Through 1998: Founding Date by NTEE Major Group

	Total	Before 1940	1940–1954	1955–1969	1970–1984	1985–1992	1993–1998	Unknown
Total								
Number of organizations	224,272	4,575	13,431	23,330	64,455	53,683	60,178	4,620
Percentage of total by year	100.0	100.0	100.0	100.0	100.0	100.0	100.0	100.0
Percentage of NTEE major category	100.0	2.0	6.0	10.4	28.7	23.9	26.8	2.1
Arts, culture, and humanities								
Number of organizations	23,779	486	1,184	2,727	7,797	5,559	5,704	322
Percentage of total by year	10.6	10.6	8.8	11.7	12.1	10.4	9.5	7.0
Percentage of NTEE major category	100.0	2.0	5.0	11.5	32.8	23.4	24.0	1.4
Education								
Number of organizations	36,513	976	3,191	5,256	10,042	7,204	8,950	894
Percentage of total by year	16.3	21.3	23.8	22.5	15.6	13.4	14.9	19.4
Percentage of NTEE major category	100.0	2.7	8.7	14.4	27.5	19.7	24.5	2.4
Environment and animals								
Number of organizations	7,458	126	270	667	2,033	1,858	2,375	129
Percentage of total by year	3.3	2.8	2.0	2.9	3.2	3.5	3.9	2.8
Percentage of NTEE major category	100.0	1.7	3.6	8.9	27.3	24.9	31.8	1.7
Health								
Number of organizations	33,423	843	2,909	3,549	10,312	8,258	6,887	665
Percentage of total by year	14.9	18.4	21.7	15.2	16.0	15.4	11.4	14.4
Percentage of NTEE major category	100.0	2.5	8.7	10.6	30.9	24.7	20.6	2.0
Human services								
Number of organizations	78,021	1,347	3,997	7,665	23,268	19,391	20,821	1,532
Percentage of total by year	34.8	29.4	29.8	32.9	36.1	36.1	34.6	33.2
Percentage of NTEE major category	100.0	1.7	5.1	9.8	29.8	24.9	26.7	2.0
International and foreign affairs								
Number of organizations	2,078	35	62	154	523	626	646	32
Percentage of total by year	0.9	0.8	0.5	0.7	0.8	1.2	1.1	0.7
Percentage of NTEE major category	100.0	1.7	3.0	7.4	25.2	30.1	31.1	1.5
Other								
Number of organizations	43,000	762	1,818	3,312	10,480	10,787	14,795	1,046
Percentage of total by year	19.2	16.7	13.5	14.2	16.3	20.1	24.6	22.6
Percentage of NTEE major category	100.0	1.8	4.2	7.7	24.4	25.1	34.4	2.4

Note: Reporting public charities include only organizations that both reported (filed IRS Form 990) and were required to do so. Organizations not required to report include religious congregations and organizations with less than $25,000 in gross receipts. Owing to rounding, percentage figures may not total 100.

Sources: IRS Business Master Files (Exempt Organizations), 1999; IRS Return Transaction File, 1999 (returns received in that calendar year), as classified according to the National Taxonomy of Exempt Entities—Core Codes and adjusted by the National Center for Charitable Statistics. See Resource B for details.

FIGURE 5.4
Reporting Public Charities: Distribution and Finances by Type, 1998

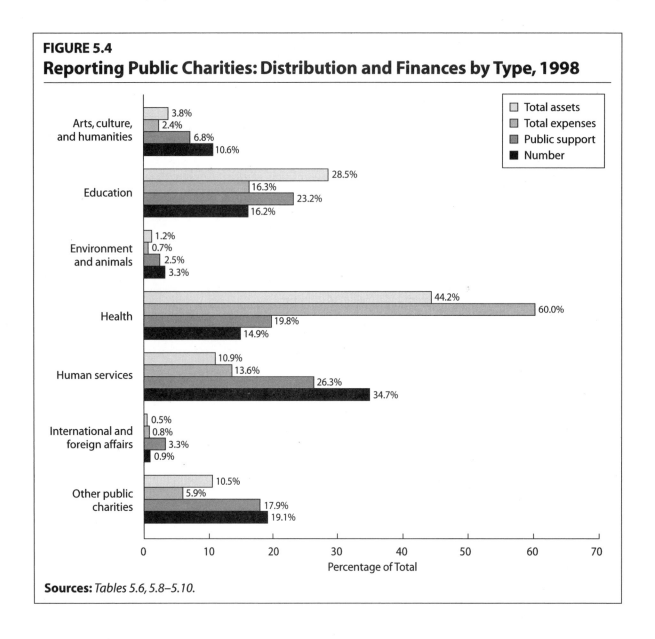

Sources: *Tables 5.6, 5.8–5.10.*

8.0 percent of total revenue. Investment income, including interest, dividends, and gains on sales of securities (stocks and bonds), was 7.7 percent of total revenue. (See Table 5.5.)

The sources of revenue change substantially, however, when the proportions are recalculated without hospitals and higher education. The remaining public charities were much more dependent on private contributions (22.3 percent) and government grants (36.3 percent, compared with 20.5 percent of revenue for all public charities). (See Figure 5.6.)

The following were some of the notable characteristics of revenue and expenses for reporting public charities in 1998:

- Total current operating expenses for all reporting public charities were $572 billion, about 92 percent of total expenses (see Table 5.5).

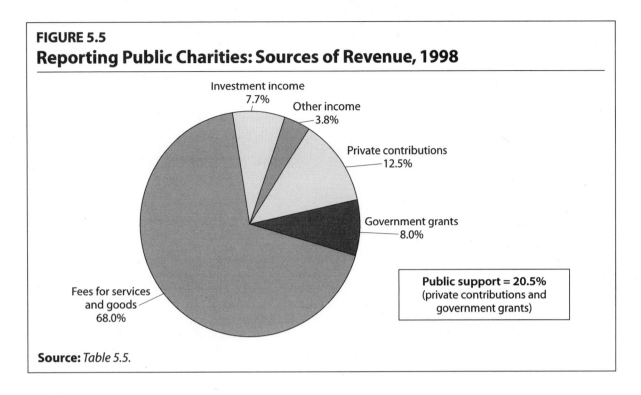

FIGURE 5.5
Reporting Public Charities: Sources of Revenue, 1998

Investment income
7.7%

Other income
3.8%

Private contributions
12.5%

Government grants
8.0%

Fees for services
and goods
68.0%

Public support = 20.5%
(private contributions and
government grants)

Source: *Table 5.5.*

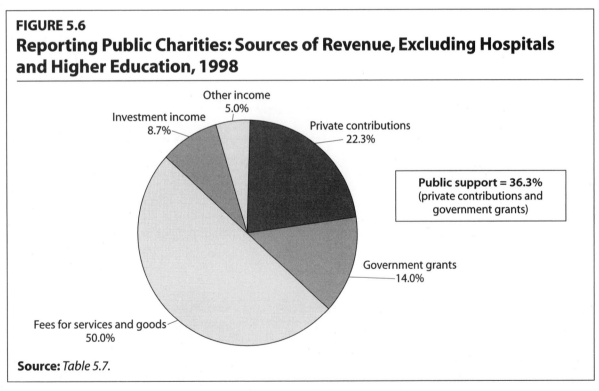

FIGURE 5.6
**Reporting Public Charities: Sources of Revenue, Excluding Hospitals
and Higher Education, 1998**

Other income
5.0%

Investment income
8.7%

Private contributions
22.3%

Public support = 36.3%
(private contributions and
government grants)

Government grants
14.0%

Fees for services and goods
50.0%

Source: *Table 5.7.*

- Paid personnel costs—wages and salaries plus fringe benefits and payroll taxes—were the single largest expense (46.4 percent) for reporting public charities ($265.2 billion). In addition, organizations included almost a third of their total operating expenses in the "other expenses" category, and some portion of that amount may be

TABLE 5.5

Reporting Public Charities: Revenue and Expenses, 1998

	All Organizations[a]		Operating Organizations[b]		Supporting Organizations[c]	
	Amount (Millions)	Percent	Amount (Millions)	Percent	Amount (Millions)	Percent
Public support	142,073.9	20.5[d]	122,990.5	19.1[d]	19,083.4	39.7[d]
Private contributions	86,599.2	12.5	68,651.2	10.6	17,948.0	37.3
Direct contributions	74,878.4	10.8	59,134.1	9.2	15,744.3	32.7
Indirect contributions	11,720.8	1.7	9,517.1	1.5	2,203.7	4.6
Government grants	55,474.6	8.0	54,339.3	8.4	1,135.4	2.4
Fees for services and goods	471,253.8	68.0	454,525.2	70.5	16,728.6	34.8
Program service revenue[e]	467,229.1	67.4	450,709.6	69.9	16,519.4	34.4
Net income from sales of inventory	4,024.7	0.6	3,815.5	0.6	209.1	0.4
Investment income	53,081.9	7.7	42,468.8	6.6	10,613.1	22.1
Dividends	15,095.2	2.2	11,823.0	1.8	3,272.2	6.8
Interest	6,410.8	0.9	5,768.4	0.9	642.5	1.3
Net gain on sale of assets	28,571.9	4.1	22,360.1	3.5	6,211.8	12.9
Other investment income	3,003.9	0.4	2,517.2	0.4	486.7	1.0
Other income	26,360.2	3.8	24,705.2	3.8	1,655.1	3.4
Dues and assessments	6,753.4	1.0	6,566.2	1.0	187.1	0.4
Net income from special events	2,337.0	-0.3	2,047.4	0.3	289.6	0.6
Other (including net rental)	17,269.8	2.5	16,091.5	2.5	1,178.3	2.5
Total revenue	692,769.7	100.0	644,689.6	100.0	48,080.1	100.0
Paid personnel	265,209.0	46.4[f]	260,780.6	47.3[f]	4,428.4	21.1[f]
Wages and salaries	220,913.8	38.6	217,299.0	39.4	3,614.9	17.2
Compensation of officers	8,270.1	1.4	7,856.0	1.4	414.1	2.0
Other wages and salaries	212,643.8	37.2	209,442.9	38.0	3,200.8	15.2
Fringe benefits and payroll taxes	44,295.1	7.7	43,481.6	7.9	813.5	3.9
Pension plan contributions	7,718.4	1.3	7,374.9	1.3	343.6	1.6
Other employee benefits	21,767.4	3.8	21,525.7	3.9	241.6	1.1
Payroll taxes	14,809.3	2.6	14,581.0	2.6	228.3	1.1
Supplies	50,405.3	8.8	48,751.3	8.8	1,654.0	7.9
Communications (printing, phone, postage)	13,639.1	2.4	13,082.8	2.4	556.3	2.6
Professional fees	8,180.0	1.4	7,653.4	1.4	526.7	2.5
Occupancy	15,335.9	2.7	14,772.2	2.7	563.7	2.7
Equipment rental and maintenance	8,243.5	1.4	7,919.3	1.4	324.2	1.5
Interest	13,039.6	2.3	12,319.8	2.2	719.9	3.4
Depreciation and depletion	27,028.9	4.7	26,100.6	4.7	928.4	4.4
Other	171,092.2	29.9	159,767.8	29.0	11,324.4	53.9
Total current operating expenses	572,173.6	100.0	551,147.7	100.0	21,025.9	100.0

Total current operating expenses	572,173.6	92.1[g]	551,147.7	93.9[g]	21,025.9	61.5[g]
Plus grants and benefits	45,735.5	7.4	33,187.7	5.7	12,547.8	36.7
Grants and allocations	32,535.6	5.2	21,666.8	3.7	10,868.8	31.8
Specific assistance to individuals	7,761.4	1.2	7,000.7	1.2	760.7	2.2
Benefits paid to members	5,438.5	0.9	4,520.1	0.8	918.3	2.7
Plus payments to affiliates	3,253.4	0.5	2,624.2	0.4	629.2	1.8
Total expenses	621,162.6	100.0	586,959.7	100.0	34,202.9	100.0
Net income (revenue minus expenses)	71,607.2	10.3[d]	57,729.9	9.0[d]	13,877.2	28.9[d]
Total assets	1,210,392.2	194.9[g]	1,064,610.4	181.4[g]	145,781.8	426.2[g]
Total liabilities	418,896.7	67.4	399,444.2	68.1	19,452.6	56.9
Net assets (assets minus liabilities)	791,495.5	127.4	665,166.2	113.3	126,329.2	369.4

Note: Reporting public charities include only organizations that both reported (filed IRS Form 990) and were required to do so. (The following were excluded: foreign organizations, government-associated organizations, organizations without state identifiers, and organizations excluded at the authors' discretion.) Organizations not required to report include religious congregations and organizations with less than $25,000 in gross receipts. Owing to rounding, column totals may not equal the sum of individual items. The table includes separate analyses for operating public charities and supporting organizations to provide a clearer picture of the distribution of funds and to avoid double-counting of the financial information for supporting organizations. See Resource B for a detailed description of the methodology. See http://www.nccs.urban.org for a full description of the National Taxonomy of Exempt Entities—Core Codes system.

[a] Number of organizations = 224,272.

[b] Number of organizations = 199,724.

[c] Number of organizations = 24,548.

[d] Percentages for revenue items and net income are expressed as percentages of total revenue.

[e] Program service revenue may include sizable income via government contracts, which the data source is unable to differentiate from funds raised via the public (that is, fees for services).

[f] Percentages for current operating expense items are expressed as percentages of total current operating expenses.

[g] Percentages for other expense items, assets, and liabilities are expressed as percentages of total expenses.

Sources: IRS Forms 990 and 990-EZ, GuideStar-NCCS National Nonprofit Organization Database, 1999 (returns received in that calendar year), as classified according to the National Taxonomy of Exempt Entities—Core Codes and adjusted by the National Center for Charitable Statistics and INDEPENDENT SECTOR. See Resource B for details.

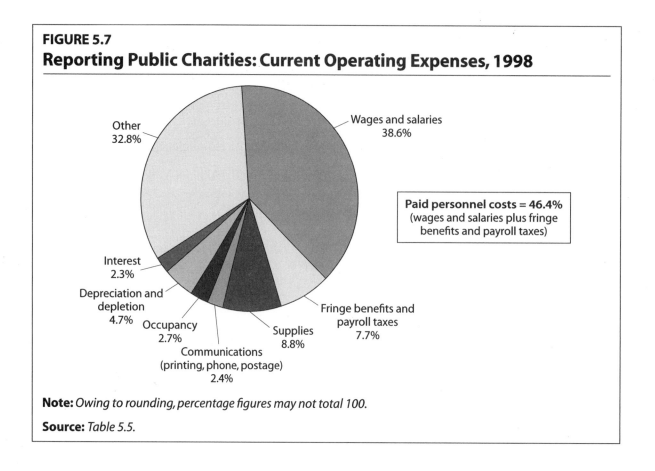

FIGURE 5.7
Reporting Public Charities: Current Operating Expenses, 1998

Other 32.8%

Wages and salaries 38.6%

Paid personnel costs = 46.4%
(wages and salaries plus fringe benefits and payroll taxes)

Interest 2.3%

Depreciation and depletion 4.7%

Occupancy 2.7%

Communications (printing, phone, postage) 2.4%

Supplies 8.8%

Fringe benefits and payroll taxes 7.7%

Note: *Owing to rounding, percentage figures may not total 100.*

Source: *Table 5.5.*

for personnel. Thus personnel costs as a percentage of total operating expenses may be even higher. Pension plan contributions, other employee benefits, and payroll taxes accounted for almost 8 percent of total current operating expenses, or 20 percent of expenditures on wages and salaries. (See Table 5.5 and Figure 5.7.)

- Two categories—(1) grants and benefits and (2) payments to affiliates—added another $49 billion to expenses, for total expenses of $621 billion (see Table 5.5).

- After all expenses were deducted from revenue, public charities were left with net income of almost $72 billion, or 10 percent of total revenue (see Table 5.5).

- Assets totaled $1.21 trillion against end-of-year liabilities of $419 billion, for net assets of $791 billion (see Table 5.5).

The relationship between assets and expenses differed substantially for operating and supporting organizations. Operating public charities had assets of $1.1 trillion, or 181 percent of total expenses, whereas supporting charities had $146 billion in assets, which represented 426 percent of their expenses (see Table 5.5). This is due to the nature and mission of supporting charities, which give a larger proportion of their total expenses as grants and allocations to operating organizations.

- Supporting public charities (about 11 percent of the total number of reporting public charities) had $48.1 billion in revenue, or about 7 percent of the total revenue for reporting public charities. These organizations primarily transfer money to the operating public charities. Public support for the supporting charities represents 40 percent of their revenue, and fees for goods and services are 35 percent. Investment income is a much higher proportion of revenue for supporting charities (22 percent) than for operating charities (7 percent). (See Table 5.5.)

- Supporting charities show a total of about $10.9 billion transferred in 1998 in the form of grants and allocations; most of this amount is probably included as revenue for the operating charities that receive this money as indirect contributions, so these funds may well be double-counted. However, the grants transferred by supporting charities represent only about 1.5 percent of the total revenue for all reporting public charities. (See Table 5.5.)

- Net assets (assets minus liabilities) were $665 billion for operating organizations (representing 113 percent of expenses) and $126 billion for supporting organizations (representing 369 percent of expenses). (See Table 5.5.)

Growth in the Number and Finances of Reporting Public Charities, 1992–1998

Growth in the Number of Reporting Public Charities, 1992–1998

- The number of reporting public charities increased by 39 percent from 1992 to 1998, with the rate of growth higher in the latter part of the time period. The rates of increase for different types of organizations varied. (See Table 5.6.)

- The highest rate of growth in reporting public charities between 1992 and 1998 occurred in two smaller categories—environment and animals (65 percent, or an increase of over 2,900 organizations to a total of 7,458) and religion-related (over 58 percent, or an increase of 4,200 organizations to a total of 11,416). (See Table 5.6.)

- The category of public and societal benefit also showed large growth (almost 58 percent between 1992 and 1998, an increase of almost 10,200 organizations). (See Table 5.6.)

TABLE 5.6

Reporting Public Charities: Change in Total Number by NTEE-CC Category, Circa 1992, 1995, 1997, and 1998

	Number of Organizations				Total Percentage Change	Average Annual Percentage Change		
	1992	1995	1997	1998	1992–1998	1992–1998	1992–1995	1995–1998
All public charities	161,125	186,871	215,237	224,272	39.2	5.7	5.1	6.3
Arts, culture, and humanities	17,290	19,567	22,772	23,779	37.5	5.5	4.2	6.7
Performing arts organizations	5,974	6,766	7,687	8,018	34.2	5.0	4.2	5.8
Historical societies and related organizations	2,515	2,885	3,543	3,752	49.2	6.9	4.7	9.2
Museums and museum activities	1,736	2,017	2,370	2,493	43.6	6.2	5.1	7.3
Other arts, culture, and humanities	7,065	7,899	9,172	9,516	34.7	5.1	3.8	6.4
Education	23,845	29,126	34,541	36,513	53.1	7.4	6.9	7.8
Higher education institutions	1,814	2,071	2,142	2,173	19.8	3.1	4.5	1.6
Student services and organizations	2,410	2,953	3,948	4,334	79.8	10.3	7.0	13.6
Elementary and secondary education	6,089	6,770	7,467	7,696	26.4	4.0	3.6	4.4
Other education	13,532	17,332	20,984	22,310	64.9	8.7	8.6	8.8
Environment and animals	4,530	5,659	6,996	7,458	64.6	8.7	7.7	9.6
Environment	2,558	3,288	4,133	4,408	72.3	9.5	8.7	10.3
Animal-related	1,972	2,371	2,863	3,050	54.7	7.5	6.3	8.8
Health	29,045	31,019	33,127	33,427	15.1	2.4	2.2	2.5
Nursing services	2,205	2,389	2,479	2,482	12.6	2.0	2.7	1.3
Hospitals and primary treatment facilities	5,029	5,013	5,195	5,236	4.0	0.7	(0.1)	1.4
Treatment facilities—outpatient	1,778	2,122	2,412	2,493	40.2	5.8	6.1	5.5
Mental health	6,210	6,515	6,844	6,815	9.7	1.6	1.6	1.5
Disease-specific—general	4,210	4,167	4,277	4,328	2.8	0.5	(0.3)	1.3
Disease-specific—research	1,285	1,499	1,765	1,805	40.5	5.8	5.3	6.4
Other health	8,328	9,314	10,155	10,268	23.3	3.6	3.8	3.3

Human services	56,867	65,723	74,918	78,021	37.2	5.4	4.9	5.9
Crime and legal-related	2,876	3,336	3,933	4,076	41.7	6.0	5.1	6.9
Employment and job-related	2,871	3,079	3,361	3,407	18.7	2.9	2.4	3.4
Food, agriculture, and nutrition	1,847	1,993	2,134	2,166	17.3	2.7	2.6	2.8
Housing and shelter	7,256	9,284	10,979	11,600	59.9	8.1	8.6	7.7
Public safety and disaster preparedness	1,741	2,279	2,768	3,000	72.3	9.5	9.4	9.6
Recreation and sports	8,934	11,408	13,669	14,329	60.4	8.2	8.5	7.9
Youth development	4,906	5,290	5,931	6,185	26.1	3.9	2.5	5.3
Children and youth services	4,994	5,618	6,050	6,255	25.3	3.8	4.0	3.6
Family services	2,721	2,924	3,054	3,073	12.9	2.0	2.4	1.7
Residential and custodial care	4,528	4,894	5,154	5,171	14.2	2.2	2.6	1.9
Services promoting independence	6,390	6,853	7,581	7,825	22.5	3.4	2.4	4.5
Other human services	7,803	8,765	10,304	10,934	40.1	5.8	4.0	7.6
International and foreign affairs	1,606	1,829	2,054	2,078	29.4	4.4	4.4	4.3
Public and societal benefit	17,607	21,848	26,296	27,780	57.8	7.9	7.5	8.3
Civil rights and advocacy	1,146	1,416	1,645	1,713	49.5	6.9	7.3	6.6
Community improvement	6,231	7,740	9,184	9,614	54.3	7.5	7.5	7.5
Philanthropy and voluntarism	7,016	8,992	11,386	12,346	76.0	9.9	8.6	11.1
Science and technology	1,289	1,435	1,587	1,589	23.3	3.5	3.6	3.5
Social science	555	651	711	713	28.5	4.3	5.5	3.1
Other public and societal benefit	1,370	1,614	1,783	1,805	31.8	4.7	5.6	3.8
Religion-related	7,219	8,478	10,570	11,416	58.2	7.9	5.5	10.4
Unknown or unclassified	3,116	3,622	3,963	3,800	22.0	3.4	5.1	1.6

Note: *Reporting public charities include only organizations that both reported (filed IRS Form 990) and were required to do so. Organizations not required to report include religious congregations and organizations with less than $25,000 in gross receipts. Owing to rounding, percentage figures may not total 100. The average annual percentage change is a compound rate that assumes a constant growth rate over time.*

Sources: *IRS Business Master Files (Exempt Organizations), 1993, 1996, 1998, 1999; IRS Return Transaction File, 1993, 1996, 1998, 1999 (returns received in those calendar years), as classified according to the National Taxonomy of Exempt Entities—Core Codes and adjusted by the National Center for Charitable Statistics. See Resource B for details.*

- The category with the largest number of operating public charities—human services—grew by over 21,000 organizations to a total of 78,021; this represented a change of 37 percent (see Table 5.6).

- The number of health organizations grew by 15 percent, from about 29,000 in 1992 to more than 33,000 in 1998. In this subsector, however, the number of outpatient treatment facilities and disease-specific research organizations each grew by 40 percent, whereas the number of hospitals and disease-specific general organizations lagged, with growth rates of 4 percent or less over the six-year period. (See Table 5.6.)

Growth in the Revenue of Reporting Public Charities, 1992–1998

Total revenue for reporting public charities increased from $471.6 billion in 1992 to $692.8 billion in 1998, at an average annual rate of 6.6 percent. This totaled 47.0 percent over the time period; in constant dollars the increase was 31.0 percent. Again, rates of increase varied for the different types of charities. (See Figure 5.8 and Table 5.7.)

As Table 5.7 shows, the trends in revenue for reporting public charities between 1992 and 1998 included:

- Among the different types of charities, the revenue of religion-related charities grew the most (95 percent, or 79 percent after adjustment for inflation) over the time period but represented only 9 percent of the total.

- The subsector with the largest proportion (57 percent) of total revenue—health—had the smallest revenue growth rate from 1992 to 1998 (an increase of 36 percent, or 20 percent in constant dollars).

- Education organizations, with 18.5 percent of the revenue in 1998, grew by 56 percent between 1992 and 1998.

- Human services, with its large number of organizations representing only 13 percent of total revenue, grew to $91.7 billion, for an increase of 71.5 percent (55.5 percent in constant dollars).

- Arts, culture, and humanities organizations grew from revenue of $11.6 billion in 1992 to $19.4 billion in 1998, but this still represented less than 3 percent of the total. The growth rate, however, was over 67 percent (51 percent in constant dollars).

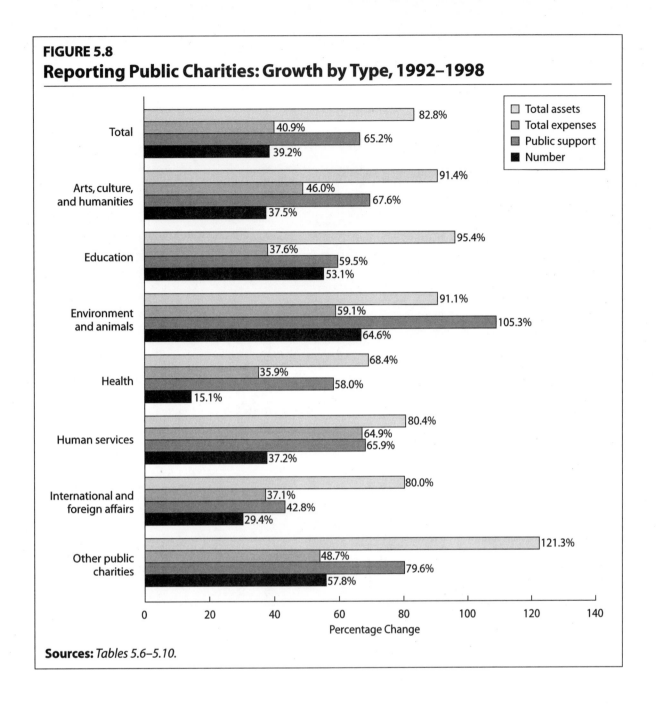

FIGURE 5.8
Reporting Public Charities: Growth by Type, 1992–1998

Legend:
- ☐ Total assets
- ☐ Total expenses
- ■ Public support
- ■ Number

Total
- Total assets: 82.8%
- Total expenses: 40.9%
- Public support: 65.2%
- Number: 39.2%

Arts, culture, and humanities
- Total assets: 91.4%
- Total expenses: 46.0%
- Public support: 67.6%
- Number: 37.5%

Education
- Total assets: 95.4%
- Total expenses: 37.6%
- Public support: 59.5%
- Number: 53.1%

Environment and animals
- Total assets: 91.1%
- Total expenses: 59.1%
- Public support: 105.3%
- Number: 64.6%

Health
- Total assets: 68.4%
- Total expenses: 35.9%
- Public support: 58.0%
- Number: 15.1%

Human services
- Total assets: 80.4%
- Total expenses: 64.9%
- Public support: 65.9%
- Number: 37.2%

International and foreign affairs
- Total assets: 80.0%
- Total expenses: 37.1%
- Public support: 42.8%
- Number: 29.4%

Other public charities
- Total assets: 121.3%
- Total expenses: 48.7%
- Public support: 79.6%
- Number: 57.8%

Percentage Change (x-axis: 0, 20, 40, 60, 80, 100, 120, 140)

Sources: *Tables 5.6–5.10.*

Growth in Public Support of Reporting Public Charities, 1992–1998

Public support is a major component of revenue for many reporting public charities. It consists of private contributions from individuals, foundations, corporations, and other public charities, as well as government grants. It does not include government contracts and program service revenue.

As Table 5.8 shows, trends in public support for reporting public charities between 1992 and 1998 included:

TABLE 5.7

Reporting Public Charities: Change in Total Revenue by NTEE-CC Category, Circa 1992, 1995, 1997, and 1998

	Total Revenue (Millions of Dollars)				Total Percentage Change	Average Annual Percentage Change		
	1992	1995	1997	1998	1992–1998	1992–1998	1992–1995	1995–1998
All public charities	471,561.9	573,376.0	663,193.0	692,769.7	46.9	6.6	6.7	6.5
Arts, culture, and humanities	11,599.9	14,140.0	17,501.8	19,407.6	67.3	9.0	6.8	11.1
Performing arts organizations	3,379.2	4,118.9	5,074.7	5,553.9	64.4	8.6	6.8	10.5
Historical societies and related organizations	788.8	994.9	1,333.8	1,590.8	101.7	12.4	8.0	16.9
Museums and museum activities	2,468.0	3,180.8	4,318.0	4,822.9	95.4	11.8	8.8	14.9
Other arts, culture, and humanities	4,963.9	5,845.5	6,775.3	7,440.0	49.9	7.0	5.6	8.4
Education	82,414.3	96,617.8	115,943.0	128,808.2	56.3	7.7	5.4	10.1
Higher education institutions	63,255.7	71,283.2	84,759.5	93,174.2	47.3	6.7	4.1	9.3
Student services and organizations	2,412.5	3,394.4	4,264.8	4,600.4	90.7	11.4	12.1	10.7
Elementary and secondary education	8,442.1	11,004.6	13,578.4	15,389.3	82.3	10.5	9.2	11.8
Other education	8,304.0	10,935.6	13,340.3	15,644.3	88.4	11.1	9.6	12.7
Environment and animals	3,418.7	4,376.9	5,614.3	6,325.7	85.0	10.8	8.6	13.1
Environment	1,805.9	2,376.0	3,070.0	3,473.4	92.3	11.5	9.6	13.5
Animal-related	1,612.8	2,000.9	2,544.3	2,852.4	76.9	10.0	7.5	12.5
Health	288,797.4	349,636.4	389,840.1	392,516.0	35.9	5.2	6.6	3.9
Nursing services	9,809.7	13,140.9	14,620.2	14,801.5	50.9	7.1	10.2	4.0
Hospitals and primary treatment facilities	227,145.5	269,307.7	294,428.5	289,083.3	27.3	4.1	5.8	2.4
Treatment facilities—outpatient	10,799.7	15,968.4	19,782.0	22,082.0	104.5	12.7	13.9	11.4
Mental health	8,628.4	11,180.0	12,510.0	13,322.2	54.4	7.5	9.0	6.0
Disease-specific—general	5,794.9	7,301.5	8,231.0	8,627.0	48.9	6.9	8.0	5.7
Disease-specific—research	3,289.2	4,929.2	5,722.6	6,414.6	95.0	11.8	14.4	9.2
Other health	23,330.0	27,808.5	34,545.8	38,185.4	63.7	8.6	6.0	11.1

Human services	53,486.4	68,436.2	84,516.0	91,745.3	71.5	9.4	8.6	10.3
Crime and legal-related	2,169.8	2,628.5	2,956.1	3,383.1	55.9	7.7	6.6	8.8
Employment and job-related	3,864.1	4,860.6	5,603.5	6,188.5	60.2	8.2	7.9	8.4
Food, agriculture, and nutrition	1,160.2	1,512.2	2,269.4	2,597.4	123.9	14.4	9.2	19.8
Housing and shelter	4,085.2	6,055.4	8,223.7	8,891.1	117.6	13.8	14.0	13.7
Public safety and disaster preparedness	418.7	576.7	678.8	759.1	81.3	10.4	11.3	9.6
Recreation and sports	2,847.1	4,015.4	5,655.2	5,253.9	84.5	10.8	12.1	9.4
Youth development	2,449.9	3,150.7	3,780.4	4,175.0	70.4	9.3	8.7	9.8
Children and youth services	3,393.2	4,717.7	5,813.3	6,499.9	91.6	11.4	11.6	11.3
Family services	2,482.7	3,040.2	3,377.9	3,636.3	46.5	6.6	7.0	6.1
Residential and custodial care	10,964.2	14,702.4	16,883.5	18,038.4	64.5	8.7	10.3	7.1
Services promoting independence	8,478.7	10,711.4	12,311.9	13,487.2	59.1	8.0	8.1	8.0
Other human services	11,172.7	12,465.0	16,962.2	18,835.4	68.6	9.1	3.7	14.8
International and foreign affairs	4,082.2	5,000.4	5,564.5	5,791.2	41.9	6.0	7.0	5.0
Public and societal benefit	23,619.8	29,657.8	37,179.8	40,267.9	70.5	9.3	7.9	10.7
Civil rights and advocacy	529.3	744.7	941.9	1,039.6	96.4	11.9	12.1	11.8
Community improvement	4,428.9	6,156.9	7,387.0	8,340.1	88.3	11.1	11.6	10.6
Philanthropy and voluntarism	10,694.4	13,569.7	18,154.6	20,262.0	89.5	11.2	8.3	14.3
Science and technology	5,350.8	5,882.2	6,380.4	6,145.0	14.8	2.3	3.2	1.5
Social science	584.3	786.5	1,244.7	1,264.8	116.4	13.7	10.4	17.2
Other public and societal benefit	2,032.1	2,517.8	3,071.2	3,216.4	58.3	8.0	7.4	8.5
Religion-related	3,229.7	4,251.2	5,552.8	6,288.7	94.7	11.7	9.6	13.9
Unknown or unclassified	913.5	1,259.3	1,480.6	1,619.2	77.3	10.0	11.3	8.7

Note: Reporting public charities include only organizations that both reported (filed IRS Form 990) and were required to do so. Organizations not required to report include religious congregations and organizations with less than $25,000 in gross receipts. Owing to rounding, percentage figures may not total 100. The average annual percentage change is a compound rate that assumes a constant growth rate over time.

Sources: IRS Business Master Files (Exempt Organizations), 1993, 1996, 1998, 1999; IRS Return Transaction File, 1993, 1996, 1998, 1999 (returns received in those calendar years), as classified according to the National Taxonomy of Exempt Entities—Core Codes and adjusted by the National Center for Charitable Statistics. See Resource B for details.

TABLE 5.8

Reporting Public Charities: Change in Public Support by NTEE-CC Category, Circa 1992, 1995, 1997, and 1998

	Public Support (Millions of Dollars)				Total Percentage Change	Average Annual Percentage Change		
	1992	1995	1997	1998	1992–1998	1992–1998	1992–1995	1995–1998
All public charities	86,100.7	106,790.8	126,897.6	142,231.2	65.2	8.7	7.4	10.0
Arts, culture, and humanities	5,665.4	6,936.4	8,537.8	9,494.0	67.6	9.0	7.0	11.0
Performing arts organizations	1,318.9	1,631.5	2,069.0	2,263.5	71.6	9.4	7.3	11.5
Historical societies and related organizations	361.7	462.4	688.4	860.1	137.8	15.5	8.5	23.0
Museums and museum activities	1,212.2	1,664.2	2,162.5	2,388.2	97.0	12.0	11.1	12.8
Other arts, culture, and humanities	2,772.7	3,178.4	3,617.9	3,982.1	43.6	6.2	4.7	7.8
Education	20,667.8	24,038.6	28,239.2	32,973.9	59.5	8.1	5.2	11.1
Higher education institutions	14,745.2	16,165.1	18,690.0	21,142.0	43.4	6.2	3.1	9.4
Student services and organizations	569.9	785.8	1,009.0	1,273.3	123.4	14.3	11.3	17.5
Elementary and secondary education	2,024.5	2,572.8	3,269.8	3,759.1	85.7	10.9	8.3	13.5
Other education	3,328.2	4,514.9	5,270.4	6,799.5	104.3	12.6	10.7	14.6
Environment and animals	1,762.5	2,407.5	3,163.2	3,618.8	105.3	12.7	11.0	14.6
Environment	1,030.1	1,407.9	1,836.6	2,108.1	104.7	12.7	11.0	14.4
Animal-related	732.4	999.6	1,326.6	1,510.8	106.3	12.8	10.9	14.8
Health	17,806.7	22,502.4	26,095.3	28,138.0	58.0	7.9	8.1	7.7
Nursing services	557.0	643.4	773.4	786.4	41.2	5.9	4.9	6.9
Hospitals and primary treatment facilities	4,919.9	6,287.3	6,692.5	7,049.5	43.3	6.2	8.5	3.9
Treatment facilities—outpatient	1,314.2	1,614.6	2,342.8	2,146.2	63.3	8.5	7.1	10.0
Mental health	3,706.7	4,645.2	5,020.5	5,313.5	43.3	6.2	7.8	4.6
Disease-specific—general	2,588.9	3,370.0	3,985.6	4,425.9	71.0	9.3	9.2	9.5
Disease-specific—research	1,441.3	1,813.6	2,383.8	2,642.1	83.3	10.6	8.0	13.4
Other health	3,278.7	4,128.3	4,896.8	5,774.5	76.1	9.9	8.0	11.8

Human services	22,687.8	27,900.2	33,687.5	37,641.3	65.9	8.8	7.1	10.5
Crime and legal-related	1,428.5	1,660.0	1,930.2	2,204.4	54.3	7.5	5.1	9.9
Employment and job-related	1,794.0	2,117.8	2,281.6	2,576.8	43.6	6.2	5.7	6.8
Food, agriculture, and nutrition	785.5	1,087.6	1,732.9	2,035.2	159.1	17.2	11.5	23.2
Housing and shelter	1,360.9	2,114.3	3,290.5	3,428.0	151.9	16.6	15.8	17.5
Public safety and disaster preparedness	158.7	238.8	294.3	318.9	100.9	12.3	14.6	10.1
Recreation and sports	828.6	1,292.4	1,489.2	1,560.0	88.3	11.1	16.0	6.5
Youth development	1,237.1	1,474.6	1,807.0	2,226.3	80.0	10.3	6.0	14.7
Children and youth services	1,697.2	2,268.0	2,658.8	3,028.7	78.5	10.1	10.1	10.1
Family services	1,227.6	1,444.7	1,588.4	1,736.8	41.5	6.0	5.6	6.3
Residential and custodial care	2,003.8	2,280.1	2,575.5	2,819.5	40.7	5.9	4.4	7.3
Services promoting independence	4,354.1	5,186.4	5,638.1	6,186.2	42.1	6.0	6.0	6.1
Other human services	5,811.8	6,735.4	8,401.2	9,520.5	63.8	8.6	5.0	12.2
International and foreign affairs	3,336.3	4,057.7	4,388.0	4,764.6	42.8	6.1	6.7	5.5
Public and societal benefit	11,893.8	16,099.3	19,047.4	21,363.0	79.6	10.3	10.6	9.9
Civil rights and advocacy	418.5	580.4	733.3	822.7	96.6	11.9	11.5	12.3
Community improvement	2,460.0	3,473.9	4,133.0	4,550.3	85.0	10.8	12.2	9.4
Philanthropy and voluntarism	7,058.7	9,514.3	10,990.5	12,525.5	77.4	10.0	10.5	9.6
Science and technology	1,045.7	1,309.3	1,407.7	1,506.8	44.1	6.3	7.8	4.8
Social science	262.5	358.8	704.4	746.2	184.3	19.0	11.0	27.7
Other public and societal benefit	648.4	862.7	1,078.5	1,211.4	86.8	11.0	10.0	12.0
Religion-related	1,895.6	2,331.2	3,136.1	3,573.3	88.5	11.1	7.1	15.3
Unknown or unclassified	384.7	517.4	603.2	664.3	72.7	9.5	10.4	8.7

Note: Reporting public charities include only organizations that both reported (filed IRS Form 990) and were required to do so. Organizations not required to report include religious congregations and organizations with less than $25,000 in gross receipts. Owing to rounding, percentage figures may not total 100. The average annual percentage change is a compound rate that assumes a constant growth rate over time.

Sources: IRS Business Master Files (Exempt Organizations), 1993, 1996, 1998, 1999; IRS Return Transaction File, 1993, 1996, 1998, 1999 (returns received in those calendar years), as classified according to the National Taxonomy of Exempt Entities—Core Codes and adjusted by the National Center for Charitable Statistics. See Resource B for details.

- Although revenue of public charities increased by 47 percent in current dollars between 1992 and 1998, public support grew by 65 percent (49 percent in constant dollars).

- The average annual rate of growth of public support over the six-year period among public charities was 8.7 percent, but the average annual rate between 1992 and 1995 (7.4 percent) was significantly lower than the increase per year between 1995 and 1998 (10.0 percent).

- The environment and animals subsector showed the highest rate of increase in public support among the major categories, with a 105 percent increase (89 percent if adjusted for inflation) over the period. The subsector had $3.6 billion in public support in 1998, which represented about 2.5 percent of the total public support for public charities.

- Human services organizations received 26 percent of total public support in 1998, and the rate of increase between 1992 and 1998 (66 percent) was the same as for the entire sector.

- With $33 billion in public support, the education subsector had a 23 percent share of total public support in 1998, but the growth rate of 60 percent (44 percent in constant dollars) was less than for the sector as a whole. The difference in the annual rates of growth between the first three years of the period (5 percent) and the second three years (11 percent) was particularly pronounced.

- Public support for the health subsector represented only 20 percent of total public support in 1998; the growth of 58 percent was less than that of the sector as a whole between 1992 and 1998. And, unlike most of the other subsectors, the rate of growth in the health subsector was almost the same between 1995 and 1998 (7.9 percent) than between 1992 and 1995 (8.1 percent).

Growth in the Expenses of Reporting Public Charities, 1992–1998

Total expenses for reporting public charities include program, fundraising, management, and general expenses, as well as payments to affiliates. Table 5.9 shows trends in total expenses for reporting public charities between 1992 and 1998.

- At the same time that total revenue for the sector grew by 47 percent to $673 billion, total expenses grew somewhat less, by 41 percent, to

$621 billion. This represented an increase of 25 percent after adjusting for inflation over the six-year period. The average increase in current dollars was 5.9 percent per year.

- Over 60 percent of the expenses ($373 billion) were in the health subsector in 1998, but the growth rate was only 36 percent in current dollars between 1992 and 1998, somewhat less than for all public charities.

- Education expenses made up 16 percent of total expenses of all public charities, and the increase between 1992 and 1998 was 38 percent in current dollars, again slightly less than for the sector as a whole.

- Expenses in both the environment and animals subsector (growing by 59 percent, in current dollars) and in the religion-related subsector (growing by 78 percent, in current dollars) grew much more than the entire group between 1992 and 1998, but each represented less than 1 percent of total expenses.

- Growth in human services organizations was the second highest among the subsectors. The increase from $51.2 billion in 1992 to $84.5 billion in 1998 was 65 percent over the six-year period (49 percent in constant dollars). Despite the strong growth, total human services expenses represented less than 14 percent of the total for the sector.

Growth in the Assets of Reporting Public Charities, 1992–1998

Total assets for reporting public charities represent the value of cash, investments, real estate, accounts receivable, and inventories at the end of the organizations' fiscal years. Table 5.10 shows trends in total assets for reporting public charities between 1992 and 1998.

Substantial growth was achieved in this six-year time period, as assets increased from $662 billion in 1992 to $1.2 trillion in 1998. This was an increase of 83 percent (67 percent in constant dollars), with an annual rate of growth of 10.6 percent. Almost all the categories of charities showed a greater rate of increase in the last three years of the time period.

Net assets, defined as total assets minus liabilities, grew even more strongly, from $395.6 billion in 1992 to $791.5 billion in 1998. This represented a robust 100 percent increase, particularly healthy when compared with an inflation rate of only 16 percent. Table 5.11 shows trends in net assets for reporting public charities between 1992 and 1998.

- Over 44 percent of the sector's assets ($535 billion) were held by health organizations, and 29 percent ($346 billion) were held by

TABLE 5.9

Reporting Public Charities: Change in Total Expenses by NTEE-CC Category, Circa 1992, 1995, 1997, and 1998

	Total Expenses (Millions of Dollars)				Total Percentage Change	Average Annual Percentage Change		
	1992	1995	1997	1998	1992–1998	1992–1998	1992–1995	1995–1998
All public charities	440,873.4	530,301.2	598,537.3	621,162.6	40.9	5.9	6.3	5.4
Arts, culture, and humanities	10,398.0	12,261.8	13,833.4	15,183.2	46.0	6.5	5.6	7.4
Performing arts organizations	3,203.1	3,759.3	4,329.1	4,729.3	47.6	6.7	5.5	8.0
Historical societies and related organizations	650.8	768.6	928.8	1,085.2	66.8	8.9	5.7	12.2
Museums and museum activities	1,916.0	2,385.8	2,768.0	3,053.2	59.4	8.1	7.6	8.6
Other arts, culture, and humanities	4,628.2	5,348.0	5,807.6	6,315.4	36.5	5.3	4.9	5.7
Education	73,712.4	86,409.6	95,521.0	101,444.0	37.6	5.5	5.4	5.5
Higher education institutions	56,758.9	64,400.4	69,597.5	73,193.0	29.0	4.3	4.3	4.4
Student services and organizations	2,063.4	2,733.7	3,403.0	3,646.2	76.7	10.0	9.8	10.1
Elementary and secondary education	7,473.4	9,732.2	11,241.1	12,050.1	61.2	8.3	9.2	7.4
Other education	7,416.6	9,543.2	11,279.4	12,554.7	69.3	9.2	8.8	9.6
Environment and animals	2,980.3	3,639.4	4,204.5	4,742.5	59.1	8.0	6.9	9.2
Environment	1,569.8	1,881.7	2,196.4	2,490.5	58.6	8.0	6.2	9.8
Animal-related	1,410.5	1,757.7	2,008.1	2,251.9	59.7	8.1	7.6	8.6
Health	274,638.3	329,580.8	368,141.0	373,221.2	35.9	5.2	6.3	4.2
Nursing services	9,547.7	12,838.3	14,159.9	14,342.5	50.2	7.0	10.4	3.8
Hospitals and primary treatment facilities	216,256.0	254,184.0	278,763.8	275,654.3	27.5	4.1	5.5	2.7
Treatment facilities—outpatient	10,398.5	15,616.3	19,646.2	22,709.8	118.4	13.9	14.5	13.3
Mental health	8,416.6	10,732.8	12,134.0	12,838.2	52.5	7.3	8.4	6.2
Disease-specific—general	5,534.4	6,909.6	7,620.2	8,251.5	49.1	6.9	7.7	6.1
Disease-specific—research	2,692.8	3,389.6	3,904.2	4,424.0	64.3	8.6	8.0	9.3
Other health	21,792.4	25,910.2	31,912.8	35,000.8	60.6	8.2	5.9	10.5

Human services	51,238.4	64,840.4	78,315.0	84,490.8	64.9	8.7	8.2	9.2
Crime and legal-related	2,097.8	2,519.3	2,805.8	3,090.8	47.3	6.7	6.3	7.1
Employment and job-related	3,756.8	4,680.9	5,303.8	5,839.9	55.4	7.6	7.6	7.7
Food, agriculture, and nutrition	1,117.3	1,447.5	2,140.6	2,465.7	120.7	14.1	9.0	19.4
Housing and shelter	3,935.8	5,527.5	6,808.5	7,559.0	92.1	11.5	12.0	11.0
Public safety and disaster preparedness	373.2	503.7	598.3	668.6	79.2	10.2	10.5	9.9
Recreation and sports	2,585.7	3,722.7	5,338.6	4,750.4	83.7	10.7	12.9	8.5
Youth development	2,286.7	2,880.9	3,253.3	3,540.5	54.8	7.6	8.0	7.1
Children and youth services	3,271.7	4,559.0	5,588.5	6,172.6	88.7	11.2	11.7	10.6
Family services	2,390.9	2,927.8	3,201.3	3,484.1	45.7	6.5	7.0	6.0
Residential and custodial care	10,489.8	13,973.9	15,804.6	16,785.9	60.0	8.2	10.0	6.3
Services promoting independence	8,229.7	10,358.5	11,758.4	12,793.3	55.5	7.6	8.0	7.3
Other human services	10,703.0	11,738.8	15,713.4	17,340.0	62.0	8.4	3.1	13.9
International and foreign affairs	3,913.0	4,781.8	5,153.5	5,364.1	37.1	5.4	6.9	3.9
Public and societal benefit	20,177.3	23,847.0	27,270.3	30,009.6	48.7	6.8	5.7	8.0
Civil rights and advocacy	511.6	702.7	851.3	924.1	80.6	10.4	11.2	9.6
Community improvement	4,159.5	5,655.4	6,726.9	7,548.4	81.5	10.4	10.8	10.1
Philanthropy and voluntarism	8,034.9	8,843.5	10,220.2	11,886.8	47.9	6.7	3.2	10.4
Science and technology	5,086.3	5,602.9	5,614.3	5,548.5	9.1	1.5	3.3	-0.3
Social science	542.1	724.1	1,056.4	1,098.1	102.6	12.5	10.1	14.9
Other public and societal benefit	1,842.9	2,318.4	2,801.2	3,003.7	63.0	8.5	8.0	9.0
Religion-related	2,938.8	3,757.3	4,738.5	5,230.9	78.0	10.1	8.5	11.7
Unknown or unclassified	876.9	1,183.2	1,360.3	1,476.2	68.3	9.1	10.5	7.7

Note: Reporting public charities include only organizations that both reported (filed IRS Form 990) and were required to do so. Organizations not required to report include religious congregations and organizations with less than $25,000 in gross receipts. Owing to rounding, percentage figures may not total 100. The average annual percentage change is a compound rate that assumes a constant growth rate over time.

Sources: IRS Business Master Files (Exempt Organizations), 1993, 1996, 1998, 1999; IRS Return Transaction File, 1993, 1996, 1998, 1999 (returns received in those calendar years), as classified according to the National Taxonomy of Exempt Entities—Core Codes and adjusted by the National Center for Charitable Statistics. See Resource B for details.

TABLE 5.10

Reporting Public Charities: Change in Total Assets by NTEE-CC Category, Circa 1992, 1995, 1997, and 1998

	Total Assets (Millions of Dollars)				Total Percentage Change	Average Annual Percentage Change		
	1992	1995	1997	1998	1992–1998	1992–1998	1992–1995	1995–1998
All public charities	662,199.0	842,833.2	1,090,337.8	1,210,392.2	82.8	10.6	8.4	12.8
Arts, culture, and humanities	24,288.3	31,043.8	40,577.6	46,481.4	91.4	11.4	8.5	14.4
Performing arts organizations	4,737.1	6,139.6	8,221.8	9,369.3	97.8	12.0	9.0	15.1
Historical societies and related organizations	2,680.7	3,469.8	4,469.0	5,225.1	94.9	11.8	9.0	14.6
Museums and museum activities	9,168.9	12,085.2	16,416.4	18,895.2	106.1	12.8	9.6	16.1
Other arts, culture, and humanities	7,701.7	9,349.1	11,470.5	12,991.8	68.7	9.1	6.7	11.6
Education	177,140.4	220,301.9	305,889.2	346,167.2	95.4	11.8	7.5	16.3
Higher education institutions	132,205.7	159,548.4	223,150.6	252,906.2	91.3	11.4	6.5	16.6
Student services and organizations	13,545.3	19,192.0	24,522.5	25,159.4	85.7	10.9	12.3	9.4
Elementary and secondary education	16,468.4	22,200.9	32,428.5	36,465.8	121.4	14.2	10.5	18.0
Other education	14,921.0	19,360.6	25,787.5	31,635.8	112.0	13.3	9.1	17.8
Environment and animals	8,027.6	10,577.3	13,256.5	15,339.6	91.1	11.4	9.6	13.2
Environment	4,930.1	6,550.1	8,044.2	9,332.1	89.3	11.2	9.9	12.5
Animal-related	3,097.6	4,027.2	5,212.3	6,007.5	93.9	11.7	9.1	14.3
Health	317,892.6	401,903.5	489,538.3	535,345.5	68.4	9.1	8.1	10.0
Nursing services	9,492.5	12,330.8	14,932.9	16,494.7	73.8	9.6	9.1	10.2
Hospitals and primary treatment facilities	250,824.0	312,490.3	373,822.8	405,540.5	61.7	8.3	7.6	9.1
Treatment facilities—outpatient	6,890.9	10,178.1	13,328.6	15,557.3	125.8	14.5	13.9	15.2
Mental health	6,183.2	7,581.1	8,955.1	9,633.4	55.8	7.7	7.0	8.3
Disease-specific—general	6,194.9	7,596.9	9,648.1	10,751.2	73.6	9.6	7.0	12.3
Disease-specific—research	12,587.8	16,818.2	22,749.7	23,713.8	88.4	11.1	10.1	12.1
Other health	25,719.4	34,908.2	46,101.2	53,654.4	108.6	13.0	10.7	15.4

Human services	73,599.9	93,610.8	119,130.6	132,745.6	80.4	10.3	8.3	12.3
Crime and legal-related	1,393.6	1,745.6	2,180.1	2,573.6	84.7	10.8	7.8	13.8
Employment and job-related	2,682.0	3,299.2	4,130.9	4,630.9	72.7	9.5	7.1	12.0
Food, agriculture, and nutrition	803.4	1,068.7	1,406.0	1,606.6	100.0	12.2	10.0	14.6
Housing and shelter	14,447.4	19,733.2	26,319.4	29,751.8	105.9	12.8	11.0	14.7
Public safety and disaster preparedness	853.2	1,230.7	1,541.3	1,754.3	105.6	12.8	13.0	12.5
Recreation and sports	3,409.8	4,842.2	5,932.7	6,602.0	93.6	11.6	12.4	10.9
Youth development	3,994.3	4,877.7	6,276.8	7,030.8	76.0	9.9	6.9	13.0
Children and youth services	2,345.2	3,096.6	4,040.1	4,646.6	98.1	12.1	9.7	14.5
Family services	1,589.2	2,038.3	2,565.9	2,805.4	76.5	9.9	8.6	11.2
Residential and custodial care	22,921.2	29,238.3	34,192.5	37,044.7	61.6	8.3	8.5	8.2
Services promoting independence	6,165.4	7,974.3	9,811.4	11,002.3	78.5	10.1	9.0	11.3
Other human services	12,995.4	14,466.0	20,733.4	23,296.8	79.3	10.2	3.6	17.2
International and foreign affairs	3,367.3	4,572.3	5,627.8	6,060.2	80.0	10.3	10.7	9.8
Public and societal benefit	50,920.9	70,738.4	102,717.7	112,673.1	121.3	14.2	11.6	16.8
Civil rights and advocacy	414.1	567.2	799.1	945.5	128.4	14.8	11.1	18.6
Community improvement	6,628.4	9,593.9	12,076.9	14,135.7	113.3	13.5	13.1	13.8
Philanthropy and voluntarism	33,455.9	46,051.5	72,555.4	79,492.1	137.6	15.5	11.2	20.0
Science and technology	5,867.6	7,748.4	8,900.3	9,000.7	53.4	7.4	9.7	5.1
Social science	904.8	1,239.8	1,908.8	2,060.7	127.8	14.7	11.1	18.5
Other public and societal benefit	3,650.1	5,537.7	6,477.1	7,038.3	92.8	11.6	14.9	8.3
Religion-related	5,908.7	8,537.9	11,557.5	13,242.8	124.1	14.4	13.1	15.8
Unknown or unclassified	1,053.2	1,547.2	2,042.6	2,337.0	121.9	14.2	13.7	14.7

Note: Reporting public charities include only organizations that both reported (filed IRS Form 990) and were required to do so. Organizations not required to report include religious congregations and organizations with less than $25,000 in gross receipts. Owing to rounding, percentage figures may not total 100. The average annual percentage change is a compound rate that assumes a constant growth rate over time.

Sources: IRS Business Master Files (Exempt Organizations), 1993, 1996, 1998, 1999; IRS Return Transaction File, 1993, 1996, 1998, 1999 (returns received in those calendar years), as classified according to the National Taxonomy of Exempt Entities—Core Codes and adjusted by the National Center for Charitable Statistics. See Resource B for details.

TABLE 5.11

Reporting Public Charities: Change in Net Assets by NTEE-CC Category, Circa 1992, 1995, 1997, and 1998

	Net Assets (Millions of Dollars)				Total Percentage Change	Average Annual Percentage Change		
	1992	1995	1997	1998	1992–1998	1992–1998	1992–1995	1995–1998
All public charities	395,644.3	515,421.9	709,015.6	791,495.4	100.1	12.3	9.2	15.4
Arts, culture, and humanities	18,707.1	24,708.0	34,561.9	39,622.5	111.8	13.3	9.7	17.0
Performing arts organizations	3,120.5	4,140.6	6,390.5	7,395.1	137.0	15.5	9.9	21.3
Historical societies and related organizations	2,368.9	3,137.6	4,073.8	4,747.5	100.4	12.3	9.8	14.8
Museums and museum activities	7,449.0	10,192.0	14,567.3	16,732.9	124.6	14.4	11.0	18.0
Other arts, culture, and humanities	5,768.6	7,237.8	9,530.4	10,747.1	86.3	10.9	7.9	14.1
Education	129,086.4	160,501.8	229,891.7	262,384.7	103.3	12.5	7.5	17.8
Higher education institutions	101,058.1	122,178.5	174,754.6	198,553.5	96.5	11.9	6.5	17.6
Student services and organizations	2,865.9	5,042.8	6,706.5	7,830.5	173.2	18.2	20.7	15.8
Elementary and secondary education	13,092.2	17,439.3	26,746.2	30,112.2	130.0	14.9	10.0	20.0
Other education	12,070.2	15,841.3	21,684.5	25,888.5	114.5	13.6	9.5	17.8
Environment and animals	5,694.9	7,642.6	10,822.1	12,627.7	121.7	14.2	10.3	18.2
Environment	3,249.9	4,537.2	6,522.8	7,670.2	136.0	15.4	11.8	19.1
Animal-related	2,444.9	3,105.4	4,299.3	4,957.4	102.8	12.5	8.3	16.9
Health	163,929.3	214,913.5	273,303.0	298,227.4	81.9	10.5	9.4	11.5
Nursing services	3,352.8	4,350.4	5,958.1	6,812.7	103.2	12.5	9.1	16.1
Hospitals and primary treatment facilities	122,881.3	160,726.0	200,508.0	216,967.6	76.6	9.9	9.4	10.5
Treatment facilities—outpatient	3,480.2	5,022.9	6,416.6	6,807.1	95.6	11.8	13.0	10.7
Mental health	3,358.6	4,316.8	5,264.1	5,677.7	69.0	9.1	8.7	9.6
Disease-specific—general	3,901.5	4,875.9	6,245.0	7,038.8	80.4	10.3	7.7	13.0
Disease-specific—research	10,985.8	13,685.3	18,176.0	18,930.6	72.3	9.5	7.6	11.4
Other health	15,969.2	21,936.1	30,735.2	35,992.8	125.4	14.5	11.2	17.9

Human services	34,767.7	43,883.9	61,568.0	69,975.3	101.3	12.4	8.1	16.8
Crime and legal-related	850.9	1,126.3	1,556.1	1,881.6	121.1	14.1	9.8	18.7
Employment and job-related	1,768.3	2,169.9	2,829.3	3,209.1	81.5	10.4	7.1	13.9
Food, agriculture, and nutrition	565.8	801.9	1,099.7	1,267.1	124.0	14.4	12.3	16.5
Housing and shelter	1,929.8	3,453.3	6,587.0	8,003.4	314.7	26.8	21.4	32.3
Public safety and disaster preparedness	651.9	983.3	1,252.0	1,425.4	118.7	13.9	14.7	13.2
Recreation and sports	2,587.9	3,400.6	4,592.5	5,089.1	96.6	11.9	9.5	14.4
Youth development	3,271.5	4,169.1	5,553.1	6,232.2	90.5	11.3	8.4	14.3
Children and youth services	1,684.7	2,094.0	2,855.6	3,294.3	95.5	11.8	7.5	16.3
Family services	1,135.7	1,440.6	1,932.1	2,099.1	84.8	10.8	8.2	13.4
Residential and custodial care	7,704.8	9,607.3	12,464.8	13,942.9	81.0	10.4	7.6	13.2
Services promoting independence	3,478.3	4,589.3	5,976.7	6,827.4	96.3	11.9	9.7	14.2
Other human services	9,138.1	10,048.3	14,869.1	16,703.7	82.8	10.6	3.2	18.5
International and foreign affairs	2,181.2	3,107.9	4,244.7	4,635.0	112.5	13.4	12.5	14.3
Public and societal benefit	36,487.7	53,240.0	84,262.1	92,086.2	152.4	16.7	13.4	20.0
Civil rights and advocacy	256.0	357.1	587.9	710.5	177.5	18.5	11.7	25.8
Community improvement	3,391.2	4,956.1	6,546.4	7,725.7	127.8	14.7	13.5	15.9
Philanthropy and voluntarism	26,623.4	39,906.5	66,628.0	72,369.6	171.8	18.1	14.4	21.9
Science and technology	3,743.1	4,836.7	6,138.4	6,277.8	67.7	9.0	8.9	9.1
Social science	632.9	849.5	1,375.6	1,507.9	138.3	15.6	10.3	21.1
Other public and societal benefit	1,841.1	2,334.2	2,985.8	3,494.7	89.8	11.3	8.2	14.4
Religion-related	4,227.6	6,686.2	9,189.8	10,545.0	149.4	16.5	16.5	16.4
Unknown or unclassified	562.6	737.8	1,172.4	1,391.5	147.4	16.3	9.5	23.6

Note: Reporting public charities include only organizations that both reported (filed IRS Form 990) and were required to report include religious congregations and organizations with less than $25,000 in gross receipts. Owing to rounding, percentage figures may not total 100. The average annual percentage change is a compound rate that assumes a constant growth rate over time.

Sources: IRS Business Master Files (Exempt Organizations), 1993, 1996, 1998, 1999; IRS Return Transaction File, 1993, 1996, 1998, 1999 (returns received in those calendar years), as classified according to the National Taxonomy of Exempt Entities—Core Codes and adjusted by the National Center for Charitable Statistics. See Resource B for details.

the education subsector. However, health organizations' assets grew by only 68 percent in current dollars over the six-year period, whereas education institutions' assets increased in value by over 95 percent.

- Religion-related organizations, with a change of 124 percent (108 percent in constant dollars), and public and societal benefit organizations, with a change of 121 percent (105 percent in constant dollars), showed much higher increases in total assets than the other types of charities, but together, the two subsectors held only 10 percent of the total assets of all charities.

- The different types of organizations had wide variations in changes in net assets, ranging from a slower rate of increase of 82 percent for the health subsector (66 percent after adjustment for inflation) to 152 percent for the public and societal benefit subsector (136 percent in constant dollars). Net assets for health organizations, however, reached $298 billion, representing 38 percent of the total for the sector, whereas public and societal benefit organizations held $92 billion, less than 12 percent of the total for the sector.

- Over 33 percent of the net assets of the sector ($262 billion) were held by the education subsector, with a rate of increase of 103 percent, which mirrored that of the group as a whole.

- There was a marked difference in the rate of change in net assets between the first three-year period (a 9.2 percent annual increase) and the second three-year period (a remarkable 15.4 percent annual increase). Almost all the subsectors realized a much greater rate of increase in net assets between 1995 and 1998.

Trends in Reporting Public Charities by Major Subsector

This section describes each of the major subsectors and highlights some of the significant findings from the detailed tables that accompany this chapter. The discussion is based on detailed 1998 financial tables (presented in the following sections) and on the previous trend tables (Tables 5.6–5.11) covering the period 1992 to 1998.

Arts, Culture, and Humanities

Table 5.12 shows the revenue and expenses of reporting public charities in the arts, culture, and humanities subsector in 1998.

- The 24,000 arts, culture, and humanities organizations represent 11 percent of reporting public charities but only 2.4 percent of total expenses. Major segments include the performing arts, museums (art, historical, and other), visual arts, historical societies, and humanities organizations such as literary societies.

- The number of arts organizations grew by more than 37 percent between 1992 and 1998, approximately the same pace as for reporting public charities as a whole. Of the total, about 5 percent were supporting organizations, compared with 11 percent for the sector as a whole.

- Total revenue and public support both grew by 9 percent per year, for a cumulative increase of 67 percent during the period (51 percent after inflation). This compares with growth rates (in current dollars) of 47 percent in total revenue and 65 percent in public support for all reporting public charities.

- Private contributions accounted for more than 39 percent of total revenue in 1998, fees for goods and services (for example, ticket sales) for 30 percent, and investment income for 13 percent. Private contributions were a higher proportion only for the environment and animals category (47 percent) and the international and foreign affairs category (62 percent). Fees as a source of revenue were relatively low (compared with the health, education, and human services subsectors), but investment income was relatively high.

Education

Table 5.13 shows the revenue and expenses of reporting public charities in the education subsector in 1998.

- The education subsector includes some of the nonprofit sector's largest institutions, as all nonprofit, nongovernmental universities, are legally defined as "public charities" in the United States. At the same time, there are thousands of parent-teacher associations and organizations, booster clubs, and other organizations involved in preschool, primary, and secondary education, as well as more than 4,000 private primary and secondary schools. It should be noted that *most* of the more than 21,000 religious or parochial schools are closely tied to religious congregations and are *not* required to register or to file a separate Form 990 with the IRS (U.S. Department of Education, National Center for Education Statistics, 1999).

- The nearly 37,000 education organizations represent 16 percent of reporting public charities and 16 percent of total expenses. However,

TABLE 5.12

Reporting Public Charities: Revenue and Expenses for NTEE-CC Arts, Culture, and Humanities Category, 1998

	All Organizations[a]		Operating Organizations[b]		Supporting Organizations[c]	
	Amount (Millions)	Percent	Amount (Millions)	Percent	Amount (Millions)	Percent
Public support	9,494.0	48.9[d]	8,989.9	48.7[d]	504.1	52.5[d]
Private contributions	7,661.8	39.5	7,216.3	39.1	445.5	46.4
Direct contributions	7,320.9	37.7	6,884.9	37.3	436.0	45.4
Indirect contributions	340.9	1.8	331.3	1.8	9.5	1.0
Government grants	1,832.3	9.4	1,773.6	9.6	58.6	6.1
Fees for services and goods	5,817.6	30.0	5,697.0	30.9	120.6	12.6
Program service revenue[e]	5,225.2	26.9	5,115.5	27.7	109.7	11.4
Net income from sales of inventory	592.4	3.1	581.5	3.2	10.9	1.1
Investment income	2,550.1	13.1	2,278.6	12.4	271.6	28.3
Dividends	652.9	3.4	560.2	3.0	92.7	9.7
Interest	211.0	1.1	195.2	1.1	15.7	1.6
Net gain on sale of assets	1,598.9	8.2	1,451.2	7.9	147.8	15.4
Other investment income	87.3	0.4	72.0	0.4	15.4	1.6
Other income	1,545.9	8.0	1,482.1	8.0	63.7	6.6
Dues and assessments	655.0	3.4	631.5	3.4	23.5	2.4
Net income from special events	244.1	1.3	222.8	1.2	21.3	2.2
Other (including net rental)	646.8	3.3	627.8	3.4	19.0	2.0
Total revenue	19,407.6	100.0	18,447.6	100.0	960.0	100.0
Paid personnel	5,397.6	39.0	5,254.7	39.1[f]	142.9	34.6[f]
Wages and salaries	4,572.3	33.0	4,448.7	33.1	123.6	29.9
Compensation of officers	476.8	3.4	461.2	3.4	15.6	3.8
Other wages and salaries	4,095.5	29.6	3,987.5	29.7	108.0	26.2
Fringe benefits and payroll taxes	825.3	6.0	806.0	6.0	19.3	4.7
Pension plan contributions	151.4	1.1	147.4	1.1	4.0	1.0
Other employee benefits	338.2	2.4	331.2	2.5	7.0	1.7
Payroll taxes	335.6	2.4	327.4	2.4	8.2	2.0
Supplies	256.9	1.9	250.3	1.9	6.6	1.6
Communications (printing, phone, postage)	677.1	4.9	660.2	4.9	16.9	4.1
Professional fees	583.2	4.2	561.1	4.2	22.0	5.3
Occupancy	541.1	3.9	529.2	3.9	11.9	2.9
Equipment rental and maintenance	187.3	1.4	180.4	1.3	6.8	1.6
Interest	151.4	1.1	143.4	1.1	8.0	1.9
Depreciation and depletion	619.9	4.5	594.3	4.4	25.5	6.2

Other	5,431.9	39.2	5,260.0	39.2	172.0	41.7
Total current operating expenses	13,846.4	100.0	13,433.7	100.0	412.7	100.0
Total current operating expenses	13,846.4	91.2[g]	13,433.7	92.3[g]	412.7	66.1[g]
Plus grants and benefits	1,286.6	8.5	1,081.3	7.4	205.3	32.9
Grants and allocations	1,236.6	8.1	1,039.3	7.1	197.4	31.6
Specific assistance to individuals	36.0	0.2	34.4	0.2	1.5	0.2
Benefits paid to members	14.0	0.1	7.6	0.1	6.4	1.0
Plus payments to affiliates	50.2	0.3	43.7	0.3	6.5	1.0
Total expenses	15,183.2	100.0	14,558.6	100.0	624.6	100.0
Net income (revenue minus expenses)	4,224.4	21.8[d]	3,888.9	21.1[d]	335.5	34.9[d]
Total assets	46,481.4	306.1[g]	42,528.9	292.1[g]	3,952.4	632.8[g]
Total liabilities	6,858.8	45.2	6,546.6	45.0	312.2	50.0
Net assets (assets minus liabilities)	39,622.5	261.0	35,982.3	247.2	3,640.2	582.8

Note: *Reporting public charities include only organizations that both reported (filed IRS Form 990) and were required to do so. (The following were excluded: foreign organizations, government-associated organizations, organizations without state identifiers, and organizations excluded at the authors' discretion.) Organizations not required to report include religious congregations and organizations with less than $25,000 in gross receipts. Owing to rounding, column totals may not equal the sum of individual items. The table includes separate analyses for operating public charities and supporting organizations to provide a clearer picture of the distribution of funds and to avoid double-counting of the financial information for supporting organizations. See Resource B for a detailed description of the methodology. See http://www.nccs.urban.org for a full description of the National Taxonomy of Exempt Entities—Core Codes system.*

[a] *Number of organizations = 23,779.*
[b] *Number of organizations = 22,634.*
[c] *Number of organizations = 1,145.*
[d] *Percentages for revenue items and net income are expressed as percentages of total revenue.*
[e] *Program service revenue may include sizable income via government contracts, which the data source is unable to differentiate from funds raised via the public (that is, fees for services).*
[f] *Percentages for current operating expense items are expressed as percentages of total current operating expenses.*
[g] *Percentages for other expense items, assets, and liabilities are expressed as percentages of total expenses.*

Sources: *IRS Forms 990 and 990-EZ, GuideStar-NCCS National Nonprofit Organization Database, 1999 (returns received in that calendar year), as classified according to the National Taxonomy of Exempt Entities—Core Codes and adjusted by the National Center for Charitable Statistics and INDEPENDENT SECTOR. See Resource B for details.*

TABLE 5.13

Reporting Public Charities: Revenue and Expenses for NTEE-CC Education Category, 1998

	All Organizations[a]		Operating Organizations[b]		Supporting Organizations[c]	
	Amount (Millions)	Percent	Amount (Millions)	Percent	Amount (Millions)	Percent
Public support	32,973.9	25.6[d]	30,522.6	24.5[d]	2,451.3	55.7[d]
Private contributions	20,249.7	15.7	17,898.6	14.4	2,351.1	53.4
Direct contributions	19,146.3	14.9	17,200.2	13.8	1,946.0	44.2
Indirect contributions	1,103.4	0.9	698.3	0.6	405.1	9.2
Government grants	12,724.2	9.9	12,624.0	10.1	100.2	2.3
Fees for services and goods	68,883.5	53.5	68,252.4	54.9	631.1	14.3
Program service revenue[e]	68,376.9	53.1	67,812.0	54.5	565.0	12.8
Net income from sales of inventory	506.5	0.4	440.4	0.4	66.2	1.5
Investment income	20,210.8	15.7	19,077.6	15.3	1,133.1	25.8
Dividends	4,588.7	3.6	4,289.7	3.4	299.0	6.8
Interest	1,214.4	0.9	1,150.8	0.9	63.6	1.4
Net gain on sale of assets	13,167.6	10.2	12,471.3	10.0	696.2	15.8
Other investment income	1,240.1	1.0	1,165.7	0.9	74.3	1.7
Other income	6,740.0	5.2	6,555.1	5.3	184.9	4.2
Dues and assessments	732.5	0.6	698.2	0.6	34.3	0.8
Net income from special events	436.5	0.3	373.9	0.3	62.6	1.4
Other (including net rental)	5,571.1	4.3	5,483.1	4.4	88.1	2.0
Total revenue	128,808.2	100.0	124,407.7	100.0	4,400.4	100.0
Paid personnel	49,100.0	54.0[f]	48,673.4	54.4[f]	426.6	31.0[f]
Wages and salaries	40,164.8	44.2	39,797.9	44.4	366.9	26.7
Compensation of officers	1,396.6	1.5	1,353.5	1.5	43.1	3.1
Other wages and salaries	38,768.2	42.6	38,444.4	42.9	323.8	23.5
Fringe benefits and payroll taxes	8,935.1	9.8	8,875.5	9.9	59.6	4.3
Pension plan contributions	2,264.6	2.5	2,246.7	2.5	17.9	1.3
Other employee benefits	4,122.7	4.5	4,099.7	4.6	23.0	1.7
Payroll taxes	2,547.8	2.8	2,529.0	2.8	18.8	1.4
Supplies	5,156.6	5.7	5,129.0	5.7	27.7	2.0
Communications (printing, phone, postage)	3,469.8	3.8	3,417.3	3.8	52.4	3.8
Professional fees	1,828.6	2.0	1,751.0	2.0	77.6	5.6
Occupancy	3,432.0	3.8	3,406.0	3.8	26.0	1.9
Equipment rental and maintenance	1,371.0	1.5	1,357.6	1.5	13.5	1.0
Interest	2,788.8	3.1	2,661.0	3.0	127.8	9.3
Depreciation and depletion	4,484.4	4.9	4,452.0	5.0	32.4	2.4
Other	19,296.5	21.2	18,704.6	20.9	591.9	43.0
Total current operating expenses	90,927.7	100.0	89,551.7	100.0	1,375.9	100.0

Total current operating expenses	90,927.7	89.6[g]	89,551.7	90.5[g]	1,375.9	55.5[g]
Plus grants and benefits	10,138.7	10.0	9,322.9	9.4	815.8	32.9
Grants and allocations	9,313.5	9.2	8,519.6	8.6	793.9	32.0
Specific assistance to individuals	771.8	0.8	757.7	0.8	14.1	0.6
Benefits paid to members	53.4	0.1	45.6	0.0	7.8	0.3
Plus payments to affiliates	377.6	0.4	90.5	0.1	287.1	11.6
Total expenses	101,444.0	100.0	98,965.2	100.0	2,478.9	100.0
Net income (revenue minus expenses)	27,364.1	21.2[d]	25,442.5	20.5[d]	1,921.6	43.7[d]
Total assets	346,167.2	341.2[g]	329,161.7	332.6[g]	17,005.5	686.0[g]
Total liabilities	83,782.5	82.6	81,919.4	82.8	1,863.1	75.2
Net assets (assets minus liabilities)	262,384.7	258.6	247,242.3	249.8	15,142.4	610.9

Note: *Reporting public charities include only organizations that both reported (filed IRS Form 990) and were required to do so. (The following were excluded: foreign organizations, government-associated organizations, organizations without state identifiers, and organizations excluded at the authors' discretion.) Organizations not required to report include religious congregations and organizations with less than $25,000 in gross receipts. Owing to rounding, column totals may not equal the sum of individual items. The table includes separate analyses for operating public charities and supporting organizations to provide a clearer picture of the distribution of funds and to avoid double-counting of the financial information for supporting organizations. See Resource B for a detailed description of the methodology. See http://www.nccs.urban.org for a full description of the National Taxonomy of Exempt Entities—Core Codes system.*

[a] *Number of organizations = 36,513.*

[b] *Number of organizations = 32,529.*

[c] *Number of organizations = 3,984.*

[d] *Percentages for revenue items and net income are expressed as percentages of total revenue.*

[e] *Program service revenue may include sizable income via government contracts, which the data source is unable to differentiate from funds raised via the public (that is, fees for services).*

[f] *Percentages for current operating expense items are expressed as percentages of total current operating expenses.*

[g] *Percentages for other expense items, assets, and liabilities are expressed as percentages of total expenses.*

Sources: *IRS Forms 990 and 990-EZ, GuideStar-NCCS National Nonprofit Organization Database, 1999 (returns received in that calendar year), as classified according to the National Taxonomy of Exempt Entities—Core Codes and adjusted by the National Center for Charitable Statistics and INDEPENDENT SECTOR. See Resource B for details.*

the education subsector includes organizations of widely varying sizes. Although colleges and universities account for less than 7 percent of the number of education organizations, they represent more than three-fourths of total revenue, public support, expenses, and assets of education organizations.

- The number of education organizations grew by 53 percent between 1992 and 1998, greater than the 39 percent for the group of public charities as a whole. However, there were differences in growth rates in the subsector. Higher education institutions and elementary and secondary education institutions grew only at the rates of 20 and 26 percent, respectively, whereas student services organizations grew at a rate of nearly 80 percent.

- Fees for services and goods, primarily tuition payments, accounted for a much higher percentage of revenue (54 percent) for education organizations than for other types of public charities, except for health organizations. Private contributions accounted for 16 percent, far less than the comparable proportion for other subsectors, whereas investment income was a larger proportion at 16 percent.

Environment and Animals

Table 5.14 shows the revenue and expenses of reporting public charities in the environment and animals subsector in 1998.

- This group of about 7,400 public charities accounts for 3 percent of the total number of organizations, and 0.8 percent of total expenses, of all public charities. (There are another 1,500 organizations in the environment and animals category that are tax exempt under section 501(c)(4) of the Internal Revenue Code, called "social welfare" organizations; these organizations are not included in this analysis.)

- The number of organizations in the environment and animals subsector grew by 65 percent between 1992 and 1998, which represents much higher growth than in most other subsectors.

- Between 1992 and 1998 the rate of growth in total revenue for charities in the environment and animals category was 85 percent, compared with 47 percent for all reporting public charities. Public support grew by 105 percent, compared with 65 percent for the whole independent sector.

- Private contributions accounted for 47 percent of revenue, whereas the proportion from fees for services and goods was 23 percent. Most subsectors had much lower shares of revenue from private sources and much higher shares of revenue from fees.

Health

Table 5.15 shows the revenue and expenses of reporting public charities in the health subsector in 1998.

- The 33,400 nonprofit health care organizations have a range of activities, covering direct delivery of services (hospitals, nursing homes, community health centers), research, and mental health. Health organizations represent 15 percent of all reporting public charities, 57 percent of total revenue, 70 percent of total fees for services and goods, and 62 percent of total current operating expenses.

- With the smallest increase in the number of organizations of any major category (only 15 percent), it was also at or near the bottom in growth of total revenue, public support, expenses, assets, and net assets between 1992 and 1998.

- Hospitals represented at least two-thirds of the health subsector in 1998, but their rate of growth has tended to lag behind other segments of the health subsector. The slow growth rate is probably a result of several factors affecting the hospital industry, such as pressure from government and managed care organizations to limit charges and curtail admissions. In addition, some nonprofit hospitals have been acquired by for-profit hospital chains or converted from nonprofit to for-profit status.

- All health organizations have relied on payments for services to a far greater extent than any other subsector, with 86 percent of their revenue in 1998 originating from this source. Other revenue sources—private contributions, government grants, and investment income—did not reach the 5 percent level.

Human Services

Table 5.16 shows the revenue and expenses of reporting public charities in the human services subsector in 1998.

- The 78,000 human services organizations constitute more than one-third of all reporting public charities. However, most of them are small, so the subsector accounts for only 14 percent of public charities' expenses. Human services include a broad array of activities, ranging from traditional social services to job training, legal aid, housing, youth development, disaster assistance, and food distribution. Although many serve predominantly low-income populations, others serve broader categories, such as youth or the elderly.

- The number of human services organizations grew at about the same rate (37 percent) as reporting public charities as a group (39 percent) between 1992 and 1998.

TABLE 5.14

Reporting Public Charities: Revenue and Expenses for NTEE-CC Environment and Animals Category, 1998

	All Organizations[a]		Operating Organizations[b]		Supporting Organizations[c]	
	Amount (Millions)	Percent	Amount (Millions)	Percent	Amount (Millions)	Percent
Public support	3,618.8	57.2[d]	3,505.6	57.7[d]	113.2	45.7[d]
Private contributions	2,962.7	46.8	2,853.9	47.0	108.8	43.9
Direct contributions	2,855.4	45.1	2,758.3	45.4	97.1	39.2
Indirect contributions	107.4	1.7	95.7	1.6	11.7	4.7
Government grants	656.1	10.4	651.7	10.7	4.4	1.8
Fees for services and goods	1,462.2	23.1	1,406.5	23.1	55.6	22.5
Program service revenue[e]	1,280.6	20.2	1,240.1	20.4	40.5	16.4
Net income from sales of inventory	181.5	2.9	166.4	2.7	15.1	6.1
Investment income	673.1	10.6	627.4	10.3	45.7	18.4
Dividends	168.3	2.7	149.1	2.5	19.2	7.8
Interest	74.0	1.2	66.9	1.1	7.2	2.9
Net gain on sale of assets	397.6	6.3	379.9	6.2	17.8	7.2
Other investment income	33.1	0.5	31.6	0.5	1.5	0.6
Other income	571.6	9.0	538.4	8.9	33.2	13.4
Dues and assessments	249.3	3.9	236.3	3.9	13.1	5.3
Net income from special events	98.3	1.6	93.7	1.5	4.6	1.9
Other (including net rental)	224.0	3.5	208.4	3.4	15.5	6.3
Total revenue	6,325.7	100.0	6,078.0	100.0	247.7	100.0
Paid personnel	1,752.4	40.8[f]	1,711.1	41.0[f]	41.3	33.5[f]
Wages and salaries	1,475.5	34.3	1,439.0	34.5	36.5	29.6
Compensation of officers	149.0	3.5	145.0	3.5	4.0	3.3
Other wages and salaries	1,326.4	30.9	1,293.9	31.0	32.5	26.3
Fringe benefits and payroll taxes	276.9	6.4	272.1	6.5	4.8	3.9
Pension plan contributions	41.1	1.0	40.1	1.0	1.0	0.8
Other employee benefits	131.0	3.0	129.5	3.1	1.5	1.2
Payroll taxes	104.8	2.4	102.5	2.5	2.3	1.9
Supplies	125.9	2.9	123.9	3.0	2.1	1.7
Communications (printing, phone, postage)	299.6	7.0	293.6	7.0	6.0	4.9
Professional fees	240.3	5.6	225.6	5.4	14.7	11.9
Occupancy	131.8	3.1	129.3	3.1	2.6	2.1
Equipment rental and maintenance	57.4	1.3	55.2	1.3	2.2	1.8
Interest	34.9	0.8	34.0	0.8	0.9	0.8
Depreciation and depletion	168.3	3.9	164.8	3.9	3.4	2.8

Other	1,486.2	34.6	1,436.1	34.4	50.1	40.6
Total current operating expenses	4,296.8	100.0	4,173.5	100.0	123.3	100.0
Total current operating expenses	4,296.8	90.6[g]	4,173.5	91.1[g]	123.3	75.3[g]
Plus grants and benefits	435.0	9.2	397.1	8.7	37.9	23.1
Grants and allocations	415.3	8.8	378.2	8.3	37.1	22.7
Specific assistance to individuals	13.7	0.3	13.6	0.3	0.1	0.1
Benefits paid to members	6.0	0.1	5.3	0.1	0.7	0.4
Plus payments to affiliates	10.7	0.2	8.2	0.2	2.5	1.5
Total expenses	4,742.5	100.0	4,578.8	100.0	163.7	100.0
Net income (revenue minus expenses)	1,583.3	25.0[d]	1,499.2	24.7[d]	84.0	33.9[d]
Total assets	15,339.6	323.5[g]	14,424.1	315.0[g]	915.5	559.3[g]
Total liabilities	2,711.9	57.2	2,652.3	57.9	59.6	36.4
Net assets (assets minus liabilities)	12,627.7	266.3	11,771.8	257.1	855.9	522.9

Note: *Reporting public charities include only organizations that both reported (filed IRS Form 990) and were required to do so. (The following were excluded: foreign organizations, government-associated organizations, organizations without state identifiers, and organizations excluded at the authors' discretion.) Organizations not required to report include religious congregations and organizations with less than $25,000 in gross receipts. Owing to rounding, column totals may not equal the sum of individual items. The table includes separate analyses for operating public charities and supporting organizations to provide a clearer picture of the distribution of funds and to avoid double-counting of the financial information for supporting organizations. See Resource B for a detailed description of the methodology. See http://www.nccs.urban.org for a full description of the National Taxonomy of Exempt Entities—Core Codes system.*

[a] *Number of organizations = 7,458.*

[b] *Number of organizations = 7,188.*

[c] *Number of organizations = 270.*

[d] *Percentages for revenue items and net income are expressed as percentages of total revenue.*

[e] *Program service revenue may include sizable income via government contracts, which the data source is unable to differentiate from funds raised via the public (that is, fees for services).*

[f] *Percentages for current operating expense items are expressed as percentages of total current operating expenses.*

[g] *Percentages for other expense items, assets, and liabilities are expressed as percentages of total expenses.*

Sources: *IRS Forms 990 and 990-EZ, GuideStar-NCCS National Nonprofit Organization Database, 1999 (returns received in that calendar year), as classified according to the National Taxonomy of Exempt Entities—Core Codes and adjusted by the National Center for Charitable Statistics and INDEPENDENT SECTOR. See Resource B for details.*

TABLE 5.15

Reporting Public Charities: Revenue and Expenses for NTEE-CC Health Category, 1998

	All Organizations[a]		Operating Organizations[b]		Supporting Organizations[c]	
	Amount (Millions)	Percent	Amount (Millions)	Percent	Amount (Millions)	Percent
Public support	28,253.3	7.2[d]	25,873.9	6.9[d]	2,379.4	12.0[d]
Private contributions	16,284.0	4.1	14,091.8	3.8	2,192.3	11.1
Direct contributions	11,683.3	3.0	10,051.7	2.7	1,631.7	8.2
Indirect contributions	4,600.7	1.2	4,040.1	1.1	560.6	2.8
Government grants	11,969.3	3.0	11,782.1	3.2	187.2	0.9
Fees for services and goods	337,228.2	85.9	322,600.9	86.6	14,627.3	73.8
Program service revenue[e]	335,910.1	85.6	321,355.6	86.2	14,554.5	73.4
Net income from sales of inventory	1,318.1	0.3	1,245.3	0.3	72.8	0.4
Investment income	17,212.5	4.4	14,867.1	4.0	2,345.4	11.8
Dividends	5,961.3	1.5	5,155.4	1.4	805.9	4.1
Interest	3,489.3	0.9	3,256.5	0.9	232.8	1.2
Net gain on sale of assets	6,695.4	1.7	5,536.0	1.5	1,159.4	5.8
Other investment income	1,066.5	0.3	919.2	0.2	147.2	0.7
Other income	9,822.0	2.5	9,351.4	2.5	470.6	2.4
Dues and assessments	1,807.5	0.5	1,800.8	0.5	6.7	0.0
Net income from special events	505.5	0.1	429.2	0.1	76.3	0.4
Other (including net rental)	7,509.0	1.9	7,121.4	1.9	387.6	2.0
Total revenue	392,516.0	100.0	372,693.3	100.0	19,822.7	100.0
Paid personnel	159,509.5	44.6[f]	157,419.0	45.9[f]	2,090.5	14.7[f]
Wages and salaries	133,229.5	37.3	131,596.4	38.3	1,633.1	11.5
Compensation of officers	3,303.3	0.9	3,208.7	0.9	94.7	0.7
Other wages and salaries	129,926.1	36.3	128,387.8	37.4	1,538.4	10.8
Fringe benefits and payroll taxes	26,280.0	7.4	25,822.6	7.5	457.4	3.2
Pension plan contributions	4,205.5	1.2	3,940.8	1.1	264.7	1.9
Other employee benefits	13,432.8	3.8	13,336.6	3.9	96.2	0.7
Payroll taxes	8,641.8	2.4	8,545.2	2.5	96.5	0.7
Supplies	41,016.9	11.5	39,515.1	11.5	1,501.8	10.5
Communications (printing, phone, postage)	4,571.5	1.3	4,330.8	1.3	240.8	1.7
Professional fees	2,886.3	0.8	2,680.8	0.8	205.6	1.4
Occupancy	6,565.4	1.8	6,237.3	1.8	328.1	2.3
Equipment rental and maintenance	5,328.6	1.5	5,077.8	1.5	250.8	1.8
Interest	7,377.5	2.1	6,923.0	2.0	454.5	3.2
Depreciation and depletion	17,641.6	4.9	16,938.9	4.9	702.7	4.9
Other	112,629.8	31.5	104,157.9	30.3	8,471.9	59.5
Total current operating expenses	357,527.1	100.0	343,280.6	100.0	14,246.6	100.0

Total current operating expenses	357,527.1	95.8[g]	343,280.6	96.5[g]	14,246.6	81.7[g]
Plus grants and benefits	13,617.2	3.6	10,513.2	3.0	3,104.0	17.8
Grants and allocations	6,161.7	1.7	4,352.3	1.2	1,809.4	10.4
Specific assistance to individuals	2,858.4	0.8	2,422.2	0.7	436.2	2.5
Benefits paid to members	4,597.2	1.2	3,738.8	1.1	858.4	4.9
Plus payments to affiliates	2,076.9	0.6	1,991.6	0.6	85.2	0.5
Total expenses	373,221.2	100.0	355,785.4	100.0	17,435.8	100.0
Net income (revenue minus expenses)	19,294.8	4.9[d]	16,907.9	4.5[d]	2,386.9	12.0[d]
Total assets	535,345.5	143.4[g]	499,832.1	140.5[g]	35,513.4	203.7[g]
Total liabilities	237,118.0	63.5	228,396.7	64.2	8,721.3	50.0
Net assets (assets minus liabilities)	298,227.4	79.9	271,435.3	76.3	26,792.1	153.7

Note: Reporting public charities include only organizations that both reported (filed IRS Form 990) and were required to do so. (The following were excluded: foreign organizations, government-associated organizations, organizations without state identifiers, and organizations excluded at the authors' discretion.) Organizations not required to report include religious congregations and organizations with less than $25,000 in gross receipts. Owing to rounding, column totals may not equal the sum of individual items. The table includes separate analyses for operating public charities and supporting organizations to provide a clearer picture of the distribution of funds and to avoid double-counting of the financial information for supporting organizations. See Resource B for a detailed description of the methodology. See http://www.nccs.urban.org for a full description of the National Taxonomy of Exempt Entities—Core Codes system.

[a] Number of organizations = 33,427.
[b] Number of organizations = 29,824.
[c] Number of organizations = 3,603.
[d] Percentages for revenue items and net income are expressed as percentages of total revenue.
[e] Program service revenue may include sizable income via government contracts, which the data source is unable to differentiate from funds raised via the public (that is, fees for services).
[f] Percentages for current operating expense items are expressed as percentages of total current operating expenses.
[g] Percentages for other expense items, assets, and liabilities are expressed as percentages of total expenses.

Sources: IRS Forms 990 and 990-EZ, GuideStar-NCCS National Nonprofit Organization Database, 1999 (returns received in that calendar year), as classified according to the National Taxonomy of Exempt Entities—Core Codes and adjusted by the National Center for Charitable Statistics and INDEPENDENT SECTOR. See Resource B for details.

TABLE 5.16

Reporting Public Charities: Revenue and Expenses for NTEE-CC Human Services Category, 1998

	All Organizations[a]		Operating Organizations[b]		Supporting Organizations[c]	
	Amount (Millions)	Percent	Amount (Millions)	Percent	Amount (Millions)	Percent
Public support	37,484.0	40.9[d]	36,898.4	40.9[d]	585.6	40.7[d]
Private contributions	16,505.8	18.0	16,069.3	17.8	436.6	30.4
Direct contributions	13,372.7	14.6	12,994.2	14.4	378.5	26.3
Indirect contributions	3,133.1	3.4	3,075.1	3.4	58.0	4.0
Government grants	20,978.2	22.9	20,829.2	23.1	149.0	10.4
Fees for services and goods	45,593.5	49.7	45,250.1	50.1	343.4	23.9
Program service revenue[e]	44,492.9	48.5	44,165.4	48.9	327.5	22.8
Net income from sales of inventory	1,100.6	1.2	1,084.7	1.2	15.9	1.1
Investment income	3,809.9	4.2	3,408.2	3.8	401.8	27.9
Dividends	1,065.2	1.2	962.5	1.1	102.7	7.1
Interest	846.0	0.9	802.1	0.9	43.9	3.1
Net gain on sale of assets	1,641.9	1.8	1,408.4	1.6	233.4	16.2
Other investment income	256.9	0.3	235.2	0.3	21.7	1.5
Other income	4,857.8	5.3	4,750.4	5.3	107.4	7.5
Dues and assessments	2,245.2	2.4	2,217.9	2.5	27.3	1.9
Net income from special events	877.4	1.0	846.9	0.9	30.5	2.1
Other (including net rental)	1,735.2	1.9	1,685.7	1.9	49.5	3.4
Total revenue	91,745.3	100.0	90,307.1	100.0	1,438.1	100.0
Paid personnel	38,878.6	50.6[f]	38,633.9	50.7[f]	244.7	37.7[f]
Wages and salaries	32,711.4	42.6	32,506.3	42.7	205.1	31.6
Compensation of officers	1,841.5	2.4	1,816.2	2.4	25.2	3.9
Other wages and salaries	30,869.9	40.2	30,690.1	40.3	179.8	27.7
Fringe benefits and payroll taxes	6,167.2	8.0	6,127.5	8.0	39.7	6.1
Pension plan contributions	720.1	0.9	714.7	0.9	5.4	0.8
Other employee benefits	2,870.8	3.7	2,850.5	3.7	20.3	3.1
Payroll taxes	2,576.3	3.4	2,562.3	3.4	14.0	2.2
Supplies	3,099.0	4.0	3,080.0	4.0	19.0	2.9
Communications (printing, phone, postage)	2,550.9	3.3	2,529.3	3.3	21.6	3.3
Professional fees	1,333.3	1.7	1,312.8	1.7	20.4	3.1
Occupancy	3,619.7	4.7	3,592.7	4.7	27.0	4.2
Equipment rental and maintenance	968.1	1.3	959.4	1.3	8.7	1.3
Interest	2,098.4	2.7	2,070.1	2.7	28.3	4.3
Depreciation and depletion	3,147.0	4.1	3,114.8	4.1	32.2	5.0
Other	21,166.1	27.5	20,918.2	27.4	248.0	38.2
Total current operating expenses	76,861.1	100.0	76,211.2	100.0	649.9	100.0

Total current operating expenses	76,861.1	91.0[g]	76,211.2	91.3[g]	649.9	64.6[g]
Plus grants and benefits	7,309.6	8.7	6,987.2	8.4	322.4	32.1
Grants and allocations	3,784.3	4.5	3,505.6	4.2	278.7	27.7
Specific assistance to individuals	2,954.1	3.5	2,913.1	3.5	41.0	4.1
Benefits paid to members	571.2	0.7	568.5	0.7	2.7	0.3
Plus payments to affiliates	320.1	0.4	286.6	0.3	33.5	3.3
Total expenses	84,490.8	100.0	83,485.0	100.0	1,005.8	100.0
Net income (revenue minus expenses)	7,254.4	7.9[d]	6,822.1	7.6[d]	432.4	30.1[d]
Total assets	132,745.6	157.1[g]	127,790.1	153.1[g]	4,955.5	492.7[g]
Total liabilities	62,770.2	74.3	61,970.5	74.2	799.7	79.5
Net assets (assets minus liabilities)	69,975.4	82.8	65,819.6	78.8	4,155.8	413.2

Note: *Reporting public charities include only organizations that both reported (filed IRS Form 990) and were required to do so. (The following were excluded: foreign organizations, government-associated organizations, organizations without state identifiers, and organizations excluded at the authors' discretion.) Organizations not required to report include religious congregations and organizations with less than $25,000 in gross receipts. Owing to rounding, column totals may not equal the sum of individual items. The table includes separate analyses for operating public charities and supporting organizations to provide a clearer picture of the distribution of funds and to avoid double-counting of the financial information for supporting organizations. See Resource B for a detailed description of the methodology. See http://www.nccs.urban.org for a full description of the National Taxonomy of Exempt Entities—Core Codes system.*

[a] *Number of organizations = 78,021.*
[b] *Number of organizations = 75,673.*
[c] *Number of organizations = 2,348.*
[d] *Percentages for revenue items and net income are expressed as percentages of total revenue.*
[e] *Program service revenue may include sizable income via government contracts, which the data source is unable to differentiate from funds raised via the public (that is, fees for services).*
[f] *Percentages for current operating expense items are expressed as percentages of total current operating expenses.*
[g] *Percentages for other expense items, assets, and liabilities are expressed as percentages of total expenses.*

Sources: *IRS Forms 990 and 990-EZ, GuideStar-NCCS National Nonprofit Organization Database, 1999 (returns received in that calendar year), as classified according to the National Taxonomy of Exempt Entities—Core Codes and adjusted by the National Center for Charitable Statistics and Independent Sector. See Resource B for details.*

- Total revenue grew by 72 percent (56 percent in constant dollars) between 1992 and 1998, but there was wide variation among the types of human services organizations. Family services charities grew the least (about 47 percent), whereas revenue for charities in the food, agriculture, and nutrition category increased the most (124 percent).

- The human services charities rely more heavily on government grants than other subsectors do. Government grants averaged 23 percent of total revenue for human services, compared with an average of 8 percent for all public charities. Only 18 percent of human services revenue came from private contributions, and almost 50 percent came from fees for services and payments for goods.

International and Foreign Affairs

Table 5.17 shows the revenue and expenses of reporting public charities in the international and foreign affairs subsector in 1998.

- The activities of the 2,000 international and foreign affairs organizations, the smallest of the subsectors discussed here, include international relief, international economic development, cultural exchanges, policy research, and advocacy.

- The total number of these organizations grew by 29 percent between 1992 and 1998, compared with 39 percent for the group as a whole.

- Total revenue grew by 42 percent, versus 47 percent for all public charities, between 1992 and 1998; growth in public support was only 43 percent, compared with the 65 percent increase for all charities combined.

- With 62 percent of its revenue from private contributions, this subsector relies far more heavily on private contributions than any other subsector does. Government grants represent the second largest source of revenue (20 percent).

Other Subsectors

Table 5.18 shows the revenue and expenses of reporting public charities in other subsectors in 1998. These other subsectors cover a diverse array of organizations, including public and societal benefit organizations, religion-related organizations, and unknown or unclassified organizations.

The most dramatic growth in numbers in this group was in philanthropy and volunteerism, a group that also led in increases in total assets (138 percent) between 1992 and 1998. Direct contributions provided 37 percent of revenues for this subsector, more than for any other group of charities.

Private Foundations

Supplemental analysis was conducted on selected financial data of private foundations using the IRS SOI sample of exempt organizations. Table 5.19 shows the tremendous growth among private foundations between 1992 and 1997. Total revenue for private foundations more than doubled during this five-year period as did their total net worth (in constant dollars), which increased from $100 billion in 1992 to $209 billion in 1997.

Largest Organizations by NTEE-CC Category

Table 5.20 lists the ten largest charities by revenue size for each of the major NTEE-CC categories. Some organizations clearly dominate their categories, such as the American Red Cross among the human services organizations, Kaiser Foundations Health Plan among the health organizations, and Common Fund among the organizations that engage in public and societal benefit. As a group, the largest organizations under health and education far outweigh their counterparts in revenue size in all other NTEE categories.

Geographical Distribution of Reporting Public Charities

Tables 5.21 and 5.22 show the geographical distribution of reporting public charities by state.

Although the U.S. population grew from 259 million residents in 1992 to 275 million in 1998, a change of only 6 percent, the number of active public charities grew by 39 percent. Again, these public charities do not include the small organizations and most religious congregations. They are located in every state, in widely varying numbers, from 2,000 in Wyoming to over 81,000 in California (this discussion excludes organizations in the U.S. territories).

- The ten states with the largest number of reporting public charities in 1998 were California, New York, Texas, Pennsylvania, Ohio, Illinois, Florida, Massachusetts, Michigan, and New Jersey, the same as in 1992. These are also the states with the largest populations. Georgia is an exception, ranking tenth in population in 1998 and eighteenth in number of reporting public charities.

TABLE 5.17

Reporting Public Charities: Revenue and Expenses for NTEE-CC International and Foreign Affairs Category, 1998

	All Organizations[a]		Operating Organizations[b]		Supporting Organizations[c]	
	Amount (Millions)	Percent	Amount (Millions)	Percent	Amount (Millions)	Percent
Public support	4,764.6	82.3[d]	4,419.6	82.5[d]	345.0	80.0[d]
Private contributions	3,606.4	62.3	3,263.3	60.9	343.1	79.6
Direct contributions	2,891.9	49.9	2,549.8	47.6	342.1	79.3
Indirect contributions	714.5	12.3	713.5	13.3	1.1	0.2
Government grants	1,158.2	20.0	1,156.4	21.6	1.8	0.4
Fees for services and goods	592.6	10.2	589.8	11.0	2.8	0.6
Program service revenue[e]	594.7	10.3	592.0	11.0	2.6	0.6
Net income from sales of inventory	(2.1)	0.0	(2.2)	0.0	0.1	0.0
Investment income	324.2	5.6	242.6	4.5	81.6	18.9
Dividends	116.1	2.0	95.8	1.8	20.3	4.7
Interest	38.3	0.7	32.9	0.6	5.4	1.3
Net gain on sale of assets	162.7	2.8	107.0	2.0	55.7	12.9
Other investment income	7.0	0.1	6.9	0.1	0.2	0.0
Other income	109.9	1.9	108.0	2.0	1.8	0.4
Dues and assessments	39.8	0.7	38.8	0.7	1.0	0.2
Net income from special events	8.2	0.1	7.6	0.1	0.7	0.2
Other (including net rental)	61.8	1.1	61.7	1.2	0.1	0.0
Total revenue	5,791.2	100.0	5,360.1	100.0	431.1	100.0
Paid personnel	746.2	26.0[f]	732.4	26.0[f]	13.8	26.5[f]
Wages and salaries	612.6	21.4	601.0	21.3	11.6	22.3
Compensation of officers	93.3	3.3	90.5	3.2	2.8	5.3
Other wages and salaries	519.3	18.1	510.5	18.1	8.8	17.0
Fringe benefits and payroll taxes	133.6	4.7	131.4	4.7	2.2	4.2
Pension plan contributions	26.8	0.9	26.7	0.9	0.1	0.3
Other employee benefits	68.3	2.4	67.0	2.4	1.2	2.4
Payroll taxes	38.5	1.3	37.6	1.3	0.8	1.6
Supplies	82.5	2.9	82.1	2.9	0.4	0.7
Communications (printing, phone, postage)	272.2	9.5	262.5	9.3	9.7	18.6
Professional fees	101.1	3.5	98.0	3.5	3.1	5.9
Occupancy	90.0	3.1	88.0	3.1	2.0	3.9
Equipment rental and maintenance	21.8	0.8	21.6	0.8	0.2	0.5
Interest	32.8	1.1	31.5	1.1	1.3	2.5
Depreciation and depletion	76.1	2.7	75.6	2.7	0.5	0.9

Other	1,444.7	50.4	1,423.7	50.6	21.0	40.5
Total current operating expenses	2,867.3	100.0	2,815.4	100.0	51.9	100.0
Total current operating expenses	2,867.3	53.5[g]	2,815.4	56.5[g]	51.9	13.5[g]
Plus grants and benefits	2,489.8	46.4	2,157.4	43.3	332.5	86.5
Grants and allocations	2,073.6	38.7	1,741.4	35.0	332.2	86.4
Specific assistance to individuals	413.4	7.7	413.2	8.3	0.2	0.1
Benefits paid to members	2.8	0.1	2.8	0.1	0.1	0.0
Plus payments to affiliates	6.9	0.1	6.9	0.1	0.0	0.0
Total expenses	5,364.1	100.0	4,979.7	100.0	384.4	100.0
Net income (revenue minus expenses)	427.2	7.4[d]	380.4	7.1[d]	46.7	10.8[d]
Total assets	6,060.2	113.0[g]	5,311.4	106.7[g]	748.8	194.8[g]
Total liabilities	1,425.2	26.6	1,364.7	27.4	60.5	15.7
Net assets (assets minus liabilities)	4,635.0	86.4	3,946.6	79.3	688.3	179.1

Note: Reporting public charities include only organizations that both reported (filed IRS Form 990) and were required to do so. (The following were excluded: foreign organizations, government-associated organizations, organizations without state identifiers, and organizations excluded at the authors' discretion.) Organizations not required to report include religious congregations and organizations with less than $25,000 in gross receipts. Owing to rounding, column totals may not equal the sum of individual items. The table includes separate analyses for operating public charities and supporting organizations to provide a clearer picture of the distribution of funds and to avoid double-counting of the financial information for supporting organizations. See Resource B for a detailed description of the methodology. See http://www.nccs.urban.org for a full description of the National Taxonomy of Exempt Entities—Core Codes system.

[a] Number of organizations = 2,078.
[b] Number of organizations = 2,003.
[c] Number of organizations = 75.
[d] Percentages for revenue items and net income are expressed as percentages of total revenue.
[e] Program service revenue may include sizable income via government contracts, which the data source is unable to differentiate from funds raised via the public (that is, fees for services).
[f] Percentages for current operating expense items are expressed as percentages of total current operating expenses.
[g] Percentages for other expense items, assets, and liabilities are expressed as percentages of total expenses.

Sources: IRS Forms 990 and 990-EZ, GuideStar-NCCS National Nonprofit Organization Database, 1999 (returns received in that calendar year), as classified according to the National Taxonomy of Exempt Entities—Core Codes and adjusted by the National Center for Charitable Statistics and INDEPENDENT SECTOR. See Resource B for details.

TABLE 5.18

Reporting Public Charities: Revenue and Expenses for Other NTEE-CC Categories, 1998

	All Organizations[a]		Operating Organizations[b]		Supporting Organizations[c]	
	Amount (Millions)	Percent	Amount (Millions)	Percent	Amount (Millions)	Percent
Public support	25,552.0	53.1[d]	12,780.4	46.7[d]	12,704.8	61.1[d]
Private contributions	19,466.4	40.5	7,258.2	26.5	12,070.6	58.1
Direct contributions	17,731.6	36.9	6,695.0	24.4	10,913.0	52.5
Indirect contributions	1,734.8	3.6	563.1	2.1	1,157.6	5.6
Government grants	6,085.6	12.7	5,522.2	20.2	634.2	3.1
Fees for services and goods	11,763.7	24.5	10,728.5	39.2	947.8	4.6
Program service revenue[e]	11,429.8	23.8	10,429.1	38.1	919.7	4.4
Net income from sales of inventory	333.9	0.7	299.4	1.1	28.1	0.1
Investment income	8,126.9	16.9	1,967.3	7.2	6,334.0	30.5
Dividends	2,489.1	5.2	610.3	2.2	1,932.2	9.3
Interest	524.0	1.1	263.9	1.0	273.9	1.3
Net gain on sale of assets	4,808.4	10.0	1,006.4	3.7	3,901.4	18.8
Other investment income	305.5	0.6	86.6	0.3	226.4	1.1
Other income	2,662.8	5.5	1,919.7	7.0	793.4	3.8
Dues and assessments	1,016.9	2.1	942.8	3.4	81.3	0.4
Net income from special events	165.0	0.3	73.4	0.3	93.6	0.5
Other (including net rental)	1,480.8	3.1	903.5	3.3	618.4	3.0
Total revenue	48,105.4	100.0	27,395.8	100.0	20,779.9	100.0
Paid personnel	9,710.1	38.0[f]	8,356.1	38.5[f]	1,468.7	35.3[f]
Wages and salaries	8,052.6	31.5	6,909.6	31.9	1,238.2	29.7
Compensation of officers	996.7	3.9	780.9	3.6	228.7	5.5
Other wages and salaries	7,055.9	27.6	6,128.7	28.3	1,009.5	24.2
Fringe benefits and payroll taxes	1,657.5	6.5	1,446.5	6.7	230.5	5.5
Pension plan contributions	304.9	1.2	258.4	1.2	50.5	1.2
Other employee benefits	794.5	3.1	711.1	3.3	92.5	2.2
Payroll taxes	558.0	2.2	477.0	2.2	87.6	2.1
Supplies	660.0	2.6	571.1	2.6	96.4	2.3
Communications (printing, phone, postage)	1,777.6	7.0	1,589.0	7.3	208.9	5.0
Professional fees	1,192.8	4.7	1,024.1	4.7	183.2	4.4
Occupancy	944.5	3.7	789.8	3.6	166.1	4.0
Equipment rental and maintenance	305.8	1.2	267.4	1.2	42.0	1.0
Interest	548.9	2.1	456.9	2.1	99.0	2.4
Depreciation and depletion	881.4	3.5	760.0	3.5	131.6	3.2
Other	9,517.3	37.3	7,867.4	36.3	1,769.5	42.5
Total current operating expenses	25,538.4	100.0	21,681.7	100.0	4,165.5	100.0

Total current operating expenses	25,538.4	70.6[g]	21,681.7	88.1[g]	4,165.5	34.4[g]
Plus grants and benefits	10,230.8	28.3	2,728.7	11.1	7,730.0	63.8
Grants and allocations	9,336.2	25.8	2,130.6	8.7	7,420.1	61.3
Specific assistance to individuals	703.4	1.9	446.6	1.8	267.5	2.2
Benefits paid to members	191.3	0.5	151.5	0.6	42.4	0.4
Plus payments to affiliates	403.5	1.1	196.6	0.8	214.3	1.8
Total expenses	36,172.8	100.0	24,607.0	100.0	12,109.8	100.0
Net income (revenue minus expenses)	11,932.6	24.8[d]	2,788.8	10.2[d]	8,670.2	41.7[d]
Total assets	126,664.0	350.2[g]	45,562.2	185.2[g]	82,690.7	682.8[g]
Total liabilities	23,236.5	64.2	16,593.9	67.4	7,636.2	63.1
Net assets (assets minus liabilities)	103,427.5	285.9	28,968.3	117.7	75,054.5	619.8

Note: *Reporting public charities include only organizations that both reported (filed IRS Form 990) and were required to do so. (The following were excluded: foreign organizations, government-associated organizations, organizations without state identifiers, and organizations excluded at the authors' discretion.) Organizations not required to report include religious congregations and organizations with less than $25,000 in gross receipts. Owing to rounding, column totals may not equal the sum of individual items. The table includes separate analyses for operating public charities and supporting organizations to provide a clearer picture of the distribution of funds and to avoid double-counting of the financial information for supporting organizations. See Resource B for a detailed description of the methodology. See http://www.nccs.urban.org for a full description of the National Taxonomy of Exempt Entities—Core Codes system.*

[a] *Number of organizations = 42,996.*
[b] *Number of organizations = 29,873.*
[c] *Number of organizations = 13,123.*
[d] *Percentages for revenue items and net income are expressed as percentages of total revenue.*
[e] *Program service revenue may include sizable income via government contracts, which the data source is unable to differentiate from funds raised via the public (that is, fees for services).*
[f] *Percentages for current operating expense items are expressed as percentages of total current operating expenses.*
[g] *Percentages for other expense items, assets, and liabilities are expressed as percentages of total expenses.*

Sources: *IRS Forms 990 and 990-EZ, GuideStar-NCCS National Nonprofit Organization Database, 1999 (returns received in that calendar year), as classified according to the National Taxonomy of Exempt Entities—Core Codes and adjusted by the National Center for Charitable Statistics and Independent Sector. See Resource B for details.*

TABLE 5.19

Private Foundations: Summary of Selected Financial Data, Circa 1982, 1987, 1992, and 1997

	Billions of Dollars					Ratio of:		Excess as a Percentage of:[b]	
	Total Revenue	**Expenses**	**Total Assets**[a]	**Liabilities**	**Net Worth**	**Liabilities to Assets**	**Revenue to Assets**	**Revenue**	**Net Worth**
Current Dollars									
1997	56.1	22.7	284.4	9.5	274.9	0.03	0.20	59.5	12.1
1992	23.6	14.5	154.0	6.8	147.2	0.04	0.15	38.6	6.2
1987	17.1	9.1	93.8	3.4	90.4	0.04	0.18	46.8	8.8
1982	9.0	5.5	48.2	2.4	45.8	0.05	0.19	38.9	7.6
Constant 1987 dollars[c]									
1997	42.7	17.3	216.4	7.2	209.2	0.03	0.20	59.5	12.1
1992	19.5	12.0	127.4	5.6	100.7	0.04	0.15	38.6	6.2
1987	17.1	9.1	93.8	3.4	90.4	0.04	0.18	46.8	8.8
1982	10.7	6.6	57.5	2.9	65.2	0.05	0.19	38.9	7.6

Note: *Organizations contained in the weighted sample were required to file Form 990-PF, Return of Private Foundation, and Form 990, Return of Organization Exempt from Income Tax, the information return, and did so. Year represents the year of filing.*

[a] *Figures represent the book value of total assets.*

[b] *Excess is the difference between total revenue and expenses.*

[c] *Based on implicit price deflators for gross domestic product, where 1992 = 120.9, 1982 = 83.8, and 1997 = 76.1.*

Sources: *IRS Statistics of Income Exempt Organizations Sample File, 1982, 1987, 1992, 1997. See Resource B for details.*

- The fewest charities were found in Wyoming, Nevada, North Dakota, Idaho, and Delaware, all states that also ranked low in population.

- The District of Columbia is unique, as it was the location of over 3,000 reporting public charities, with a rank of 24 when grouped with the states but with a population rank of 50 out of 51.

- The South was the home of 30 percent of all reporting public charities in 1998, followed by the Midwest (24 percent), the Northeast (23 percent), and the West (22 percent).

The density of reporting public charities, as measured by the number of organizations per 10,000 residents, provides an indication of the level of the development of the nonprofit sector. Again, these reporting public charities do not include small organizations and religious congregations, so the densities may be understated.

- The density of reporting public charities (those that filed Form 990) increased by nearly one-third between 1992 and 1998. In 1992 there were 6.2 for every 10,000 people in the United States. By 1998 there were 8.2.

- The Northeast had the highest density of reporting public charities per 10,000 residents (10.0), followed by the Midwest (8.7), the West (8.3), and the South (7.1).

- The District of Columbia had a very high density of 59 reporting public charities per 10,000 residents. As the nation's capital, it is the location of many national and international charities and also has a small number of residents. This combination produces a density that is very different from that of a typical state.

- The lowest concentration of reporting public charities tended to be in East South Central and West South Central states, but Nevada and Utah in the Mountain states were also very low in density.

- The rates of growth in the number of reporting public charities between 1992 and 1998 did vary among the regions and the states, but there were few changes in the rankings.

- Although the overall rate of growth over the six years was 39 percent, the Northeast and Midwest regions grew the slowest (34 percent and 37 percent, respectively); the South grew the fastest (44 percent), followed by the West (41 percent).

- The Mountain region experienced the most growth in numbers of reporting public charities between 1992 and 1998 (50 percent), compared with a national average of 39 percent.

- Almost all regions showed an increase in the average annual rate of growth between 1995 and 1998 as compared with the period 1992 to 1995.

Financial Trends in Reporting Public Charities by State

Table 5.23 shows trends in total revenue for reporting public charities by state between 1992 and 1998. Total revenue for reporting public charities by state showed healthy increases over the six-year period. Overall growth in revenue between 1992 and 1998 was an impressive 47 percent in current dollars, significantly higher than the rate of inflation of nearly 16 percent. The average annual increase for all reporting public charities was 6.6 percent. The Northeast region received $213 billion in 1998 (31 percent of the total), followed by the South (with 27 percent), the Midwest (with 24 percent), and the West (with 18 percent). These proportions were virtually unchanged from 1992. The revenue of reporting public charities in two states was much higher than the rest in 1998—New York, with $77 billion (11 percent of total revenue), and California, with $75 billion (also 11 percent).

TABLE 5.20

Largest Reporting Public Charities by NTEE-CC Major Category and Total Revenue, Circa 1998

Rank	Name	Total Revenue (Millions of Dollars)
Arts, culture, and humanities		
1	Public Broadcasting Service (VA)	446.2
2	Metropolitan Museum of Art (NY)	345.9
3	Corporation for Public Broadcasting (DC)	281.3
4	Metropolitan Opera Association Inc. (NY)	194.0
5	Art Institute of Chicago (IL)	188.4
6	American Museum of Natural History (NY)	159.8
7	Childrens Television Workshop (NY)	158.1
8	Museum of Modern Art (NY)	150.9
9	Colonial Williamsburg Foundation (VA)	135.8
10	Museum of Fine Arts (MA)	134.0
Education		
1	Harvard College (MA)	3,598.1
2	University of Pennsylvania (PA)	2,608.9
3	Stanford University (CA)	2,022.2
4	Duke University (NC)	1,920.4
5	Columbia University (NY)	1,872.1
6	California Institute of Technology (CA)	1,854.3
7	Emory University (GA)	1,842.5
8	Johns Hopkins University (MD)	1,805.4
9	Yale University (CT)	1,798.2
10	Cornell University (NY)	1,784.3
Human services		
1	American Red Cross (VA)	2,057.8
2	Evangelical Lutheran Good Samaritan Society (SD)	703.6
3	Legal Services Corporation (DC)	285.0
4	National Collegiate Athletic Association (KS)	272.3
5	Boy Scouts of America National Council (TX)	192.6
6	Adult Communities in Total Services Inc. (PA)	152.1
7	General Assembly of Christian Church Disciples (MO)	147.3
8	Macomb Oakland Regional Center (MI)	141.5
9	Resource Health Care America Inc. Group Return (GA)	140.0
10	Father Flanagan's Boys Home (NE)	138.3
International and foreign affairs		
1	Maharishi Global Development Fund (NY)	430.5
2	Cooperative for Assistance and Relief Everywhere (GA)	385.5
3	World Vision International (CA)	376.8
4	United Israel Appeal Inc. (NY)	251.7
5	Foster Parents Plan International Inc. (RI)	227.7
6	Feed the Children Inc. (OK)	203.7
7	World Vision Inc. (WA)	188.4
8	Institute for the Advancement of Education in Jaffa (NY)	161.3
9	United States Committee for UNICEF (NY)	157.7
10	Food for the Poor Inc. (FL)	134.5

Note: *Reporting public charities include only organizations that both reported (filed IRS Form 990) and were required to do so. Organizations not required to report include religious congregations and organizations with less than $25,000 in gross receipts.*

TABLE 5.20 (continued)

Largest Reporting Public Charities by NTEE-CC Major Category and Total Revenue, Circa 1998

Rank	Name	Total Revenue (Millions of Dollars)
Environment and animals		
1	Nature Conservancy Inc. (VA)	493.8
2	New York Zoological Society (NY)	126.2
3	Zoological Society of San Diego (CA)	126.0
4	World Wildlife Fund Inc. (DC)	112.0
5	Ducks Unlimited Inc. (TN)	108.6
6	Trust for Public Land (CA)	88.4
7	National Wildlife Federation (VA)	82.4
8	National Fish and Wildlife Foundation (DC)	75.9
9	National Audubon Society Inc. (NY)	73.2
10	Humane Society of the United States (DC)	54.0
Health		
1	Kaiser Foundation Health Plan Inc. (CA)	11,129.0
2	Kaiser Foundation Hospitals (CA)	3,878.0
3	Howard Hughes Medical Institute (MD)	1,676.8
4	Mercy Health Services (MI)	1,580.9
5	Health Insurance Plan of Greater New York (NY)	1,556.1
6	IHC Health Services Inc. (UT)	1,437.0
7	Harvard Pilgrim Health Care Inc. (MA)	1,287.2
8	Clarian Health Partners Inc. (IN)	1,256.7
9	Hackensack University Medical Center (NJ)	1,248.7
10	Cleveland Clinic Foundation (OH)	1,212.6
Public and societal benefit		
1	Common Fund for Non-Profit Organizations (CT)[a]	2,214.6
2	Fidelity Investments Charitable Gift Fund (MA)	670.2
3	Mitre Corporation (MA)	526.1
4	National Geographic Society (DC)	494.9
5	Electric Power Research Institute Inc. (CA)	422.5
6	Underwriters Laboratories Inc. (IL)	407.2
7	Aerospace Corporation (CA)	366.7
8	American Chemical Company (DC)	316.3
9	Southwest Research Institute (TX)	305.5
10	Universities Research Association Inc. (DC)	271.9
Religion-related		
1	Christian Broadcasting Network Inc. (VA)	238.9
2	American Bible Society (NY)	155.0
3	Trinity Christian Center of Santa Ana Inc. (CA)	151.8
4	Focus on the Family (CO)	110.9
5	Billy Graham Evangelistic Association (MN)	106.1
6	Marvin M. Schwan Charitable Foundation (MO)	75.7
7	Promise Keepers (CO)	44.9
8	In Touch Ministries Inc. (GA)	38.0
9	Coral Ridge Ministries Media Inc. (FL)	31.9
10	RBC Ministries (MI)	28.7

[a] *This organization was formerly classified under "education." For purposes of this study, it has since been reclassified under "public and societal benefit" because of changes in its mission statement that have broadened its client base to include hospitals, other nonprofits, and foundations, in addition to educational institutions.*

Sources: *IRS Business Master Files (Exempt Organizations), 1999; IRS Return Transaction File, 1999 (returns received in that calendar year).*

TABLE 5.21

Public Charities, Population, and Density by State, Circa 1992 and 1998

	Number of Active Public Charities[a]		Rank		Number of Reporting Public Charities		Rank	
	1992	1998	1992	1998	1992	1998	1992	1998
United States	508,347	711,460			161,125	224,272		
Northeast	106,417	147,211			38,714	51,84		
New England	32,687	44,488			12,687	16,996		
Connecticut	7,786	10,302	22	23	2,922	3,781	20	22
Maine	3,012	4,099	38	39	1,175	1,639	35	35
Massachusetts	14,593	19,971	9	9	5,908	7,756	8	8
New Hampshire	2,624	3,761	41	42	996	1,445	38	38
Rhode Island	2,516	3,458	43	43	906	1,274	40	40
Vermont	2,156	2,897	45	46	780	1,101	43	43
Middle Atlantic	73,730	102,723			26,027	34,849		
New Jersey	13,630	19,351	10	10	4,327	6,173	10	10
New York	38,718	53,225	2	2	13,339	17,360	2	2
Pennsylvania	21,382	30,147	6	5	8,361	11,316	4	4
Midwest	127,575	174,230			39,774	54,459		
East North Central	82,143	111,470			26,373	35,908		
Illinois	21,658	29,149	5	7	6,870	9,175	6	6
Indiana	11,495	15,689	15	16	3,550	4,919	16	15
Michigan	15,659	21,870	8	8	5,019	6,850	9	9
Ohio	22,511	30,096	4	6	7,369	10,052	5	5
Wisconsin	10,820	14,666	18	20	3,565	4,912	15	16
West North Central	45,432	62,760			13,401	18,551		
Iowa	7,499	10,101	24	24	2,071	2,849	25	26
Kansas	5,962	8,260	30	31	1,774	2,413	29	30
Minnesota	11,004	15,603	17	17	3,723	5,372	13	13
Missouri	12,713	17,405	11	13	3,282	4,467	18	19
Nebraska	4,308	6,040	33	33	1,273	1,788	33	33
North Dakota	1,963	2,557	48	49	641	815	45	50
South Dakota	1,983	2,794	47	47	637	847	46	48
South	157,842	228,044			46,956	67,527		
South Atlantic	82,730	121,647			26,624	38,435		
Delaware	1,696	2,334	50	50	605	848	48	47
District of Columbia	6,512	7,851	27	32	2,376	3,077	23	24
Florida	20,088	31,980	7	4	6,055	8,995	7	7
Georgia	9,990	15,187	20	19	3,111	4,624	19	18
Maryland	10,552	15,304	19	18	3,417	4,900	17	17
North Carolina	12,592	18,128	12	11	4,146	6,056	12	12
South Carolina	5,658	8,878	32	27	1,609	2,338	32	32
Virginia	12,448	17,552	13	12	4,291	6,138	11	11
West Virginia	3,194	4,433	37	37	1,014	1,459	37	37
East South Central	26,850	37,632			7,178	10,330		
Alabama	6,040	8,516	29	29	1,767	2,552	30	28
Kentucky	6,337	8,563	28	28	1,900	2,660	27	27
Mississippi	3,311	4,858	36	36	936	1,335	39	39
Tennessee	11,162	15,695	16	15	2,575	3,783	22	21
West South Central	48,262	68,765			13,154	18,762		
Arkansas	4,134	5,741	34	34	1,221	1,711	34	34
Louisiana	5,878	8,336	31	30	1,688	2,369	31	31
Oklahoma	7,113	9,759	25	26	1,818	2,439	28	29
Texas	31,137	44,929	3	3	8,427	12,243	3	3
West	116,083	161,211			35,591	50,243		
Mountain	30,939	45,246			8,950	13,416		
Arizona	6,598	9,760	26	25	2,008	2,934	26	25
Colorado	9,242	13,318	21	21	2,845	4,329	21	20
Idaho	2,286	3,270	44	45	564	850	49	46
Montana	2,973	3,987	39	41	844	1,208	41	41
Nevada	2,119	3,399	46	44	507	833	50	49
New Mexico	3,740	5,156	35	35	1,112	1,623	36	36
Utah	2,561	4,356	42	38	628	1,043	47	44
Wyoming	1,420	2,000	51	51	442	596	51	51
Pacific	85,144	115,965			26,641	36,827		
Alaska	1,857	2,559	49	48	652	920	44	45
California	60,543	81,629	1	1	19,305	25,969	1	1
Hawaii	2,814	4,025	40	40	790	1,137	42	42
Oregon	7,770	10,858	23	22	2,302	3,591	24	23
Washington	12,160	16,894	14	14	3,592	5,210	14	14
U.S. Territories	430	764			90	198		

Note: *Reporting public charities include only organizations that both reported (filed IRS Form 990) and were required to do so. Organizations not required to report include religious congregations and organizations with less than $25,000 in gross receipts. Owing to rounding, percentage figures may not total 100.*

[a] *The total number of active public charities as reported in the IRS Business Master Files (Exempt Organizations) is diminished here by the number of organizations without geographical identifiers.*

Population (Thousands)		Rank		Reporting Public Charities per 10,000 Residents			Rank	
1992	1998	1992	1998	1992	1998	Total Change 1992–1998	1992	1998
259,041	274,618			6.2	8.2	1.9		
51,069	51,686			7.6	10.0	2.5		
13,188	13,429			9.6	12.7	3.0		
3,275	3,273	27	29	8.9	11.6	2.6	12	12
5,993	6,144	13	13	9.9	12.6	2.8	6	8
1,236	1,248	39	39	9.5	13.1	3.6	8	5
1,113	1,186	41	42	9.0	12.2	3.2	11	10
1,001	988	43	43	9.1	12.9	3.8	9	6
570	591	50	49	13.7	18.6	5.0	2	2
37,882	38,257			6.9	9.1	2.2		
7,811	8,096	9	9	5.5	7.6	2.1	36	35
18,090	18,159	2	3	7.4	9.6	2.2	19	19
11,981	12,002	5	6	7.0	9.4	2.4	23	22
60,711	62,951			6.6	8.7	2.1		
42,766	44,257			6.2	8.1	1.9		
11,635	12,070	6	5	5.9	7.6	1.7	33	34
5,649	5,908	14	14	6.3	8.3	2.0	30	29
9,470	9,820	8	8	5.3	7.0	1.7	37	37
11,008	11,238	7	7	6.7	8.9	2.3	28	28
5,005	5,222	18	18	7.1	9.4	2.3	20	23
17,945	18,693			7.5	9.9	2.5		
2,807	2,861	30	30	7.4	10.0	2.6	18	18
2,526	2,639	32	32	7.0	9.1	2.1	21	25
4,472	4,726	20	20	8.3	11.4	3.0	14	14
5,194	5,438	15	16	6.3	8.2	1.9	29	30
1,602	1,661	36	38	7.9	10.8	2.8	16	17
635	638	47	47	10.1	12.8	2.7	5	7
709	731	45	46	9.0	11.6	2.6	10	11
88,102	95,349			5.3	7.1	1.8		
45,062	48,927			5.9	7.9	1.9		
690	744	46	45	8.8	11.4	2.6	13	13
584	521	49	50	40.7	59.0	18.3	1	1
13,505	14,908	4	4	4.5	6.0	1.5	45	46
6,759	7,637	11	10	4.6	6.1	1.5	44	45
4,903	5,130	19	19	7.0	9.6	2.6	25	21
6,832	7,546	10	11	6.1	8.0	2.0	32	32
3,601	3,840	25	26	4.5	6.1	1.6	46	44
6,383	6,789	12	12	6.7	9.0	2.3	27	27
1,805	1,812	35	35	5.6	8.1	2.4	35	31
15,520	16,469			4.6	6.3	1.6		
4,139	4,351	22	23	4.3	5.9	1.6	47	47
3,756	3,934	24	25	5.1	6.8	1.7	42	40
2,610	2,751	31	31	3.6	4.9	1.3	50	50
5,014	5,433	17	17	5.1	7.0	1.8	40	38
27,520	29,953			4.8	6.3	1.5		
2,394	2,538	33	33	5.1	6.7	1.6	41	41
4,271	4,363	21	22	4.0	5.4	1.5	48	48
3,204	3,339	28	27	5.7	7.3	1.6	34	36
17,650	19,712	3	2	4.8	6.2	1.4	43	43
55,139	60,263			6.5	8.3	1.9		
14,413	16,805			6.2	8.0	1.8		
3,867	4,667	23	21	5.2	6.3	1.1	39	42
3,460	3,969	26	24	8.2	10.9	2.7	15	16
1,066	1,231	42	40	5.3	6.9	1.6	38	39
822	880	44	44	10.3	13.7	3.5	4	4
1,331	1,744	38	36	3.8	4.8	1.0	49	51
1,581	1,734	37	37	7.0	9.4	2.3	22	24
1,821	2,101	34	34	3.4	5.0	1.5	51	49
463	480	51	51	9.5	12.4	2.9	7	9
40,726	43,458			6.5	8.5	1.9		
587	615	48	48	11.1	15.0	3.8	3	3
30,876	32,683	1	1	6.3	7.9	1.7	31	33
1,150	1,190	40	41	6.9	9.6	2.7	26	20
2,974	3,282	29	28	7.7	10.9	3.2	17	15
5,139	5,688	16	15	7.0	9.2	2.2	24	26
4,020	4,370			0.2	0.5	0.2	0.2	0.2

Sources: *IRS Business Master Files (Exempt Organizations), 1993, 1999; IRS Return Transaction File, 1993, 1999 (returns received in those calendar years). See Resource B for details. Population figures are based on U.S. Bureau of the Census, 2001.*

TABLE 5.22

Reporting Public Charities: Total Number by State, Circa 1992, 1995, 1997, and 1998

	Number of Organizations				Total Percentage Change		Average Annual Percentage Change		
	1992	1995	1997	1998	1992–1998	1992–1998	1992–1995	1995–1998	
United States	161,125	186,871	215,237	224,272	39.2	5.7	5.1	6.3	
Northeast	38,714	44,125	49,881	51,846	33.9	5.0	4.5	5.5	
New England	12,687	14,392	16,342	16,996	34.0	5.0	4.3	5.7	
Connecticut	2,922	3,243	3,661	3,781	29.4	4.4	3.5	5.2	
Maine	1,175	1,378	1,573	1,639	39.5	5.7	5.5	6.0	
Massachusetts	5,908	6,661	7,497	7,756	31.3	4.6	4.1	5.2	
New Hampshire	996	1,131	1,337	1,445	45.1	6.4	4.3	8.5	
Rhode Island	906	1,059	1,228	1,274	40.6	5.8	5.3	6.4	
Vermont	780	920	1,046	1,101	41.2	5.9	5.7	6.2	
Middle Atlantic	26,027	29,733	33,539	34,850	33.9	5.0	4.5	5.4	
New Jersey	4,327	5,123	5,851	6,173	42.7	6.1	5.8	6.4	
New York	13,339	15,003	16,787	17,361	30.2	4.5	4.0	5.0	
Pennsylvania	8,361	9,607	10,901	11,316	35.3	5.2	4.7	5.6	
Midwest	39,774	45,889	52,375	54,459	36.9	5.4	4.9	5.9	
East North Central	26,373	30,351	34,505	35,908	36.2	5.3	4.8	5.8	
Illinois	6,870	7,816	8,899	9,175	33.6	4.9	4.4	5.5	
Indiana	3,550	4,107	4,716	4,919	38.6	5.6	5.0	6.2	
Michigan	5,019	5,827	6,588	6,850	36.5	5.3	5.1	5.5	
Ohio	7,369	8,486	9,589	10,052	36.4	5.3	4.8	5.8	
Wisconsin	3,565	4,115	4,713	4,912	37.8	5.5	4.9	6.1	
West North Central	13,401	15,538	17,870	18,551	38.4	5.6	5.1	6.1	
Iowa	2,071	2,400	2,766	2,849	37.6	5.5	5.0	5.9	
Kansas	1,774	2,089	2,360	2,413	36.0	5.3	5.6	4.9	
Minnesota	3,723	4,400	5,122	5,372	44.3	6.3	5.7	6.9	
Missouri	3,282	3,721	4,272	4,467	36.1	5.3	4.3	6.3	
Nebraska	1,273	1,509	1,741	1,788	40.5	5.8	5.8	5.8	
North Dakota	641	720	792	815	27.1	4.1	4.0	4.2	
South Dakota	637	699	817	847	33.0	4.9	3.1	6.6	
South	46,956	55,541	64,630	67,527	43.8	6.2	5.8	6.7	
South Atlantic	26,624	31,525	36,677	38,435	44.4	6.3	5.8	6.8	
Delaware	605	711	804	848	40.2	5.8	5.5	6.0	
District of Columbia	2,376	2,691	2,991	3,077	29.5	4.4	4.2	4.6	
Florida	6,055	7,229	8,535	8,995	48.6	6.8	6.1	7.6	

Georgia	3,665	3,111	4,348	4,624	48.6	6.8	5.6	8.1
Maryland	4,048	3,417	4,713	4,900	43.4	6.2	5.8	6.6
North Carolina	4,973	4,146	5,793	6,056	46.1	6.5	6.3	6.8
South Carolina	1,908	1,609	2,224	2,338	45.3	6.4	5.8	7.0
Virginia	5,110	4,291	5,872	6,138	43.0	6.1	6.0	6.3
West Virginia	1,190	1,014	1,397	1,459	43.9	6.3	5.5	7.0
East South Central	8,514	7,178	9,880	10,330	43.9	6.3	5.9	6.7
Alabama	2,059	1,767	2,413	2,552	44.4	6.3	5.2	7.4
Kentucky	2,308	1,900	2,621	2,660	40.0	5.8	6.7	4.8
Mississippi	1,093	936	1,251	1,335	42.6	6.1	5.3	6.9
Tennessee	3,054	2,575	3,595	3,783	46.9	6.6	5.9	7.4
West South Central	15,502	13,154	18,073	18,762	42.6	6.1	5.6	6.6
Arkansas	1,462	1,221	1,679	1,711	40.1	5.8	6.2	5.4
Louisiana	2,036	1,688	2,353	2,369	40.3	5.8	6.4	5.2
Oklahoma	2,079	1,818	2,352	2,439	34.2	5.0	4.6	5.5
Texas	9,925	8,427	11,689	12,243	45.3	6.4	5.6	7.2
West	41,177	35,591	48,176	50,242	41.2	5.9	5.0	6.9
Mountain	10,792	8,950	12,752	13,416	49.9	7.0	6.4	7.5
Arizona	2,351	2,008	2,808	2,934	46.1	6.5	5.4	7.7
Colorado	3,510	2,845	4,069	4,329	52.2	7.2	7.3	7.2
Idaho	680	564	821	850	50.7	7.1	6.4	7.7
Montana	963	844	1,144	1,208	43.1	6.2	4.5	7.8
Nevada	613	507	753	833	64.3	8.6	6.5	10.8
New Mexico	1,355	1,112	1,595	1,623	46.0	6.5	6.8	6.2
Utah	799	628	982	1,043	66.1	8.8	8.4	9.3
Wyoming	521	442	580	596	34.8	5.1	5.6	4.6
Pacific	30,385	26,641	35,424	36,826	38.2	5.5	4.5	6.6
Alaska	763	652	879	920	41.1	5.9	5.4	6.4
California	21,699	19,305	25,109	25,968	34.5	5.1	4.0	6.2
Hawaii	938	790	1,104	1,137	43.9	6.3	5.9	6.6
Oregon	2,765	2,302	3,354	3,591	56.0	7.7	6.3	9.1
Washington	4,220	3,592	4,978	5,210	45.0	6.4	5.5	7.3
U.S. Territories	139	90	175	198	120.0	14.0	15.6	12.5

Note: Reporting public charities include only organizations that both reported (filed IRS Form 990) and were required to report include religious congregations and organizations with less than $25,000 in gross receipts. Owing to rounding, percentage figures may not total 100. The average annual percentage change is a compound rate that assumes a constant growth rate over time.

Sources: IRS Business Master Files (Exempt Organizations) 1993, 1996, 1998, 1999; IRS Return Transaction File, 1993, 1996, 1998, 1999 (returns received in those calendar years), as classified according to the National Taxonomy of Exempt Entities—Core Codes and adjusted by the National Center for Charitable Statistics. See Resource B for details.

TABLE 5.23

Reporting Public Charities: Total Revenue by State, Circa 1992, 1995, 1997, and 1998

	Total Revenue (Millions of Dollars)				Total Percentage Change	Average Annual Percentage Change		
	1992	1995	1997	1998	1992–1998	1992–1998	1992–1995	1995–1998
United States	471,561.9	573,376.0	663,193.0	692,769.7	46.9	6.6	6.7	6.5
Northeast	147,096.1	179,973.5	205,598.7	213,202.0	44.9	6.4	7.0	5.8
New England	44,587.8	53,159.4	64,753.1	67,679.9	51.8	7.2	6.0	8.4
Connecticut	10,538.9	11,575.8	15,016.8	15,016.7	42.5	6.1	3.2	9.1
Maine	2,196.0	2,802.0	3,737.6	4,101.4	86.8	11.0	8.5	13.5
Massachusetts	24,961.3	30,168.6	36,109.6	38,069.9	52.5	7.3	6.5	8.1
New Hampshire	2,567.1	3,264.0	3,789.8	4,152.6	61.8	8.3	8.3	8.4
Rhode Island	3,164.2	3,870.1	4,414.5	4,587.9	45.0	6.4	6.9	5.8
Vermont	1,160.3	1,478.9	1,684.8	1,751.4	50.9	7.1	8.4	5.8
Middle Atlantic	102,508.2	126,814.0	140,845.5	145,522.1	42.0	6.0	7.4	4.7
New Jersey	15,040.8	18,409.2	20,801.8	22,276.9	48.1	6.8	7.0	6.6
New York	54,419.5	66,036.5	73,797.6	76,986.7	41.5	6.0	6.7	5.2
Pennsylvania	33,048.0	42,368.4	46,246.1	46,258.5	40.0	5.8	8.6	3.0
Midwest	114,955.7	140,917.7	161,276.6	169,436.0	47.4	6.7	7.0	6.3
East North Central	80,814.6	98,419.8	111,694.7	116,842.6	44.6	6.3	6.8	5.9
Illinois	24,525.4	29,602.1	32,292.4	32,931.2	34.3	5.0	6.5	3.6
Indiana	10,210.4	12,350.7	14,441.6	15,808.8	54.8	7.6	6.5	8.6
Michigan	16,756.0	21,188.5	24,294.1	25,154.0	50.1	7.0	8.1	5.9
Ohio	21,266.6	25,073.8	28,536.6	29,741.4	39.9	5.7	5.6	5.9
Wisconsin	8,056.2	10,204.7	12,130.0	13,207.3	63.9	8.6	8.2	9.0
West North Central	34,141.0	42,497.8	49,581.9	52,593.4	54.0	7.5	7.6	7.4
Iowa	3,953.2	5,578.4	5,959.3	5,959.7	50.8	7.1	12.2	2.2
Kansas	3,045.7	3,840.8	4,570.3	4,946.3	62.4	8.4	8.0	8.8
Minnesota	9,199.7	11,713.9	13,484.7	14,660.1	59.4	8.1	8.4	7.8
Missouri	12,560.8	14,503.1	17,042.9	16,687.7	32.9	4.8	4.9	4.8
Nebraska	2,405.7	2,890.1	3,910.5	4,712.1	95.9	11.9	6.3	17.7
North Dakota	1,456.3	1,970.9	2,258.9	3,170.3	117.7	13.8	10.6	17.2
South Dakota	1,519.7	2,000.6	2,355.3	2,457.3	61.7	8.3	9.6	7.1
South	121,836.4	150,870.6	177,286.3	185,092.0	51.9	7.2	7.4	7.1
South Atlantic	74,205.8	92,490.4	107,610.1	114,321.2	54.1	7.5	7.6	7.3
Delaware	847.6	1,223.6	1,396.8	1,467.1	73.1	9.6	13.0	6.2
District of Columbia	8,506.0	10,155.9	11,341.7	12,562.0	47.7	6.7	6.1	7.3
Florida	16,565.1	21,125.8	24,879.3	24,428.4	47.5	6.7	8.4	5.0

Georgia	8,726.9	12,502.7	16,682.0	17,405.4	99.4	12.2	12.7	11.7
Maryland	9,997.5	12,744.9	15,278.7	16,568.4	65.7	8.8	8.4	9.1
North Carolina	10,111.2	12,979.3	14,372.3	15,402.8	52.3	7.3	8.7	5.9
South Carolina	4,006.4	4,783.9	4,484.5	4,747.8	18.5	2.9	6.1	(0.3)
Virginia	12,675.3	13,707.4	15,540.3	18,238.7	43.9	6.3	2.6	10.0
West Virginia	2,769.9	3,266.8	3,634.5	3,500.6	26.4	4.0	5.7	2.3
East South Central	17,809.3	22,013.9	26,252.5	27,891.6	56.6	7.8	7.3	8.2
Alabama	3,591.4	4,167.5	5,098.6	5,059.2	40.9	5.9	5.1	6.7
Kentucky	4,681.2	6,294.0	7,022.7	7,337.5	56.7	7.8	10.4	5.2
Mississippi	1,893.5	2,694.4	3,094.7	3,156.3	66.7	8.9	12.5	5.4
Tennessee	7,643.2	8,858.0	11,036.6	12,338.7	61.4	8.3	5.0	11.7
West South Central	29,821.3	36,366.2	43,423.7	42,879.2	43.8	6.2	6.8	5.6
Arkansas	2,645.6	3,444.0	4,246.1	3,933.6	48.7	6.8	9.2	4.5
Louisiana	4,522.7	5,292.3	5,770.3	5,906.2	30.6	4.5	5.4	3.7
Oklahoma	3,531.7	4,196.6	4,920.9	5,132.7	45.3	6.4	5.9	6.9
Texas	19,121.1	23,433.4	28,486.3	27,906.7	45.9	6.5	7.0	6.0
West	87,372.6	100,745.7	118,056.3	123,944.0	41.9	6.0	4.9	7.2
Mountain	16,150.9	20,148.3	24,596.6	24,096.3	49.2	6.9	7.6	6.1
Arizona	4,524.9	6,358.1	7,152.6	7,454.7	64.7	8.7	12.0	5.4
Colorado	5,426.2	6,124.8	8,780.8	7,407.2	36.5	5.3	4.1	6.5
Idaho	661.4	768.8	1,045.4	1,060.2	60.3	8.2	5.1	11.3
Montana	1,230.3	1,635.5	1,808.9	1,983.3	61.2	8.3	10.0	6.6
Nevada	637.7	829.2	1,002.4	1,055.1	65.5	8.8	9.1	8.4
New Mexico	1,424.6	1,968.6	2,053.2	1,983.1	39.2	5.7	11.4	0.2
Utah	2,055.1	2,182.2	2,440.1	2,793.4	35.9	5.2	2.0	8.6
Wyoming	190.8	281.1	313.4	359.4	88.4	11.1	13.8	8.5
Pacific	71,221.7	80,597.4	93,459.7	99,847.7	40.2	5.8	4.2	7.4
Alaska	610.2	840.4	1,013.2	1,108.5	81.7	10.5	11.3	9.7
California	55,658.4	61,308.1	71,909.9	75,115.2	35.0	5.1	3.3	7.0
Hawaii	1,978.4	2,404.8	2,852.6	2,690.2	36.0	5.3	6.7	3.8
Oregon	3,996.4	4,938.4	5,522.2	8,093.9	102.5	12.5	7.3	17.9
Washington	8,978.3	11,105.8	12,161.8	12,840.0	43.0	6.1	7.3	5.0
U.S. Territories	301.2	868.6	975.0	1,095.7	263.8	24.0	42.3	42.3

Note: *Reporting public charities include only organizations that both reported (filed IRS Form 990) and were required to do so. Organizations not required to report include religious congregations and organizations with less than $25,000 in gross receipts. Owing to rounding, percentage figures may not total 100. The average annual percentage change is a compound rate that assumes a constant growth rate over time.*

Sources: *IRS Business Master Files (Exempt Organizations), 1993, 1996, 1998, 1999; IRS Return Transaction File, 1993, 1996, 1998, 1999 (returns received in those calendar years), as classified according to the National Taxonomy of Exempt Entities—Core Codes and adjusted by the National Center for Charitable Statistics. See Resource B for details.*

- Revenue growth rates for the period ranged from a low of 5.8 percent per year for the charities in the Pacific region to a high of 7.8 percent for those in the East South Central region.

- Variations were much greater at the state level; the states with the lowest rates of growth in charity revenue were South Carolina (2.9 percent) and West Virginia (4 percent), whereas North Dakota (13.8 percent) and Oregon (12.5 percent) led the states with the highest change.

Table 5.24 shows trends in public support for reporting public charities by state between 1992 and 1998. Nationally, cumulative growth in public support between 1992 and 1998 was 65 percent in current dollars, or an average of 8.7 percent per year. The total public support of $142 billion in 1998 includes individual, corporate, and foundation gifts, as well as government grants. This growth in public support was substantially more than the 47 percent growth in total revenue over the six-year period.

- Public support for public charities in the South grew at the fastest rate (77 percent), followed by the West (69 percent), the Midwest (67 percent), and the Northeast (51 percent). However, in 1998 public support represented 31 percent of the total for the independent sector in the South and only 19 percent in the West. The Midwest had only 20 percent of the total, and the Northeast received 30 percent. The 1992 distribution of public support among the four regions was similar.

- Organizations in the Middle Atlantic states had the lowest growth change in public support revenue, with an average annual rate of only 6 percent, whereas charities in the East South Central region (Alabama, Kentucky, Mississippi, and Tennessee) reported the highest change, with growth rates of 12 percent per year.

- Charities in almost all regions showed an increased rate of growth in public support between 1995 and 1998 as compared with the period 1992 to 1995; the exceptions were the New England and West North Central states.

- Organizations in two states again received much more in public support than others in 1998. New York charities received $18.0 billion (almost 13 percent of total public support), and California charities received $15.6 billion (11 percent of the total).

Table 5.25 shows trends in total expenses for reporting public charities by state between 1992 and 1998. The growth in total expenses for reporting public charities over the six-year period (41 percent) was less than the growth in revenue (47 percent). The rates of growth for the four regions were quite close, with the South at 46 percent, the Midwest at 41 percent, the West at 39 percent, and the Northeast at 38 percent. However, organizations in the Northeast had the highest proportion of total expenses (30 percent), followed by those in the South (27 percent), the Midwest (24 percent), and the West (18 percent). These proportions were virtually unchanged from 1992.

- Although there were variations among the states, the charities in most of them had lower rates of increase in total expenses over the last three years of the six-year period, from 1995 to 1998.

- Expenses of charities in California and New York each reached $69.4 billion in 1998. Organizations in these two states had expenses that totaled over 22 percent of all expenses in the sector in 1998. This was a slight drop from the 24 percent of total expenses that charities in the two states represented in 1992.

Table 5.26 shows trends in total assets for reporting public charities by state between 1992 and 1998. Total assets for charities grew 83 percent between 1992 (reported as $662 billion) and 1998 (over $1.2 trillion), much more than the inflation rate (16 percent). The rate was faster than the rate of growth for revenue (47 percent in current dollars) and expenses (41 percent in current dollars).

- Organizations in the South led the asset growth at 89 percent over the six years, followed by the Northeast at 84 percent, the Midwest at 83 percent, and the West at 70 percent. However, the proportion of charity assets throughout the regions varied, with organizations in the Northeast holding 33 percent of the total. Organizations in the South had 28 percent of total assets, followed by those in the Midwest (with 24 percent) and those in the West (with only 15 percent).

- In almost all the regions, asset growth was stronger between 1995 and 1998 than it was between 1992 and 1995.

- Among the individual states, assets held by New York and California organizations again were by far the largest. New York charities' assets reached over $121 billion in 1998 (10 percent of all charity assets), and California charities' assets were $110 billion (9 percent).

Table 5.27 shows trends in net assets for reporting public charities by state between 1992 and 1998. Net assets, defined as total assets minus liabilities, for reporting public charities experienced remarkable growth in the six years, increasing from $396 billion in 1992 to $791 billion in 1998, an increase of 100 percent in current dollars. In constant dollars, the increase was 84 percent.

TABLE 5.24

Reporting Public Charities: Public Support by State, Circa 1992, 1995, 1997, and 1998

	Public Support (Millions of Dollars)				Total Percentage Change	Average Annual Percentage Change		
	1992	1995	1997	1998	1992–1998	1992–1998	1992–1995	1995–1998
United States	86,100.7	106,790.8	126,897.6	142,073.9	65.0	8.7	7.4	10.0
Northeast	28,093.4	34,297.8	37,837.7	42,365.0	50.8	7.1	6.9	7.3
New England	8,144.6	10,934.2	12,302.6	13,846.9	70.0	9.2	10.3	8.2
Connecticut	1,709.5	2,063.4	2,592.5	2,847.2	66.5	8.9	6.5	11.3
Maine	387.3	509.3	604.0	684.2	76.7	10.0	9.6	10.3
Massachusetts	4,787.3	6,793.3	7,428.4	8,416.4	75.8	9.9	12.4	7.4
New Hampshire	414.8	463.6	517.9	616.1	48.5	6.8	3.8	9.9
Rhode Island	617.2	789.4	801.9	879.2	42.4	6.1	8.5	3.7
Vermont	228.5	315.1	357.9	403.8	76.7	10.0	11.3	8.6
Middle Atlantic	19,948.8	23,363.6	25,535.0	28,518.1	43.0	6.1	5.4	6.9
New Jersey	2,251.3	2,632.5	2,957.2	3,267.1	45.1	6.4	5.4	7.5
New York	13,133.0	15,096.9	16,207.3	18,231.4	38.8	5.6	4.8	6.5
Pennsylvania	4,564.5	5,634.2	6,370.6	7,019.6	53.8	7.4	7.3	7.6
Midwest	16,960.3	21,774.2	25,901.8	28,241.2	66.5	8.9	8.7	9.1
East North Central	12,084.4	15,002.1	17,536.6	19,542.5	61.7	8.3	7.5	9.2
Illinois	3,906.8	5,034.5	5,932.4	6,313.2	61.6	8.3	8.8	7.8
Indiana	1,248.4	1,708.4	2,015.8	2,486.5	99.2	12.2	11.0	13.3
Michigan	2,337.5	3,001.9	3,327.0	3,613.9	54.6	7.5	8.7	6.4
Ohio	3,500.7	3,921.7	4,680.2	5,259.6	50.2	7.0	3.9	10.3
Wisconsin	1,091.0	1,335.7	1,581.2	1,869.2	71.3	9.4	7.0	11.9
West North Central	4,875.9	6,772.1	8,365.2	8,698.7	78.4	10.1	11.6	8.7
Iowa	598.0	769.6	940.0	1,011.7	69.2	9.2	8.8	9.5
Kansas	435.3	638.7	830.1	850.4	95.3	11.8	13.6	10.0
Minnesota	1,615.6	2,283.8	2,762.1	2,654.3	64.3	8.6	12.2	5.1
Missouri	1,542.1	2,134.6	2,699.5	2,952.6	91.5	11.4	11.4	11.4
Nebraska	409.0	562.2	659.0	747.9	82.9	10.6	11.2	10.0
North Dakota	121.4	141.2	191.9	183.3	51.1	7.1	5.2	9.1
South Dakota	154.5	242.1	282.6	298.4	93.2	11.6	16.1	7.2

South	25,142.3	31,448.3	38,414.1	44,444.3	76.8	10.0	7.7	12.2
South Atlantic	16,431.2	20,657.4	25,194.1	29,284.9	78.2	10.1	7.9	12.3
Delaware	175.8	244.5	305.4	339.2	92.9	11.6	11.6	11.5
District of Columbia	3,033.6	3,850.5	4,462.4	5,012.4	65.2	8.7	8.3	9.2
Florida	3,188.3	4,117.0	5,045.1	5,565.0	74.5	9.7	8.9	10.6
Georgia	2,482.5	3,352.2	4,005.5	5,136.2	106.9	12.9	10.5	15.3
Maryland	1,701.0	2,166.1	2,471.2	2,878.1	69.2	9.2	8.4	9.9
North Carolina	1,795.3	2,329.3	2,967.8	3,458.9	92.7	11.5	9.1	14.1
South Carolina	574.3	791.8	958.9	1,018.0	77.3	10.0	11.3	8.7
Virginia	3,171.4	3,445.8	4,537.3	5,374.1	69.5	9.2	2.8	16.0
West Virginia	309.0	360.2	440.5	502.9	62.7	8.5	5.2	11.8
East South Central	3,134.5	3,909.2	4,734.6	6,053.7	93.1	11.6	7.6	15.7
Alabama	688.1	805.4	1,050.7	1,043.8	51.7	7.2	5.4	9.0
Kentucky	722.4	835.5	1,017.6	1,225.3	69.6	9.2	5.0	13.6
Mississippi	372.8	498.5	533.5	616.5	65.4	8.7	10.2	7.3
Tennessee	1,351.2	1,769.8	2,132.9	3,168.1	134.5	15.3	9.4	21.4
West South Central	5,576.6	6,881.7	8,485.4	9,105.8	63.3	8.5	7.3	9.8
Arkansas	435.4	537.0	713.8	689.0	58.2	7.9	7.2	8.7
Louisiana	695.0	864.6	972.9	1,083.3	55.9	7.7	7.5	7.8
Oklahoma	701.5	954.0	1,196.2	1,208.9	72.3	9.5	10.8	8.2
Texas	3,744.7	4,526.1	5,602.5	6,124.7	63.6	8.5	6.5	10.6
West	15,845.8	18,954.6	24,538.3	26,766.3	68.9	9.1	6.2	12.2
Mountain	3,465.2	4,289.9	5,748.8	5,947.3	71.6	9.4	7.4	11.5
Arizona	1,028.2	1,300.7	1,560.6	1,763.6	71.5	9.4	8.2	10.7
Colorado	1,147.9	1,521.7	2,355.9	2,072.8	80.6	10.4	9.9	10.9
Idaho	149.1	153.3	210.8	193.1	29.5	4.4	0.9	8.0
Montana	186.4	246.9	283.5	323.1	73.4	9.6	9.8	9.4
Nevada	144.0	174.4	282.2	273.3	89.7	11.3	6.6	16.2
New Mexico	307.0	462.7	502.1	664.2	116.4	13.7	14.6	12.8
Utah	410.1	310.6	420.0	495.3	20.8	3.2	-8.9	16.8
Wyoming	92.5	119.8	133.7	161.8	74.9	9.8	9.0	10.5
Pacific	12,380.6	14,664.7	18,789.5	20,819.0	68.2	9.0	5.8	12.4
Alaska	393.5	500.7	609.6	677.4	72.2	9.5	8.4	10.6
California	9,277.6	10,861.0	14,225.7	15,666.8	68.9	9.1	5.4	13.0
Hawaii	458.3	478.8	530.1	549.7	19.9	3.1	1.5	4.7
Oregon	709.7	868.5	1,083.2	1,346.7	89.8	11.3	7.0	15.7
Washington	1,541.5	1,955.6	2,340.8	2,578.4	67.3	9.0	8.3	9.7
U.S. Territories	58.8	315.8	205.7	257.0	336.8	27.9	75.1	(6.6)

(continued)

TABLE 5.24 (continued)

Reporting Public Charities: Public Support by State, Circa 1992, 1995, 1997, and 1998

	Public Support (Millions of Dollars)				Total Percentage Change	Average Annual Percentage Change		
	1992	1995	1997	1998	1992–1998	1992–1998	1992–1995	1995–1998
United States	75,774.3	92,961.4	110,982.7	122,990.5	62.3	8.4	7.1	9.8
Northeast	24,781.7	29,296.8	33,065.1	36,839.8	48.7	6.8	5.7	7.9
New England	7,284.8	8,858.8	10,534.6	11,710.3	60.7	8.2	6.7	9.7
Connecticut	1,415.6	1,737.9	2,169.8	2,380.0	68.1	9.0	7.1	11.1
Massachusetts	4,346.6	5,186.3	6,263.2	6,950.5	59.9	8.1	6.1	10.3
Maine	356.4	471.2	552.3	627.5	76.1	9.9	9.8	10.0
New Hampshire	382.6	424.6	478.9	566.0	47.9	6.7	3.5	10.0
Rhode Island	567.2	737.9	735.8	809.5	42.7	6.1	9.2	3.1
Vermont	216.4	300.9	334.6	376.8	74.1	9.7	11.6	7.8
Middle Atlantic	17,496.8	20,438.0	22,530.5	25,129.5	43.6	6.2	5.3	7.1
New Jersey	1,999.5	2,355.9	2,621.5	2,911.4	45.6	6.5	5.6	7.3
New York	11,388.2	12,984.6	14,163.7	15,882.4	39.5	5.7	4.5	6.9
Pennsylvania	4,109.1	5,097.5	5,745.3	6,335.7	54.2	7.5	7.4	7.5
Midwest	14,420.6	18,458.1	22,036.6	23,964.1	66.2	8.8	8.6	9.1
East North Central	10,298.5	12,848.6	15,037.3	16,614.7	61.3	8.3	7.7	8.9
Illinois	3,376.9	4,377.6	5,166.5	5,653.9	67.4	9.0	9.0	8.9
Indiana	1,046.2	1,451.1	1,727.6	1,966.7	88.0	11.1	11.5	10.7
Michigan	1,989.1	2,533.5	2,844.0	3,077.5	54.7	7.5	8.4	6.7
Ohio	2,957.4	3,361.0	3,929.8	4,265.7	44.2	6.3	4.4	8.3
Wisconsin	929.0	1,125.4	1,369.4	1,650.8	77.7	10.1	6.6	13.6
West North Central	4,122.1	5,609.5	6,999.4	7,349.4	78.3	10.1	10.8	9.4
Iowa	513.6	671.4	797.5	868.1	69.0	9.1	9.3	8.9
Kansas	374.4	566.0	715.3	747.5	99.7	12.2	14.8	9.7
Minnesota	1,328.3	1,818.2	2,270.0	2,174.9	63.7	8.6	11.0	6.2
Missouri	1,321.5	1,757.4	2,304.8	2,584.7	95.6	11.8	10.0	13.7
Nebraska	344.2	458.9	527.2	569.3	65.4	8.8	10.1	7.5
North Dakota	105.7	120.9	142.8	158.3	49.9	7.0	4.6	9.4
South Dakota	134.6	216.7	241.7	246.5	83.1	10.6	17.2	4.4
South	22,412.1	27,979.0	33,836.8	38,406.7	71.4	9.4	7.7	11.1
South Atlantic	14,720.0	18,431.6	22,239.7	25,860.9	75.7	9.8	7.8	12.0
Delaware	148.4	201.3	259.4	293.8	98.0	12.1	10.7	13.4
District of Columbia	2,802.5	3,567.9	4,176.8	4,605.1	64.3	8.6	8.4	8.9
Florida	2,810.4	3,624.4	4,430.9	4,919.2	75.0	9.8	8.8	10.7

Georgia	2,313.5	3,113.5	3,635.6	4,579.2	97.9	12.1	10.4	13.7
Maryland	1,365.5	1,865.6	2,129.2	2,421.0	77.3	10.0	11.0	9.1
North Carolina	1,595.1	2,087.2	2,613.6	3,033.1	90.1	11.3	9.4	13.3
South Carolina	488.7	654.8	767.3	885.2	81.1	10.4	10.2	10.6
Virginia	2,924.9	2,987.0	3,830.8	4,669.3	59.6	8.1	0.7	16.1
West Virginia	270.9	330.0	396.2	455.1	68.0	9.0	6.8	11.3
East South Central	2,748.1	3,445.6	4,229.9	4,612.5	67.8	9.0	7.8	10.2
Alabama	574.6	666.2	910.6	887.2	54.4	7.5	5.1	10.0
Kentucky	601.0	711.2	886.6	1,005.2	67.2	8.9	5.8	12.2
Mississippi	353.2	474.0	502.3	561.9	59.1	8.0	10.3	5.8
Tennessee	1,219.2	1,594.3	1,930.5	2,158.2	77.0	10.0	9.4	10.6
West South Central	4,944.1	6,101.7	7,367.3	7,933.2	60.5	8.2	7.3	9.1
Arkansas	407.2	495.7	618.6	584.3	43.5	6.2	6.8	5.6
Louisiana	630.4	774.5	844.7	934.7	48.3	6.8	7.1	6.5
Oklahoma	622.8	816.6	975.4	1,071.1	72.0	9.5	9.5	9.5
Texas	3,283.8	4,014.9	4,928.6	5,343.2	62.7	8.5	6.9	10.0
West	14,113.1	16,926.6	21,856.1	23,542.9	66.8	8.9	6.2	11.6
Mountain	3,105.7	3,833.0	5,133.5	5,276.1	69.9	9.2	7.3	11.2
Arizona	910.8	1,136.6	1,343.8	1,495.8	64.2	8.6	7.7	9.6
Colorado	1,040.1	1,407.3	2,192.1	1,892.1	81.9	10.5	10.6	10.4
Idaho	126.1	130.6	184.1	163.7	29.8	4.4	1.2	7.8
Montana	170.5	226.2	256.9	295.2	73.2	9.6	9.9	9.3
Nevada	123.6	147.5	229.0	237.9	92.5	11.5	6.1	17.3
New Mexico	271.9	413.5	463.3	624.8	129.8	14.9	15.0	14.7
Utah	376.9	267.0	346.0	425.5	12.9	2.0	(10.9)	16.8
Wyoming	85.9	104.2	118.1	141.1	64.3	8.6	6.7	10.6
Pacific	11,007.4	13,093.6	16,722.7	18,266.8	66.0	8.8	6.0	11.7
Alaska	374.0	486.0	592.3	656.4	75.5	9.8	9.1	10.5
California	8,256.3	9,665.4	12,612.3	13,667.0	65.5	8.8	5.4	12.2
Hawaii	407.1	444.9	490.0	510.0	25.3	3.8	3.0	4.7
Oregon	631.1	774.0	959.1	1,184.5	87.7	11.1	7.0	15.2
Washington	1,338.9	1,723.4	2,069.1	2,248.9	68.0	9.0	8.8	9.3
U.S. Territories	58.8	301.0	188.0	237.1	406.9	31.1	86.0	(7.6)

Note: *Reporting public charities include only organizations that both reported (filed IRS Form 990) and were required to do so. Organizations not required to report include religious congregations and organizations with less than $25,000 in gross receipts. Owing to rounding, percentage figures may not total 100. The average annual percentage change is a compound rate that assumes a constant growth rate over time.*

Sources: *IRS Business Master Files (Exempt Organizations), 1993, 1996, 1998, 1999; IRS Return Transaction File, 1993, 1996, 1998, 1999 (returns received in those calendar years), as classified according to the National Taxonomy of Exempt Entities—Core Codes and adjusted by the National Center for Charitable Statistics. See Resource B for details.*

TABLE 5.25

Reporting Public Charities: Total Expenses by State, Circa 1992, 1995, 1997, and 1998

	Total Expenses (Millions of Dollars)				Total Percentage Change	Average Annual Percentage Change		
	1992	1995	1997	1998	1992–1998	1992–1998	1992–1995	1995–1998
United States	440,873.4	530,301.2	598,537.3	621,162.6	40.9	5.9	6.3	5.4
Northeast	137,511.9	167,509.3	184,315.3	189,051.9	37.5	5.4	6.8	4.1
New England	39,957.7	47,331.4	54,737.0	56,458.2	41.3	5.9	5.8	6.1
Connecticut	8,859.4	10,193.2	11,338.5	11,216.1	26.6	4.0	4.8	3.2
Maine	2,054.4	2,636.6	3,412.8	3,705.9	80.4	10.3	8.7	12.0
Massachusetts	22,705.0	26,598.3	31,196.2	32,170.2	41.7	6.0	5.4	6.5
New Hampshire	2,296.9	2,920.8	3,267.0	3,629.0	58.0	7.9	8.3	7.5
Rhode Island	2,948.0	3,623.0	4,038.7	4,179.8	41.8	6.0	7.1	4.9
Vermont	1,094.0	1,359.6	1,483.9	1,557.1	42.3	6.1	7.5	4.6
Middle Atlantic	97,554.2	120,177.9	129,578.3	132,593.7	35.9	5.2	7.2	3.3
New Jersey	14,112.7	17,429.3	19,314.6	20,818.0	47.5	6.7	7.3	6.1
New York	52,080.9	62,531.6	67,464.1	69,376.7	33.2	4.9	6.3	3.5
Pennsylvania	31,360.6	40,217.0	42,799.6	42,399.1	35.2	5.2	8.6	1.8
Midwest	107,599.5	129,858.5	146,303.1	152,021.6	41.3	5.9	6.5	5.4
East North Central	75,879.9	91,178.0	102,009.8	104,968.3	38.3	5.6	6.3	4.8
Illinois	23,104.2	27,247.6	29,417.0	29,597.1	28.1	4.2	5.7	2.8
Indiana	9,386.0	11,208.6	12,805.5	13,608.9	45.0	6.4	6.1	6.7
Michigan	15,981.2	19,988.2	22,617.8	23,433.0	46.6	6.6	7.7	5.4
Ohio	19,854.8	23,291.2	25,981.6	26,258.6	32.3	4.8	5.5	4.1
Wisconsin	7,553.6	9,442.5	11,187.9	12,070.8	59.8	8.1	7.7	8.5
West North Central	31,719.6	38,680.5	44,293.3	47,053.3	48.3	6.8	6.8	6.7
Iowa	3,712.2	5,157.6	5,414.3	5,332.5	43.6	6.2	11.6	1.1
Kansas	2,891.2	3,533.3	4,231.2	4,573.5	58.2	7.9	6.9	9.0
Minnesota	8,515.6	10,675.9	12,084.7	13,225.9	55.3	7.6	7.8	7.4
Missouri	11,601.3	13,070.9	14,899.6	14,585.0	25.7	3.9	4.1	3.7
Nebraska	2,216.0	2,569.2	3,408.1	4,142.1	86.9	11.0	5.1	17.3
North Dakota	1,382.2	1,820.5	2,084.6	2,922.0	111.4	13.3	9.6	17.1
South Dakota	1,401.0	1,853.0	2,170.8	2,272.3	62.2	8.4	9.8	7.0
South	113,028.1	137,561.5	157,988.1	164,778.5	45.8	6.5	6.8	6.2
South Atlantic	68,930.1	83,767.0	95,557.8	101,440.3	47.2	6.7	6.7	6.6
Delaware	762.9	1,065.1	1,176.8	1,291.7	69.3	9.2	11.8	6.6
District of Columbia	8,017.1	9,451.7	10,433.1	11,350.3	41.6	6.0	5.6	6.3
Florida	15,494.5	19,473.3	22,135.4	22,105.1	42.7	6.1	7.9	4.3

Georgia	8,174.6	11,513.3	15,065.3	15,017.9	83.7	10.7	12.1	9.3
Maryland	9,264.0	10,659.2	13,084.2	14,057.4	51.7	7.2	4.8	9.7
North Carolina	9,159.9	11,796.3	13,126.5	13,972.5	52.5	7.3	8.8	5.8
South Carolina	3,631.9	4,268.6	3,820.7	4,377.8	20.5	3.2	5.5	0.8
Virginia	11,840.2	12,411.6	13,218.2	15,998.3	35.1	5.1	1.6	8.8
West Virginia	2,584.9	3,127.9	3,497.5	3,269.4	26.5	4.0	6.6	1.5
East South Central	16,485.2	20,144.5	23,608.9	24,625.4	49.4	6.9	6.9	6.9
Alabama	3,308.7	3,820.2	4,584.9	4,620.1	39.6	5.7	4.9	6.5
Kentucky	4,315.8	5,786.3	6,360.6	6,578.0	52.4	7.3	10.3	4.4
Mississippi	1,763.3	2,486.5	2,816.9	2,874.1	63.0	8.5	12.1	4.9
Tennessee	7,097.5	8,051.6	9,846.5	10,553.2	48.7	6.8	4.3	9.4
West South Central	27,612.8	33,650.0	38,821.5	38,712.8	40.2	5.8	6.8	4.8
Arkansas	2,515.0	3,241.3	3,914.9	3,613.0	43.7	6.2	8.8	3.7
Louisiana	4,158.3	4,907.2	5,165.5	5,337.0	28.3	4.2	5.7	2.8
Oklahoma	3,338.3	3,979.4	4,370.9	4,549.4	36.3	5.3	6.0	4.6
Texas	17,601.1	21,522.0	25,370.1	25,213.3	43.2	6.2	6.9	5.4
West	82,452.8	94,548.7	109,006.3	114,267.7	38.6	5.6	4.7	6.5
Mountain	15,164.9	18,596.4	22,513.5	22,047.9	45.4	6.4	7.0	5.8
Arizona	4,312.0	5,872.2	6,822.8	7,095.1	64.5	8.7	10.8	6.5
Colorado	5,070.2	5,687.8	7,966.8	6,697.2	32.1	4.7	3.9	5.6
Idaho	598.2	683.3	890.1	960.2	60.5	8.2	4.5	12.0
Montana	1,137.0	1,508.8	1,668.9	1,811.7	59.3	8.1	9.9	6.3
Nevada	573.2	750.8	848.8	919.6	60.4	8.2	9.4	7.0
New Mexico	1,321.9	1,809.0	1,799.3	1,661.5	25.7	3.9	11.0	(2.8)
Utah	1,974.5	2,042.1	2,248.7	2,586.3	31.0	4.6	1.1	8.2
Wyoming	177.9	242.5	268.0	316.3	77.8	10.1	10.9	9.3
Pacific	67,287.8	75,952.3	86,492.9	92,219.8	37.1	5.4	4.1	6.7
Alaska	574.8	760.6	930.4	1,005.0	74.8	9.8	9.8	9.7
California	52,768.3	58,030.1	66,702.2	69,411.9	31.5	4.7	3.2	6.2
Hawaii	1,773.4	2,129.2	2,408.2	2,312.8	30.4	4.5	6.3	2.8
Oregon	3,727.7	4,618.9	5,102.7	7,584.6	103.5	12.6	7.4	18.0
Washington	8,443.7	10,413.5	11,349.5	11,905.5	41.0	5.9	7.2	4.6
U.S. Territories	281.2	823.2	924.4	1,042.9	270.9	24.4	43.1	8.2

Note: Reporting public charities include only organizations that both reported (filed IRS Form 990) and were required to report include religious congregations and organizations with less than $25,000 in gross receipts. Owing to rounding, percentage figures may not total 100. The average annual percentage change is a compound rate that assumes a constant growth rate over time.

Sources: IRS Business Master Files (Exempt Organizations), 1993, 1996, 1998, 1999; IRS Return Transaction File, 1993, 1996, 1998, 1999 (returns received in those calendar years), as classified according to the National Taxonomy of Exempt Entities—Core Codes and adjusted by the National Center for Charitable Statistics. See Resource B for details.

TABLE 5.26

Reporting Public Charities: Total Assets by State, Circa 1992, 1995, 1997, and 1998

	Total Assets (Millions of Dollars)				Total Percentage Change	Average Annual Percentage Change		
	1992	1995	1997	1998	1992–1998	1992–1998	1992–1995	1995–1998
United States	662,199.0	842,833.2	1,090,337.8	1,210,392.2	82.8	10.6	8.4	12.8
Northeast	216,134.5	273,019.3	362,170.1	398,040.7	84.2	10.7	8.1	13.4
New England	82,239.5	105,110.9	147,722.4	160,142.0	94.7	11.7	8.5	15.1
Connecticut	23,999.6	30,789.0	48,790.0	48,896.5	103.7	12.6	8.7	16.7
Maine	3,039.4	3,997.5	5,819.0	6,390.6	110.3	13.2	9.6	16.9
Massachusetts	44,690.1	57,105.1	75,997.7	85,685.9	91.7	11.5	8.5	14.5
New Hampshire	4,382.7	5,695.9	7,346.4	8,497.5	93.9	11.7	9.1	14.3
Rhode Island	4,403.8	5,438.8	6,950.0	7,538.3	71.2	9.4	7.3	11.5
Vermont	1,723.9	2,084.6	2,819.2	3,133.3	81.8	10.5	6.5	14.6
Middle Atlantic	133,895.0	167,908.3	214,447.7	237,898.7	77.7	10.1	7.8	12.3
New Jersey	18,373.3	23,288.3	29,603.1	33,715.1	83.5	10.6	8.2	13.1
New York	73,046.7	89,465.5	109,146.4	121,108.3	65.8	8.8	7.0	10.6
Pennsylvania	42,475.0	55,154.4	75,698.2	83,075.3	95.6	11.8	9.1	14.6
Midwest	158,579.4	208,248.5	261,611.7	289,384.7	82.5	10.5	9.5	11.6
East North Central	108,349.5	143,133.3	180,205.8	202,240.0	86.7	11.0	9.7	12.2
Illinois	34,065.4	45,623.1	57,664.5	62,852.0	84.5	10.7	10.2	11.3
Indiana	14,858.4	19,348.7	24,657.2	29,006.6	95.2	11.8	9.2	14.4
Michigan	18,243.5	23,401.0	29,213.9	32,790.2	79.7	10.3	8.7	11.9
Ohio	30,898.1	41,124.5	52,477.9	58,754.0	90.2	11.3	10.0	12.6
Wisconsin	10,284.2	13,636.1	16,192.4	18,837.2	83.2	10.6	9.9	11.4
West North Central	50,229.8	65,115.2	81,405.9	87,144.7	73.5	9.6	9.0	10.2
Iowa	6,346.6	9,223.9	11,240.8	12,347.5	94.6	11.7	13.3	10.2
Kansas	3,907.3	4,791.6	5,832.1	6,689.1	71.2	9.4	7.0	11.8
Minnesota	13,069.5	17,862.5	21,110.0	23,424.2	79.2	10.2	11.0	9.5
Missouri	17,508.4	21,844.2	28,665.6	29,985.6	71.3	9.4	7.7	11.1
Nebraska	5,005.1	5,872.5	7,816.2	7,833.0	56.5	7.8	5.5	10.1
North Dakota	1,685.0	2,116.2	2,606.3	3,413.7	102.6	12.5	7.9	17.3
South Dakota	2,707.9	3,404.4	4,134.9	3,451.7	27.5	4.1	7.9	0.5
South	178,993.3	229,733.1	299,104.4	338,919.4	89.3	11.2	8.7	13.8
South Atlantic	109,037.5	142,116.3	184,445.7	209,990.1	92.6	11.5	9.2	13.9
Delaware	2,238.5	3,060.1	3,625.4	4,006.7	79.0	10.2	11.0	9.4
District of Columbia	10,334.6	12,842.9	16,731.5	17,683.0	71.1	9.4	7.5	11.2
Florida	24,518.4	32,124.6	39,007.4	44,302.8	80.7	10.4	9.4	11.3

Georgia	12,655.7	18,491.0	26,917.0	146.4	16.2	13.5	19.0
Maryland	19,374.2	24,589.6	33,404.9	85.4	10.8	8.3	13.5
North Carolina	14,235.4	19,091.9	28,726.7	101.8	12.4	10.3	14.6
South Carolina	5,097.0	7,246.0	8,477.3	100.1	12.3	12.4	12.1
Virginia	17,507.1	21,047.2	33,312.3	90.3	11.3	6.3	16.5
West Virginia	3,076.5	3,622.9	4,652.8	51.2	7.1	5.6	8.7
East South Central	24,612.8	31,357.0	45,227.4	83.8	10.7	8.4	13.0
Alabama	4,947.1	6,039.3	8,282.1	67.4	9.0	6.9	11.1
Kentucky	6,286.0	8,145.6	11,168.7	77.7	10.1	9.0	11.1
Mississippi	2,507.7	3,548.4	5,163.5	105.9	12.8	12.3	13.3
Tennessee	10,872.1	13,623.6	18,914.0	89.6	11.3	7.8	14.8
West South Central	45,343.1	56,259.9	83,701.9	84.6	10.8	7.5	14.2
Arkansas	2,950.8	3,443.1	4,800.5	62.7	8.4	5.3	11.7
Louisiana	6,715.8	8,157.7	10,356.7	54.2	7.5	6.7	8.3
Oklahoma	5,865.7	6,657.2	9,366.8	59.7	8.1	4.3	12.1
Texas	29,810.8	38,001.9	59,177.9	98.5	12.1	8.4	15.9
West	107,071.3	129,497.0	165,314.6	69.7	9.2	6.5	11.9
Mountain	20,165.1	25,751.5	33,389.1	77.8	10.1	8.5	11.7
Arizona	4,884.4	6,822.4	8,352.7	98.5	12.1	11.8	12.4
Colorado	6,660.9	8,207.2	12,693.9	90.6	11.3	7.2	15.6
Idaho	951.6	1,211.4	1,594.8	67.6	9.0	8.4	9.6
Montana	1,653.6	2,264.6	2,744.0	65.9	8.8	11.1	6.6
Nevada	1,067.7	1,721.0	2,276.4	113.2	13.4	17.2	9.8
New Mexico	2,107.9	2,879.9	3,266.0	52.2	7.2	11.0	3.7
Utah	2,484.8	2,151.0	2,933.3	18.0	2.8	(4.7)	10.9
Wyoming	354.0	494.1	702.9	98.5	12.1	11.8	12.5
Pacific	86,906.2	103,745.5	145,807.8	67.8	9.0	6.1	12.0
Alaska	702.0	974.1	1,196.1	95.2	11.8	11.5	12.0
California	67,003.4	77,950.0	101,402.1	64.3	8.6	5.2	12.2
Hawaii	3,874.1	5,220.0	6,666.4	90.4	11.3	10.5	12.2
Oregon	4,183.6	5,493.0	6,647.6	122.0	14.2	9.5	19.1
Washington	11,143.1	14,108.4	16,013.3	58.9	8.0	8.2	7.9
U.S. Territories	1,420.5	2,335.2	2,137.1	68.3	9.1	18.0	0.8

Note: *Reporting public charities include only organizations that both reported (filed IRS Form 990) and were required to do so. Organizations not required to report include religious congregations and organizations with less than $25,000 in gross receipts. Owing to rounding, percentage figures may not total 100. The average annual percentage change is a compound rate that assumes a constant growth rate over time.*

Sources: *IRS Business Master Files (Exempt Organizations), 1993, 1996, 1998, 1999; IRS Return Transaction File, 1993, 1996, 1998, 1999 (returns received in those calendar years), as classified according to the National Taxonomy of Exempt Entities—Core Codes and adjusted by the National Center for Charitable Statistics. See Resource B for details.*

TABLE 5.27

Reporting Public Charities: Net Assets by State, Circa 1992, 1995, 1997, and 1998

	Total Assets (Millions of Dollars)				Total Percentage Change	Average Annual Percentage Change		
	1992	1995	1997	1998	1992–1998	1992–1998	1992–1995	1995–1998
United States	395,644.3	515,421.9	709,015.6	791,495.4	100.1	12.3	9.2	15.4
Northeast	131,401.4	168,991.1	242,561.7	267,119.1	103.3	12.6	8.7	16.5
New England	54,554.4	72,326.9	109,539.2	118,802.4	117.8	13.8	9.9	18.0
Connecticut	16,929.8	22,991.5	40,710.6	39,978.2	136.1	15.4	10.7	20.3
Maine	1,753.9	2,364.3	3,583.0	3,988.4	127.4	14.7	10.5	19.0
Massachusetts	28,582.8	37,985.3	53,241.6	61,347.3	114.6	13.6	9.9	17.3
New Hampshire	3,028.4	3,876.9	5,139.0	5,891.4	94.5	11.7	8.6	15.0
Rhode Island	3,069.1	3,752.7	4,924.5	5,400.0	75.9	9.9	6.9	12.9
Vermont	1,190.4	1,356.2	1,940.5	2,197.1	84.6	10.8	4.4	17.4
Middle Atlantic	76,847.1	96,664.2	133,022.5	148,316.7	93.0	11.6	7.9	15.3
New Jersey	10,462.7	13,516.9	18,814.7	21,153.8	102.2	12.4	8.9	16.1
New York	41,994.2	51,270.0	66,686.2	75,121.8	78.9	10.2	6.9	13.6
Pennsylvania	24,390.2	31,877.2	47,521.6	52,041.1	113.4	13.5	9.3	17.7
Midwest	92,791.0	124,553.0	165,823.2	187,944.4	102.5	12.5	10.3	14.7
East North Central	63,945.4	85,552.4	114,352.1	131,032.0	104.9	12.7	10.2	15.3
Illinois	20,272.9	27,618.2	37,100.4	40,963.1	102.1	12.4	10.9	14.0
Indiana	9,289.9	12,325.6	16,970.7	20,010.5	115.4	13.6	9.9	17.5
Michigan	9,873.6	12,888.9	17,301.7	19,611.3	98.6	12.1	9.3	15.0
Ohio	18,415.9	24,441.0	32,708.1	38,461.0	108.8	13.1	9.9	16.3
Wisconsin	6,093.1	8,278.7	10,271.2	11,986.1	96.7	11.9	10.8	13.1
West North Central	28,845.6	39,000.6	51,471.1	56,912.4	97.3	12.0	10.6	13.4
Iowa	3,296.5	4,586.6	6,016.3	6,782.6	105.8	12.8	11.6	13.9
Kansas	2,129.4	2,876.3	3,636.6	4,016.1	88.6	11.2	10.5	11.8
Minnesota	7,600.1	10,631.0	13,169.1	14,782.0	94.5	11.7	11.8	11.6
Missouri	10,969.6	14,768.0	20,279.7	21,570.3	96.6	11.9	10.4	13.5
Nebraska	2,877.7	3,456.3	4,946.4	5,696.3	97.9	12.1	6.3	18.1
North Dakota	851.2	1,165.7	1,476.6	1,946.5	128.7	14.8	11.0	18.6
South Dakota	1,121.1	1,516.7	1,946.3	2,118.7	89.0	11.2	10.6	11.8
South	112,943.0	148,483.3	201,032.2	227,660.1	101.6	12.4	9.5	15.3
South Atlantic	69,016.1	91,573.7	124,652.6	142,475.7	106.4	12.8	9.9	15.9
Delaware	1,156.9	1,862.1	2,356.0	2,651.7	129.2	14.8	17.2	12.5
District of Columbia	6,305.5	8,019.3	10,745.8	12,158.2	92.8	11.6	8.3	14.9
Florida	13,276.4	19,340.4	24,660.8	28,361.9	113.6	13.5	13.4	13.6

Georgia	8,596.2	12,201.3	19,457.9	22,251.0	158.8	17.2	12.4	22.2
Maryland	13,934.3	16,897.1	22,651.4	24,253.9	74.1	9.7	6.6	12.8
North Carolina	9,525.6	12,723.7	17,706.7	19,916.4	109.1	13.1	10.1	16.1
South Carolina	3,152.4	4,542.2	5,322.1	6,530.7	107.2	12.9	12.9	12.9
Virginia	11,215.1	13,642.4	18,852.7	23,284.9	107.6	12.9	6.7	19.5
West Virginia	1,853.9	2,345.1	2,899.2	3,067.0	65.4	8.8	8.2	9.4
East South Central	14,992.7	19,701.9	26,187.2	29,055.3	93.8	11.7	9.5	13.8
Alabama	2,873.0	3,709.9	4,966.6	5,241.5	82.4	10.5	8.9	12.2
Kentucky	3,820.6	5,181.8	6,481.5	7,201.5	88.5	11.1	10.7	11.6
Mississippi	1,382.7	1,933.2	2,710.9	3,031.0	119.2	14.0	11.8	16.2
Tennessee	6,916.2	8,877.0	12,028.2	13,581.3	96.4	11.9	8.7	15.2
West South Central	28,934.2	37,207.7	50,192.4	56,129.1	94.0	11.7	8.7	14.7
Arkansas	1,795.6	2,249.1	3,138.5	3,355.1	86.9	11.0	7.8	14.3
Louisiana	4,041.1	5,229.2	6,356.1	6,789.5	68.0	9.0	9.0	9.1
Oklahoma	4,090.3	4,710.1	6,425.4	7,026.5	71.8	9.4	4.8	14.3
Texas	19,007.2	25,019.4	34,272.4	38,957.9	105.0	12.7	9.6	15.9
West	58,266.4	72,822.2	98,768.3	107,867.3	85.1	10.8	7.7	14.0
Mountain	10,556.4	13,961.8	19,986.0	20,314.2	92.4	11.5	9.8	13.3
Arizona	1,809.2	2,945.4	3,800.0	4,417.3	144.2	16.0	17.6	14.5
Colorado	3,760.3	4,941.1	8,309.9	7,350.3	95.5	11.8	9.5	14.2
Idaho	605.6	741.0	1,030.2	1,093.6	80.6	10.4	7.0	13.9
Montana	861.8	1,132.8	1,414.8	1,617.1	87.6	11.1	9.5	12.6
Nevada	645.5	1,187.6	1,657.1	1,711.2	165.1	17.6	22.5	12.9
New Mexico	1,026.8	1,425.5	1,777.8	1,853.3	80.5	10.3	11.6	9.1
Utah	1,632.8	1,273.3	1,593.1	1,814.1	11.1	1.8	(8.0)	12.5
Wyoming	214.3	315.1	403.1	457.2	113.3	13.5	13.7	13.2
Pacific	47,710.0	58,860.4	78,782.3	87,553.1	83.5	10.6	7.3	14.2
Alaska	408.6	597.5	756.2	904.7	121.4	14.2	13.5	14.8
California	35,647.3	42,525.0	58,616.4	64,247.9	80.2	10.3	6.1	14.7
Hawaii	2,805.0	3,870.8	5,025.7	5,507.9	96.4	11.9	11.3	12.5
Oregon	2,485.5	3,361.9	4,327.7	5,830.2	134.6	15.3	10.6	20.1
Washington	6,363.6	8,505.2	10,056.3	11,062.4	73.8	9.7	10.2	9.2
U.S. Territories	242.4	572.3	830.1	904.6	273.1	24.5	33.2	16.5

Note: *Reporting public charities include only organizations that both reported (filed IRS Form 990) and were required to do so. Organizations not required to report include religious congregations and organizations with less than $25,000 in gross receipts. Owing to rounding, percentage figures may not total 100. The average annual percentage change is a compound rate that assumes a constant growth rate over time.*

Sources: *IRS Business Master Files (Exempt Organizations), 1993, 1996, 1998, 1999; IRS Return Transaction File, 1993, 1996, 1998, 1999 (returns received in those calendar years), as classified according to the National Taxonomy of Exempt Entities—Core Codes and adjusted by the National Center for Charitable Statistics. See Resource B for details.*

- Net assets of organizations in the Northeast, Midwest, and South showed similar growth (ranging from 102 to 103 percent), whereas growth for charities in the West was lower (85 percent). In 1998 the proportion of net assets held by charities in the West was only 14 percent, compared with 34 percent for organizations in the Northeast, 29 percent for those in the South, and 24 percent for those in the Midwest.

- Charities in all states showed higher rates of growth in net assets in the last three years of the six-year period (between 1995 and 1998).

- Net assets of organizations in four states—New York ($75 billion), California ($64 billion), Massachusetts ($61 billion), and Pennsylvania ($52 billion)—represented almost 32 percent of the total net assets for all reporting public charities in 1998. This is a slight decrease from the 33 percent proportion of all net assets that were held by charitable organizations in these four states in 1992.

Although growth patterns in numbers of organizations, total revenue, public support, total expenses, and net assets vary somewhat among the geographical regions of the United States, the overall distribution of the financial variables remained remarkably unchanged between 1992 and 1998. Charities in New York and California represent the largest proportion of most financial variables when they are analyzed on a geographical basis. Although growth rates vary, with some small states showing large increases, the overall proportions show stability over time.

References

Gronbjerg, K. A. "Using NTEE to Classify Nonprofit Organizations: An Assessment of Human Service and Regional Applications." *Voluntas*, 1994, 5(3), 301.

Haycock, N. *The Nonprofit Sector in New York City.* New York: Nonprofit Coordinating Committee of New York, 1992.

Internal Revenue Service. *Annual Report.* (Various editions.) Washington, D.C.: U.S. Government Printing Office, various years.

Internal Revenue Service. *Data Book.* (Various editions.) Washington, D.C.: U.S. Government Printing Office, various years.

Smith, D. H. "Some Challenges in Nonprofit and Voluntary Action Research." *Nonprofit and Voluntary Sector Quarterly*, 1995, 24(2), 99.

U.S. Bureau of the Census. "Population Projections." [http://www.census.gov/population/www/projections/popproj.html]. 2001.

U.S. Department of Education, National Center for Education Statistics. *Private School Universe Survey, 1997–98.* Washington, D.C.: U.S. Government Printing Office, 1999.

Resources

Resource A

National Taxonomy of Exempt Entities—Core Codes (NTEE-CC) for the Nonprofit Sector

A—Arts, Culture, and Humanities

A01 Alliance and Advocacy Organizations

A02 Management and Technical Assistance

A03 Professional Societies and Associations

A05 Research Institutes and/or Public Policy Analysis

A11 Single-Organization Support

A12 Fundraising or Fund Distribution

A19 Nonmonetary Support Not Elsewhere Classified

A20 Arts and Cultural Organizations—Multipurpose

A23 Cultural and Ethnic Awareness

A25 Arts Education

A26 Arts Councils and Agencies

A30 Media and Communications Organizations

A31 Film and Video

A32 Television

A33 Printing and Publishing

A34 Radio

A40 Visual Arts Organizations

A50 Museums and Museum Activities

A51 Art Museums

A52 Children's Museums

A54 History Museums

A56 Natural History and Natural Science Museums

A57 Science and Technology Museums

A60 Performing Arts Organizations and Activities

A61 Performing Arts Centers

A62 Dance

A63 Ballet

A65 Theater

A68 Music

A69 Symphony Orchestras

A6A Opera

A6B Singing Choral

A6C Music Groups, Bands, and Ensembles

This list of codes is from the Urban Institute, National Center for Charitable Statistics. For additional information, see http://www.nccs.urban.org. Codes marked with an asterisk (*) have been added pending approval.

A6E Performing Arts Schools

A70 Humanities Organizations

A80 Historical Societies and Related Historical Activities

A84 Commemorative Events

A90 Arts Service Organizations and Activities

A99 Arts, Culture, and Humanities Not Elsewhere Classified

B—Education

B01 Alliance and Advocacy Organizations

B02 Management and Technical Assistance

B03 Professional Societies and Associations

B05 Research Institutes and/or Public Policy Analysis

B11 Single-Organization Support

B12 Fundraising or Fund Distribution

B19 Nonmonetary Support Not Elsewhere Classified

B20 Elementary and Secondary Education (K–12)

B21 Kindergartens, Preschools, Nursery Schools, and Early Admissions

B24 Primary and Elementary Schools

B25 Secondary and High Schools

B28 Special Education Institutions and Programs

B30 Vocational and Technical Schools

B40 Higher Education Institutions

B41 Community and Junior Colleges

B42 Undergraduate Colleges (Four-Year)

B43 Universities and Technological Institutes

B50 Graduate and Professional Schools (Separate Entities)

B60 Adult and Continuing Education

B70 Libraries

B80 Student Services and Organizations of Students

B82 Scholarships, Student Financial Aid Services, and Awards

B83 Student Sororities and Fraternities

B84 Alumni Associations

B90 Educational Services and Schools— Other

B92 Remedial Reading and Reading Encouragement Programs

B94 Parent-Teacher Groups

B99 Education Not Elsewhere Classified

C—Environmental Quality, Protection, and Beautification

C01 Alliance and Advocacy Organizations

C02 Management and Technical Assistance

C03 Professional Societies and Associations

C05 Research Institutes and/or Public Policy Analysis

C11 Single-Organization Support

C12 Fundraising or Fund Distribution

C19 Nonmonetary Support Not Elsewhere Classified

C20 Pollution Abatement and Control Services

C27 Recycling Programs

C30 Natural Resources Conservation and Protection

C32 Water Resources and Wetlands Conservation and Management

C34 Land Resources Conservation

C35 Energy Resources Conservation and Development

C36 Forest Conservation

C40 Botanical, Horticultural, and Landscape Services

C41 Botanical Gardens, Arboretums, and Botanical Organizations

C42 Garden Clubs and Horticultural Programs

C50 Environmental Beautification and Aesthetics

C60 Environmental Education and Outdoor Survival Programs

C99 Environmental Quality, Protection, and Beautification Not Elsewhere Classified

D—Animal-Related Organizations and Activities

D01 Alliance and Advocacy Organizations

D02 Management and Technical Assistance

D03 Professional Societies and Associations

D05 Research Institutes and/or Public Policy Analysis

D11 Single-Organization Support

D12 Fundraising or Fund Distribution

D19 Nonmonetary Support Not Elsewhere Classified

D20 Animal Protection and Welfare

D30 Wildlife Preservation and Protection

D31 Endangered Species Protection

D32 Bird Sanctuaries and Preserves

D33 Fisheries Resources

D34 Wildlife Sanctuaries and Refuges

D40 Veterinary Services

D50 Zoos and Zoological Societies

D60 Other Services—Specialty Animals

D61 Animal Training

D99 Animal-Related Organizations and Activities Not Elsewhere Classified

E—Health (General and Rehabilitative)

E01 Alliance and Advocacy Organizations

E02 Management and Technical Assistance

E03 Professional Societies and Associations

E05 Research Institutes and/or Public Policy Analysis

E11 Single-Organization Support

E12 Fundraising or Fund Distribution

E19 Nonmonetary Support Not Elsewhere Classified

E20 Hospitals and Related Primary Medical Care Facilities

E21 Community Health Systems

E22 Hospitals—General

E24 Hospitals—Specialty

E30 Health Treatment Facilities—Primarily Outpatient

E31 Group Health Practice (Health Maintenance Organizations)

E32 Ambulatory Health Centers and Community Clinics

E40 Reproductive Health Care Facilities and Allied Services

E42 Family Planning Centers

E50 Rehabilitative Medical Services

E60 Health Support Services

E61 Blood Supply–Related

E62 Ambulance and Emergency Medical Transport Services

E65 Organ and Tissue Banks

E70 Public Health Programs (Including General Health and Wellness Promotion)

E80 Health—General and Financing

E86 Patient Services—Entertainment and Recreation

E90 Nursing Services—General

E91 Nursing and Convalescent Facilities

E92 Home Health Care

E99 Health (General and Rehabilitative) Not Elsewhere Classified

F—Mental Health and Crisis Intervention

F01 Alliance and Advocacy Organizations

F02 Management and Technical Assistance

F03 Professional Societies and Associations

F05 Research Institutes and/or Public Policy Analysis

F11 Single-Organization Support

F12 Fundraising or Fund Distribution

F19 Nonmonetary Support Not Elsewhere Classified

F20 Alcohol and Drug Abuse—Prevention and Treatment

F21 Alcohol and Drug Abuse—Prevention Only

F22 Alcohol and Drug Abuse—Treatment Only

F30 Mental Health Treatment— Multipurpose

F31 Psychiatric and Mental Health Hospitals

F32 Community Mental Health Centers

F33 Group Homes and Residential Treatment Facilities—Mental Health–Related

F40 Hot Line and Crisis Intervention Services

F42 Rape Victim Services

F50 Addictive Disorders

F52 Smoking Addiction

F53 Eating Disorders and Addiction

F54 Gambling Addiction

F60 Counseling and Support Groups

F70 Mental Health Disorders

F80 Mental Health Associations— Multipurpose

F99 Mental Health and Crisis Intervention Not Elsewhere Classified

G—Diseases, Disorders, and Medical Disciplines

G01 Alliance and Advocacy Organizations

G02 Management and Technical Assistance

G03 Professional Societies and Associations

G05 Research Institutes and/or Public Policy Analysis

G11 Single-Organization Support

G12 Fundraising or Fund Distribution

G19 Nonmonetary Support Not Elsewhere Classified

G20 Birth Defects and Genetic Diseases

G25 Down's Syndrome

G30 Cancer

G40 Diseases of Specific Organs

G41 Eye Diseases, Blindness, and Vision Impairments

G42 Ear and Throat Diseases

G43 Heart and Circulatory System Diseases and Disorders

G44 Kidney Disease

G45 Lung Disease

G48 Brain Disorders

G50 Nerve, Muscle, and Bone Diseases

G51 Arthritis

G54 Epilepsy

G60 Allergy-Related Diseases

G61 Asthma

G70 Digestive Diseases and Disorders

G80 Specifically Named Diseases

G81 AIDS

G83 Alzheimer's Disease

G84 Autism

G90 Medical Specialties

G92 Biomedicine and Bioengineering

G94 Geriatrics

G96 Neurology and Neuroscience

G98 Pediatrics

G99 Diseases, Disorders, and Medical Disciplines Not Elsewhere Classified

G9B Surgery

H—Medical Research

H01 Alliance and Advocacy Organizations

H02 Management and Technical Assistance

H03 Professional Societies and Associations

H05 Research Institutes and/or Public Policy Analysis

H11 Single-Organization Support

H12 Fundraising or Fund Distribution

H19 Nonmonetary Support Not Elsewhere Classified

H20 Birth Defects and Genetic Diseases Research

H25 Down's Syndrome Research

H30 Cancer Research

H40 Specific Organs Research

H41 Eye Diseases, Blindness, and Vision Impairments Research

H42 Ear and Throat Diseases Research

H43 Heart and Circulatory System Diseases and Disorders Research

H44 Kidney Disease Research

H45 Lung Disease Research

H48 Brain Disorders Research

H50 Nerve, Muscle, and Bone Diseases Research

H51 Arthritis Research

H54 Epilepsy Research

H60 Allergy-Related Diseases Research

H70 Digestive Diseases and Disorders Research

H80 Specifically Named Diseases Research

H81 AIDS Research

H83 Alzheimer's Disease Research

H84 Autism Research

H90 Medical Specialties Research

H92 Biomedicine and Bioengineering Research

H94 Geriatrics Research

H96 Neurology and Neuroscience Research

H98 Pediatrics Research

H99 Medical Research Not Elsewhere Classified

H9B Surgery Research

I—Crime and Legal-Related Organizations and Activities

I01 Alliance and Advocacy Organizations

I02 Management and Technical Assistance

I03 Professional Societies and Associations

I05 Research Institutes and/or Public Policy Analysis

I11 Single-Organization Support

I12 Fundraising or Fund Distribution

I19 Nonmonetary Support Not Elsewhere Classified

I20 Crime and Violence Prevention

I21 Delinquency Prevention

I23 Drunk Driving–Related

I30 Correctional Facilities

I31 Transitional Care and Halfway Houses for Offenders and Ex-Offenders

I40 Rehabilitation Services for Offenders

I43 Services to Prisoners and Families— Multipurpose

I44 Prison Alternatives

I50 Administration of Justice and Courts

I51 Dispute Resolution and Mediation Services

I60 Law Enforcement Agencies (Police Departments)

I70 Protection Against and Prevention of Neglect, Abuse, and Exploitation

I71 Prevention of Spouse Abuse

I72 Prevention of Child Abuse

I73 Prevention of Sexual Abuse

I80 Legal Services

I83 Public Interest Law and Litigation

I99 Crime and Legal-Related Organizations and Activities Not Elsewhere Classified

J—Employment and Job-Related Organizations and Activities

J01 Alliance and Advocacy Organizations

J02 Management and Technical Assistance

J03 Professional Societies and Associations

J05 Research Institutes and/or Public Policy Analysis

J11 Single-Organization Support

J12 Fundraising or Fund Distribution

J19 Nonmonetary Support Not Elsewhere Classified

J20 Employment Procurement Assistance and Job Training

J21 Vocational Counseling, Guidance, and Testing

J22 Vocational Training

J30 Vocational Rehabilitation

J32 Goodwill Industries

J33 Sheltered Remunerative Employment and Work Activity Centers

J40 Labor Unions and Organizations

J99 Employment and Job-Related Organizations and Activities Not Elsewhere Classified

K—Food, Agriculture, and Nutrition

K01 Alliance and Advocacy Organizations

K02 Management and Technical Assistance

K03 Professional Societies and Associations

K05 Research Institutes and/or Public Policy Analysis

K11 Single-Organization Support

K12 Fundraising or Fund Distribution

K19 Nonmonetary Support Not Elsewhere Classified

K20 Agricultural Programs

K25 Farmland Preservation

K26 Livestock Breeding, Development, and Management

K28 Farm Bureaus and Granges

K30 Food Service and Free Food Distribution Programs

K31 Food Banks and Pantries

K34 Congregate Meals

K35 Eateries, Agency- and Organization-Sponsored (Soup Kitchens)

K36 Meals on Wheels

K40 Nutrition Programs

K99 Food, Agriculture, and Nutrition Not Elsewhere Classified

L—Housing and Shelter

L01 Alliance and Advocacy Organizations

L02 Management and Technical Assistance

L03 Professional Societies and Associations

L05 Research Institutes and/or Public Policy Analysis

L11 Single-Organization Support

L12 Fundraising or Fund Distribution

L19 Nonmonetary Support Not Elsewhere Classified

L20 Housing Development, Construction, and Management

L21 Public Housing Facilities

L22 Senior Citizens' Housing and Retirement Communities

L25 Housing Rehabilitation

L30 Housing Search Assistance

L40 Low-Cost Temporary Housing

L41 Homeless and Temporary Shelters

L50 Housing Owners' and Renters' Organizations

L80 Housing Support Services

L81 Home Improvement and Repairs

L82 Housing Expense Reduction Support

L99 Housing and Shelter Not Elsewhere Classified

M—Public Safety, and Disaster Preparedness and Relief

M01 Alliance and Advocacy Organizations

M02 Management and Technical Assistance

M03 Professional Societies and Associations

M05 Research Institutes and/or Public Policy Analysis

M11 Single-Organization Support

M12 Fundraising or Fund Distribution

M19 Nonmonetary Support Not Elsewhere Classified

M20 Disaster Preparedness and Relief Services

M23 Search and Rescue Squads and Services

M24 Fire Prevention, Protection, and Control

M40 Safety Education

M41 First-Aid Training and Services

M42 Automotive Safety

M99 Public Safety, and Disaster Preparedness and Relief Not Elsewhere Classified

N—Recreation, Sports, Leisure, and Athletics

N01 Alliance and Advocacy Organizations

N02 Management and Technical Assistance

N03 Professional Societies and Associations

N05 Research Institutes and/or Public Policy Analysis

N11 Single-Organization Support

N12 Fundraising or Fund Distribution

N19 Nonmonetary Support Not Elsewhere Classified

N20 Recreational and Sporting Camps

N30 Physical Fitness and Community Recreational Facilities

N31 Community Recreational Centers

N32 Parks and Playgrounds

N40 Sports Training Facilities and Agencies

N50 Recreational, Pleasure, and Social Clubs

N52 Fairs, County and Other

N60 Amateur Sports Clubs and Leagues

N61 Fishing and Hunting Clubs

N62 Basketball

N63 Baseball and Softball

N64 Soccer Clubs and Leagues

N65 Football Clubs and Leagues

N66 Tennis and Racquet Sports Clubs and Leagues

N67 Swimming and Water Recreation

N68 Winter Sports (Snow and Ice)

N69 Equestrian and Riding Sports

N6A Golf

N70 Amateur Sports Competitions

N71 Olympics Committees and Related International Competitions

N72 Special Olympics

N80 Professional Athletic Leagues

N99 Recreation, Sports, Leisure, and Athletics Not Elsewhere Classified

O—Youth Development

O01 Alliance and Advocacy Organizations

O02 Management and Technical Assistance

O03 Professional Societies and Associations

O05 Research Institutes and Public Policy Analysis

O11 Single-Organization Support

O12 Fundraising or Fund Distribution

O19 Nonmonetary Support Not Elsewhere Classified

O20 Youth Centers and Clubs—Multipurpose

O21 Boys Clubs

O22 Girls Clubs

O23 Boys and Girls Clubs (Combined)

O30 Adult and Child Matching Programs

O31 Big Brothers and Big Sisters

O40 Scouting Organizations

O41 Boy Scouts of America

O42 Girl Scouts of the USA

O43 Camp Fire

O50 Youth Development Programs—Other

O51 Youth Community Service Clubs

O52 Youth Development—Agricultural

O53 Youth Development—Business

O54 Youth Development—Citizenship Programs

O55 Youth Development—Religious Leadership

O99 Youth Development Not Elsewhere Classified

P—Human Services (Multipurpose)

P01 Alliance and Advocacy Organizations

P02 Management and Technical Assistance

P03 Professional Societies and Associations

P05 Research Institutes and Public Policy Analysis

P11 Single Organization Support

P12 Fundraising or Fund Distribution

P19 Nonmonetary Support Not Elsewhere Classified

P20 Human Service Organizations

P21 American Red Cross

P22 Urban League

P24 Salvation Army

P26 Volunteers of America

P27 Young Men's and Women's Associations (YMCA, YWCA, YWHA, YMHA)

P28 Neighborhood Centers and Settlement Houses

P29 Thrift Shops

P30 Children's and Youth Services

P31 Adoption

P32 Foster Care

P33 Child Day Care

P40 Family Services

P42 Single-Parent Agencies and Services

P43 Family Violence Shelters and Services

P44 Homemakers and Home Health Aides

P45 Family Services and Adolescent Parents

P46 Family Counseling

P50 Personal Social Services

P51 Financial Counseling and Money Management

P52 Transportation (Free and Subsidized)

P58 Gift Distribution

P60 Emergency Assistance (Food, Clothing, Cash)

P61 Travelers' Aid

P62 Victims' Services

P70 Residential and Custodial Care

P72 Halfway Houses (Short-Term Residential Care)

P73 Group Homes (Long-Term Residential Care)

P74 Hospices

P75 Senior Continuing Care Communities

P80 Services to Promote the Independence of Specific Populations

P81 Senior Centers and Services

P82 Centers and Services for the Developmentally Disabled

P84 Ethnic and Immigrant Centers and Services

P85 Homeless Persons' Centers and Services

P86 Blind and Visually Impaired Centers and Services*

P87 Deaf and Hearing Impaired Centers and Services*

P99 Human Services (Multipurpose) Not Elsewhere Classified

Q—International and Foreign Affairs, and National Security

Q01 Alliance and Advocacy Organizations

Q02 Management and Technical Assistance

Q03 Professional Societies and Associations

Q05 Research Institutes and Public Policy Analysis

Q11 Single-Organization Support

Q12 Fundraising or Fund Distribution

Q19 Nonmonetary Support Not Elsewhere Classified

Q20 Promotion of International Understanding

Q21 International Cultural Exchange

Q22 International Student Exchange and Aid

Q23 International Exchanges

Q30 International Development and Relief Services

Q31 International Agricultural Development

Q32 International Economic Development

Q33 International Relief

Q40 International Peace and Security

Q41 Arms Control and Peace Organizations

Q42 United Nations Association

Q43 National Security (Domestic)

Q70 International Human Rights

Q71 International Migration and Refugee Issues

Q99 International and Foreign Affairs, and National Security Not Elsewhere Classified

R—Civil Rights, Social Action, and Advocacy

R01 Alliance and Advocacy Organizations

R02 Management and Technical Assistance

R03 Professional Societies and Associations

R05 Research Institutes and Public Policy Analysis

R11 Single-Organization Support

R12 Fundraising or Fund Distribution

R19 Nonmonetary Support Not Elsewhere Classified

R20 Civil Rights Advocacy for Specific Groups

R22 Minority Rights

R23 Disabled Persons' Rights

R24 Women's Rights

R25 Seniors' Rights

R26 Lesbian and Gay Rights

R30 Intergroup and Race Relations

R40 Voter Education and Registration

R60 Civil Liberties Advocacy

R61 Right to Life

R62 Right to Life Advocacy

R63 Censorship, Freedom of Speech, and Press Issues

R67 Right to Die and Euthanasia Issues

R99 Civil Rights, Social Action, and Advocacy Not Elsewhere Classified

S—Community Improvement and Capacity Building

S01 Alliance and Advocacy Organizations

S02 Management and Technical Assistance

S03 Professional Societies and Associations

S05 Research Institutes and Public Policy Analysis

S11 Single-Organization Support

S12 Fundraising or Fund Distribution

S19 Nonmonetary Support Not Elsewhere Classified

S20 Community and Neighborhood Development and Improvement— General

S21 Community Coalitions

S22 Neighborhood and Block Associations

S30 Economic Development

S31 Urban and Community Economic Development

S32 Rural Development

S40 Business and Industry

S41 Promotion of Business

S43 Management Services for Small Business and Entrepreneurs

S46 Boards of Trade

S47 Real Estate Organizations

S50 Nonprofit Management

S80 Community Service Clubs

S81 Women's Service Clubs

S82 Men's Service Clubs

S99 Community Improvement and Capacity Building Not Elsewhere Classified

T—Philanthropy, Voluntarism, and Grant-Making Foundations

T01 Alliance and Advocacy Organizations

T02 Management and Technical Assistance

T03 Professional Societies and Associations

T05 Research Institutes and Public Policy Analysis

T11 Single-Organization Support

T12 Fundraising or Fund Distribution

T19 Nonmonetary Support Not Elsewhere Classified

T20 Private Grant-Making Foundations

T21 Corporate Foundations

T22 Private Independent Foundations

T23 Private Operating Foundations

T30 Public Foundations

T31 Community Foundations

T40 Voluntarism Promotion

T50 Philanthropy, Charity, and Voluntarism Promotion—General

T70 Fundraising Organizations That Cross Categories

T90 Named Foundations and Trusts Not Elsewhere Classified

T99 Philanthropy, Voluntarism, and Grant-Making Foundations Not Elsewhere Classified

U—Science and Technology Research Institutes and Services

U01 Alliance and Advocacy Organizations

U02 Management and Technical Assistance

U03 Professional Societies and Associations

U05 Research Institutes and Public Policy Analysis

U11 Single-Organization Support

U12 Fundraising or Fund Distribution

U19 Nonmonetary Support Not Elsewhere Classified

U20 Science—General

U21 Marine Science and Oceanography

U30 Physical Science and Earth Sciences— Research

U31 Astronomy

U33 Chemistry and Chemical Engineering

U34 Mathematics

U36 Geology

U40 Engineering and Technology— Research

U41 Computer Science

U42 Engineering

U50 Biological and Life Sciences Research

U99 Science and Technology Research Not Elsewhere Classified

V—Social Science Research Institutes and Services

V01 Alliance and Advocacy Organizations

V02 Management and Technical Assistance

V03 Professional Societies and Associations

V05 Research Institutes and Public Policy Analysis

V11 Single-Organization Support

V12 Fundraising or Fund Distribution

V19 Nonmonetary Support Not Elsewhere Classified

V20 Social Science Research

V21 Anthropology and Sociology

V22 Economics (as a Social Science)

V23 Behavioral Science

V24 Political Science

V25 Population Studies

V26 Law, International Law, and Jurisprudence

V30 Interdisciplinary Research

V31 Black Studies

V32 Women's Studies

V33 Ethnic Studies

V34 Urban Studies

V35 International Studies

V36 Gerontology (as a Social Science)

V37 Labor Studies

V99 Social Science Research Not Elsewhere Classified

W—Public and Societal Benefit Organizations and Activities (Multipurpose and Other)

W01 Alliance and Advocacy Organizations

W02 Management and Technical Assistance

W03 Professional Societies and Associations

W05 Research Institutes and Public Policy Analysis

W11 Single-Organization Support

W12 Fundraising or Fund Distribution

W19 Nonmonetary Support Not Elsewhere Classified

W20 Government and Public Administration

W22 Public Finance, Taxation, and Monetary Policy

W24 Citizen Participation

W30 Military and Veterans' Organizations

W40 Public Transportation Systems and Services

W50 Telephone, Telegraph, and Telecommunication Services

W60 Financial Institutions and Services (Nongovernment-Related)

W61 Credit Unions

W70 Leadership Development

W80 Public Utilities

W90 Consumer Protection and Safety

W99 Public and Societal Benefit Not Elsewhere Classified

X—Religion and Spiritual Development

X01 Alliance and Advocacy Organizations

X02 Management and Technical Assistance

X03 Professional Societies and Associations

X05 Research Institutes and Public Policy Analysis

X11 Single-Organization Support

X12 Fundraising or Fund Distribution

X19 Nonmonetary Support Not Elsewhere Classified

X20 Christian

X21 Protestant

X22 Roman Catholic

X30 Jewish

X40 Islamic

X50 Buddhist

X70 Hindu

X80 Religious Media and Communications Organizations*

X81 Religious Film and Video*

X82 Religious Television*

X83 Religious Printing and Publishing*

X84 Religious Radio*

X90 Interfaith Issues

X99 Religion and Spiritual Development Not Elsewhere Classified

Y—Mutual and Membership Benefit Organizations (Other)

Y01 Alliance and Advocacy Organizations

Y02 Management and Technical Assistance

Y03 Professional Societies and Associations

Y05 Research Institutes and Public Policy Analysis

Y11 Single-Organization Support

Y12 Fundraising or Fund Distribution

Y19 Nonmonetary Support Not Elsewhere Classified

Y20 Insurance Providers and Services

Y22 Local Benevolent Life Insurance Associations, Mutual Irrigation and Telephone Companies, and Like Organizations

Y23 Mutual Insurance Company, Association

Y24 Supplemental Unemployment Compensation

Y30 Pension and Retirement Funds

Y33 Teachers Retirement Fund Association

Y34 Employee-Funded Pension Trust

Y35 Multi-Employer Pension Plans

Y40 Fraternal Beneficiary Societies

Y42 Domestic Fraternal Societies— 501(c)(10)

Y43 Voluntary Employees Beneficiary Associations—501(c)(9) (Nongovernment)

Y44 Voluntary Employees Beneficiary Associations—501(c)(9) (Government)*

Y50 Cemeteries and Burial Services

Y99 Mutual and Membership Benefit Organizations (Other) Not Elsewhere Classified

Z—Unknown or Unclassified

Z99 Unknown or Unclassified

Resource B
Technical Notes

Chapter One

What Is the Independent Sector?

Figure B.1 shows the components of the independent (or "voluntary" or "third") sector.

Table 1.4

Information on national income (excluding assigned values for volunteers and unpaid family workers) is adapted from the *Survey of Current Business*, published by the U.S. Department of Commerce, Bureau of Economic Analysis. The national income and product accounts of the United States are generally published in the July issue of the *Survey of Current Business*.

National income for the private nonprofit and government sectors is limited to compensation (that is, wages and salaries adjusted to include estimated fringe benefits) for paid employees. Nonprofit sector compensation is also based on data from the *Survey of Current Business*. Government compensation of paid employees includes that of military personnel and all civilian government employees at all levels of government engaged in various types of government activities, including government enterprises.

Assigned dollar values for volunteer time are based on volunteer hours derived from INDEPENDENT SECTOR's survey *Giving and Volunteering in the United States.* The total annual dollar value for volunteers is based on the total number of full-time-equivalent volunteers multiplied by the average gross hourly earnings for private nonagricultural employees (as reported in the *Economic Report of the President*), increased by 12 percent for benefits. Nonprofit employees would generally be working in nonagricultural industries.

Assigned dollar values for unpaid family workers are assumed to be one-half of the average annual earnings of the self-employed, multiplied by

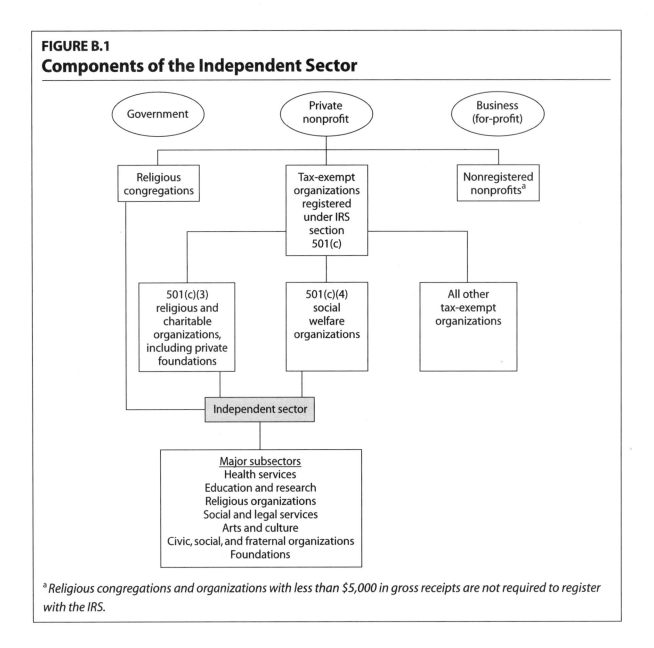

FIGURE B.1
Components of the Independent Sector

[a] Religious congregations and organizations with less than $5,000 in gross receipts are not required to register with the IRS.

the number of unpaid family workers estimated in the *Current Population Survey* of the U.S. Bureau of the Census and published annually by the U.S. Department of Labor, Bureau of Labor Statistics, in the January issue of *Employment and Earnings.* Average annual earnings of the self-employed are from the national income and product accounts of the United States.

The business (for-profit) sector includes all sectors except the private nonprofit and government sectors. In addition to the usual industry groups, such as manufacturing and wholesale and retail trade, the business sector in this table includes private households. In addition to compensation of employees, national income for business includes income of proprietors, corporate profits, and net interest.

Table 1.6

The attempt is to include all persons who are actively engaged in employment. This may include salaried workers, self-employed persons, unpaid family workers, and volunteers. Persons in the military are included in the estimates of government employment. Volunteers are converted to full-time-equivalent employment by dividing estimates of total hours volunteered by 1,700, which is a reasonable approximation of actual hours worked by a full-time employee in a year. Total employment estimates represent data generated from the statistical collection programs of both the U.S. Department of Labor and the U.S. Department of Commerce. Paid employment estimates are published annually by the U.S. Department of Commerce, Bureau of Economic Analysis, in the December issue of the *Survey of Current Business,* in two tables ("Full-Time and Part-Time Employees by Industry" and "Self-Employed Persons by Industry") that present annual data for the national income accounts.

Annual estimates of the number of paid employees in the nonprofit sector are based on detailed estimates for specific subsectors, such as hospitals, colleges, and religious organizations, and are aggregated to obtain yearly totals. Early estimates were prepared in connection with a study commissioned by Yale University's Program on Non-Profit Organizations (appearing in G. Rudney and M. Weitzman, "Significance of Employment and Earnings in the Philanthropic Sector: 1972–1982," working paper no. 77, Program on Non-Profit Organizations, Yale University, 1983). Later estimates are based on work performed at INDEPENDENT SECTOR (appearing in various editions of *Dimensions of the Independent Sector* and in this book).

Employment in the business (for-profit) sector includes all employment except that in private nonprofit organizations and the government sector. In this table business employment also includes that of private households.

Government employment encompasses all government employees, civilian and military, at all levels of government, federal, state, and local.

Table 1.7

Total earnings from work is a composite of actual earnings and assigned values imputed for volunteers and unpaid family workers. Actual earnings are from the *Survey of Current Business,* published by the U.S. Department of Commerce, Bureau of Economic Analysis, and appear annually in the December national income issue of that publication.

Table 1.8

Current operating expenditures are based on estimates of compensation of employees in nonprofit institutions, a component in the national income and product accounts of the United States, which appear in table 1.7 ("Gross

Domestic Product by Sector") in the July issue of the *Survey of Current Business,* published by the U.S. Department of Commerce, Bureau of Economic Analysis.

To estimate current operating expenditures for nonprofit institutions, compensation of employees is taken to represent 55 percent of such expenditures (consistent with the estimate employed in D. L. Hiestand, "Recent Trends in the Not-for-Profit Sector," *Research Papers,* 1977, 1, 334, sponsored by the Commission on Private Philanthropy and Public Needs). In recent years compensation of employees as a percentage of current operating expenditures has been slowly declining to about 47 to 50 percent. Therefore current operating expenditure estimates may be somewhat understated for the later years.

Nonprofit institutions, as defined by the Bureau of Economic Analysis, include organizations in the independent sector, as well as nonprofit organizations in the manufacturing of food and related products, business associations, professional membership organizations, labor unions, hotels and other lodging places, and so on.

Chapter Three

Table 3.3

Although the statistical data generated by the IRS on the charitable contribution deductions of individuals are the best available standard to use in estimating total individual giving, it is incomplete. Most important, data on the charitable contributions of taxpayers who chose to use a standard deduction (that is, nonitemizers) are lacking. Household surveys, like those conducted by INDEPENDENT SECTOR on giving and volunteering in the United States, attempt to obtain this information by asking respondents directly about their level of giving and whether they intend to itemize or not. However, INDEPENDENT SECTOR has ascertained that the data collected from these surveys are valuable in studying behavioral patterns with regard to giving and volunteering but inaccurate in estimating aggregate contributions. This is partly due to the insufficient number of respondents belonging to the highest income brackets, who contribute a significant amount to charitable giving. Respondents also tend to get confused about the type of tax form they actually filed and may not recall the amount of contribution they claimed.

A method adopted by INDEPENDENT SECTOR to complete its estimates on charitable contributions for both itemizers and nonitemizers is to use available IRS data on the charitable contributions of nonitemizers collected in 1985 and 1986. As part of an experiment carried out by the government in the early 1980s, taxpayers who did not itemize were allowed to take 50 percent of their charitable contributions as a tax deduction in 1985, and 100 percent in 1986, after which time the experiment ended. Data show that this change in tax law had a marked effect in increasing charitable contributions in 1986. The experiment also provided a basis by which to estimate charitable contributions of nonitemizers by their adjusted gross income for subsequent years. Updated IRS data on charitable contributions of itemizers serve as a broad reference on which to base nonitemizers' contributions in the same adjusted gross income categories.

Table 3.16

There are a number of reasons that the Foundation Center's count of the total number of private grant-making foundations is lower than those reported by the IRS (as shown in Table 5.1). One major reason given by the Foundation Center is a difference in definition. The Internal Revenue Code defines private foundations "only by exclusion of other nonprofit organizations." By this definition, organizations that may actually be public charities but lose that status owing to lack of public support may be counted as foundations. The Foundation Center refers to these organizations as "failed public charities." The IRS definition may also include libraries, museums, and homes for the aged that have been endowed by an individual or single family. In contrast, the Foundation Center specifically defines a private foundation as "a nongovernmental, nonprofit organization with its own funds (from either an individual, family or corporation) and program managed by its own trustees and directors, established to maintain or aid educational, social, charitable, religious, or other activities serving the common welfare, primarily by making grants to other nonprofit organizations." (For a more comprehensive explanation of the variation in count, see the Foundation Center's *Foundation Yearbook: Facts and Figures on Private and Community Foundations*, 2000, Appendix A, p. 85.)

Chapter Four

INDEPENDENT SECTOR has developed a general circular-flow model that identifies different elements present in independent sector entities engaged in carrying out their objectives (see Figure B.2). There are four major elements to the model: activities, outputs (which can be expanded eventually to include outcomes), revenue, and expenditures. Two additional components are added to the model to accommodate two phenomena primarily associated with the independent sector—volunteering (time and number of persons) and contributions (both private and government).

FIGURE B.2

Schematic of Elements Associated with the Independent Sector

Activities	→	Outputs	→	Revenue	→	Expenditures	→

	Equal to or transformed into	**Indicators**	Financed and made possible by flow of funds from such sources as	**Cash**	Used to pay for resources in such areas as	• Labor
						  Paid
						  Volunteer
							In order to support such activities as listed in the first column

• Treating patients (for example, admission, laboratory tests)		• Number of examinations		• Charitable contributions
				  Individual gifts
				  Individual bequest
				  Corporations
				  Foundations
				  Government			

		• Circulation volume				• Goods and services	

• Publishing newsletters (for example, information gathering, writing articles)		• Number of visitors		• Fees for service
				  Individuals
				  Corporations
				  Government
						• Space	

		• Number of food packages distributed				• Interest	
• Giving performances (for example, rehearsals, constructing scenery)		**Users**		• Capital account Disinvestment		• Investment	

		• Consumers				• Transfer
						  Grants and benefits
						  Specific assistance to individuals
						  Benefits paid to or for members	

		• Business		• Borrowing			
• Conducting museum tours (for example, learning about the exhibits, preparing materials for audiences)		• Government		**In-kind**			
		• Rest of the world		• Volunteers (time)			
• Distributing food packages (for example, soliciting donations, assembling packages)				• Other (for example, real estate, products, artwork)			

Contributions to Religion

Estimates for revenue for the religion subsector were developed from IN-DEPENDENT SECTOR's survey on religion, as reported in *From Belief to Commitment: The Activities and Finances of Religious Organizations in the United States.* Based on survey results, total revenues for religion in 1986 were estimated at $41.8 billion. Subsequent estimates for contributions to religion have been extrapolated by increasing the 1986 base by the annual percentage increase in contributions as reported from surveys conducted annually by the Southern Baptist Convention. The Convention is the single largest Protestant group, with about 41,000 churches and a membership of close to 16 million. The quality and timeliness of these surveys have made them a reliable data source to use in updating estimates for contributions made to religion.

Chapter Five

Chapter Five is based on analyses of data from IRS Forms 990 filed by 501(c)(3) organizations. Four different series of data files were used for the analyses; they are discussed in the following sections.

IRS Business Master Files of Tax-Exempt Organizations, 1992–1998

The IRS Business Master Files of Tax-Exempt Organizations are cumulative files that include basic descriptive information on all nonprofit organizations that have obtained recognition of their tax-exempt status from the IRS. With the major exception of religious congregations and organizations with less than $5,000 in annual gross receipts, most nonprofits must obtain this recognition. Key information drawn from these files includes organizations' names, addresses, ruling dates (the dates that they obtained recognition of their exempt status from the IRS), and National Taxonomy of Exempt Entities (NTEE) purpose codes. The 1998 file contains more than 712,000 records. This series of files provided most of the data for Table 5.1.

IRS Return Transaction Files, 1992–1998

The IRS Return Transaction Files (RTFs) contain most of the revenue items, plus a number of other variables, for all organizations filing IRS Form 990 or 990-EZ and that reported more than $25,000 in gross receipts. The 1999 RTF, which was used for the 1998 analysis in the 1992–1998 *Nonprofit Almanac* trend tables, contains data on 228,011 organizations, of which 224,272 were considered in-scope (see "Out-of-Scope Organizations," further on) and

TABLE B.1

Fiscal Years of the 1999 Return Transaction File, Circa 1998

	Number of Organizations	Percentage of Total
1996	6,563	2.9
1997	31,977	14.0
1998	167,872	73.6
1999	21,599	9.5

included in the tables. The files contain most of the revenue variables collected on the first part of IRS Form 990, with the notable exception of government grants.

The RTFs, the primary source for the National Center for Charitable Statistics (NCCS) Core Files, include data from all returns *received by the IRS* in a given calendar year, plus prior-year data from organizations that the IRS expects to file but that have not yet done so. Thus the 1999 file contains data from all returns received between January 1, 1999, and December 31, 1999, plus a substantial percentage of returns probably received in 1997 or 1998. As Table B.1 shows, nearly 74 percent of the records in the 1999 RTF (the file used for 1998 analysis) represented fiscal-year 1998 finances. When a return's data are available from the Statistics of Income (SOI) Sample, these highly reliable data replace the data from the original RTF record.

GuideStar-NCCS National Nonprofit Organization Database, 1998

The GuideStar-NCCS National Nonprofit Organization Database (GNNND) includes detailed data on more than five hundred variables from public charities that file IRS Form 990 (75 percent) and a substantially smaller number of variables for organizations filing IRS Form 990-EZ (25 percent). NCCS contracts with the IRS to obtain scanned images of all Forms 990, 990-EZ, and 990-PF received by the IRS. GuideStar and its subcontractors manually enter most variables from the forms, schedules, and attachments. If financial entries fail arithmetic checks, the data are rechecked for correspondence to the original form.

To date, the database contains more than 230,000 organizations. However, because of the newness of the data and inconsistencies between the GNNND and the RTFs, NCCS included only those records that were also

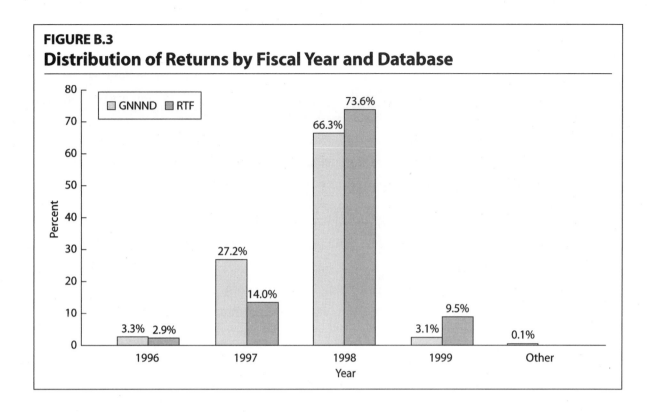

FIGURE B.3
Distribution of Returns by Fiscal Year and Database

found in the 1999 RTFs. For organizations appearing in the 1999 RTF but missing from the GNNND, RTF and SOI records were added, and values for fields not available in the RTFs were imputed so that every organization in the RTF was represented in the GNNND.

Returns of organizations that were *not* represented in the RTF were dropped from the analyses in this book in order to prevent any possibility of double-counting because the Federal Employer Identification Numbers (EINs)—the unique organization identifier used for all IRS nonprofit organization files—for some organizations were not consistently entered in the two data sources. At the time of this writing, we cannot assess the extent to which inconsistent EINs are the result of errors on the part of the IRS, GuideStar-NCCS, or the individual organizations completing their Forms 990.

Because the 1998 RTF and 1998 GNNND include some returns for fiscal years 1996, 1997, and 1999 (see Figure B.3), and because, in some cases, one file may have a 1998 return whereas the other has a return from a different year, the aggregate finances for the two files do not match perfectly. In order to ensure consistent trend data and because of the newness of the GNNND, we have chosen to use control totals from the RTF to adjust the GNNND data. As a result of these adjustments, approximately 15 percent of the organizations in the GNNND as used in this book are from the RTFs and SOI files.

IRS Statistics of Income Exempt Organizations Sample Files, 1982–1997

The IRS Statistics of Income Exempt Organizations Sample Files are annual samples developed by the IRS Statistics of Income Division and contain all large 501(c)(3) organizations—defined as those with more than $10 million in assets for 1987 and 1992 and more than $30 million in 1997—plus a random sample of smaller organizations stratified and weighted by asset level. Most financial variables on Form 990 are included in these files. The data are checked for consistency by the IRS, so the financial data are considered highly reliable for research purposes.

Classification

Tables in Chapters Four and Five that group organizations based on their primary activities use the National Taxonomy of Exempt Entities—Core Codes (NTEE-CC). This classification system has been designed to identify the primary purpose of nonprofit organizations. The current version groups 629 codes into twenty-six major groups, such as arts and culture, education, environment, health, youth development, and international activities. (Both summary and detailed information on NTEE-CC is available at http://www.nccs.urban.org.)

Identification and Correction of Errors in Financial Data

A number of steps were taken to check for financial errors in the GNNND and RTFs. (Full documentation of these procedures can be found at http://www.nccs.urban.org.) Although we cannot claim to have identified and corrected all the errors in such a large number of records, we have sought to locate and correct all major errors through the following means:

- Comparison of the largest organizations in each file
- Review of the original unedited IRS Forms 990 for large outliers, with special attention paid to the allocation of functional expenses between personnel-related expenses and the "other expense" category
- Automated procedures for locating and fixing internally inconsistent records

Out-of-Scope Organizations

Several categories of organizations were considered *out-of-scope* and excluded from the analysis in Chapter Five. These categories include mutual benefit organizations, foreign organizations, private foundations filing

TABLE B.2

Out-of-Scope Organizations by Type

	Number	Percent	Total Expenses (Millions)	Percent	Total Assets (Millions)	Percent
Total in-scope and out-of-scope organizations	228,011	100.0	702,063.0	100.0	1,477,187.3	100.0
Total in-scope organizations	224,272	98.4	621,162.6	88.5	1,210,392.2	81.9
Total out-of-scope organizations	3,739	1.6	80,900.4	11.5	266,795.1	18.1
Mutual benefit organizations	668	0.3	49,011.2	7.0	193,070.2	13.1
Organizations with foreign or missing geographical identifiers	223	0.1	8,515.2	1.2	19,792.1	1.3
Organizations with missing geographical identifiers	373	0.2	223.6	0.0	870.8	0.1
Private foundations	870	0.4	372.4	0.1	1,113.9	0.1
Total government-related organizations	1,456	0.6	7,895.4	1.1	25,344.9	1.7
Government-related organizations— public university–related	1,299	0.6	7,249.7	1.0	24,960.2	1.7
Government-related organizations— other	157	0.1	645.7	0.1	384.7	0.0
Other	149	0.1	14,882.5	2.1	26,603.2	1.8

the wrong form, organizations with missing geographical information, government-related organizations, and fundraising foundations controlled by public universities.

The out-of-scope organizations represent 1.6 percent of the total number of organizations filing Form 990 in 1998 and substantially higher percentages of total expenses and assets (see Table B.2). More than $47 billion (59 percent) of the total expenses and more than $184 billion (69 percent) of the assets of the out-of-scope organizations are attributable to two related retirement funds—the Teachers Insurance and Annuity Association and the College Retirement Equities Fund (the combined entity of which is known as "TIAA-CREF"). These types of organizations are classified as mutual benefit organizations.

Resource C

Key Data Sources and Web Sites on the Nonprofit Sector

VARIOUS DATA and information sources were used in compiling materials for this book. Most, if not all, of these resources have made their data available on the World Wide Web. Following is a list of some of the Internet links to key data and information sources that INDEPENDENT SECTOR has used for this publication as well as for general information on the U.S. nonprofit sector. Although this list is far from comprehensive, it could serve as a useful gateway to finding additional information on the nonprofit sector and its subsectors. The list is grouped into four sections: (1) general information on nonprofit organizations, (2) U.S. government agencies, (3) nonprofit news providers, and (4) Nonprofit Academic Centers Council.

General Information on Nonprofit Organizations

American Association of Fundraising Counsel Trust for Philanthropy	http://www.aafrc.org
American Council on Education	http://www.acenet.edu
American Hospital Association	http://www.ahadata.com
Americans for the Arts	http://www.artsusa.org
America's Charities	http://www.charities.org
Association of Fundraising Professionals	http://www.nsfre.org
Association of Small Foundations	http://www.smallfoundations.org
The Conference Board	http://www.conference-board.org

Council for Advancement and Support of Education	http://www.case.org
Council for Aid to Education	http://www.cae.org
Council on Foundations	http://www.cof.org
Foundation Center	http://www.fdncenter.org
Foundation Center for Independent Higher Education	http://www.fihe.org
GuideStar	http://www.guidestar.org
INDEPENDENT SECTOR	http://www.independentsector.org
Joint Center Online	http://www.jointcenter.org
National Center for Charitable Statistics	http://www.nccs.urban.org
National Charities Information Bureau	http://www.give.org
NewTithing Group	http://www.newtithing.org
Nonprofit Pathfinder	http://www.nonprofitpathfinder.org
The Taft Group	http://www.taftgroup.com
VolunteerMatch	http://www.volunteermatch.org

U.S. Government Agencies

Bureau of Economic Analysis	http://www.bea.doc.gov
Bureau of Labor Statistics	http://www.bls.gov
Bureau of the Census	http://www.census.gov
Federal Reserve Economic Data	http://www.stls.frb.org/fred/
Federal Statistics	http://www.fedstats.gov
Government Printing Office	http://www.access.gpo.gov
Internal Revenue Service	http://www.irs.ustreas.gov
National Center for Education Statistics	http://www.nces.ed.gov
National Center for Health Statistics	http://www.cdc.gov/nchs/

Nonprofit News Providers

Chronicle of Higher Education	http://www.chronicle.merit.edu
Chronicle of Philanthropy	http://www.philanthropy.com
Nonprofit Times	http://www.nptimes.com
Nonprofitxpress Bulletin	http://www.npxpress.com
Philanthropy News Network	http://www.pnnonline.org

Nonprofit Academic Centers Council

Boston College—Social Welfare Research Institute	http://www.bc.edu/swri
Case Western Reserve University—Mandel Center for Nonprofit Organizations	http://www.cwru.edu/mandelcenter/
City University of New York—Center for the Study of Philanthropy	http://www.philanthropy.org
Duke University—Center for the Study of Philanthropy and Voluntarism	http://www.pubpol.duke.edu
Georgetown University—Center for the Study of Voluntary Organizations and Services	http://www.georgetown.edu/grad/gppi/welcome.html
Grand Valley State University—Center for Philanthropy and Nonprofit Leadership	http://www.gvsu.edu
Harvard University—Hauser Center for Nonprofit Organizations	http://www.ksghauser.harvard.edu
Indiana University—Center on Philanthropy	http://www.philanthropy.iupui.edu
John Hopkins University—Center for Civil Society Studies	http://www.jhu.edu/~ccss/
New School for Social Research—Nonprofit Management Program	http://www.newschool.edu

New York University—
National Center on
Philanthropy and the Law   http://www.law.nyu.edu/ncpl/

New York University—
Robert F. Wagner
Graduate School
of Public Service   http://www.nyu.edu/wagner/

Portland State University—
Institute for Nonprofit
Management   http://www.upa.pdx.edu/PA/INPM/

Regis University—Center
for Nonprofit Leadership   http://www.regis.edu/spsgrad/

Rockefeller Archives Center   http://www.rockefeller.edu/
                                        archive.ctr/

Seattle University—Institute
of Public Service   http://www.seattleu.edu/artsci/

Seton Hall University—
Center for Public Service   http://artsci.shu.edu/cps/

Tufts University—University
College of Citizenship
and Public Service   http://www.uccps.tufts.edu

The Union Institute—
Center on Public Policy   http://www.tui.edu/OSR/cpp.htm

University of California
at Berkley—Public and
Nonprofit Management
Program   http://www.haas.berkeley.edu/
                                        PNMP/

University of Maryland
University College—
Graduate School
of Management
and Technology   http://www.umuc.edu

University of Michigan—
Program on Nonprofit
and Public Management   http://www.umich.edu/~nonproft/

University of Minnesota—
Program on Public Policy,
Philanthropy and the
Nonprofit Sector   http://www.hhh.umn.edu

University of Missouri
    Kansas City—Midwest
    Center for Nonprofit
    Leadership   http://bsbpa.umkc.edu/mwcnl//

University of Pennsylvania—
    Center for Community
    Partnerships   http://www.upenn.edu/ccp/

University of St. Thomas—
    Center for Nonprofit   http://www.gsb.stthomas.edu/
    Management   nonpro.htm/

University of San Francisco—
    Institute for Nonprofit
    Organization Management   http://www.inom.org

University of Washington—
    Graduate School of
    Public Affairs   http://www.evans.washington.edu

Yale University—Program on
    Non-Profit Organizations   http://www.yale.edu/divinity/ponpo/

York University—Nonprofit
    Management and   http://www.schulich.yorku.ca/
    Leadership Program   ssb.nsf?open

Resource D
Glossary of Terms

SOME of these definitions have been taken from other publications, including the "Glossary of Philanthropic Terms" in Council on Foundations, *Corporate Philanthropy: Philosophy, Management, Trends, Future, Background* (Washington, D.C.: Council on Foundations, 1982); U.S. Bureau of the Census, *Statistical Abstract of the United States* (Washington, D.C.: U.S. Government Printing Office, 1985); and U.S. Bureau of the Census, *Social Indicators III* (Washington, D.C.: U.S. Government Printing Office, various years). Many of the definitions from these publications have been revised to reflect their specific relationship to the independent sector. Other definitions of specific terms used to describe the functions of activities of this sector, such as *assigned value for volunteer time,* have been written by the authors.

AGI. Adjusted gross income. This is "total income" as defined by the tax code, less "statutory adjustments" (primarily business, investment, or certain other deductions, such as payments to a Keogh retirement plan or an individual retirement account).

Assets. Financial holdings of an organization, such as property or resources, cash, accounts receivable, equipment, and so on, and balances against liabilities.

Assigned value for volunteer time. The monetary value of volunteer time calculated as the total number of hours formally volunteered to organizations in a year, multiplied by the hourly wage for nonagricultural workers for that year, as published in the *Economic Report of the President,* and increased by 12 percent to estimate the value of fringe benefits.

Average. A single number of values that is often used to represent the typical value of a group of numbers. It is regarded as a measure of the "location" or "central tendency" of a group of numbers. The *arithmetic mean* is the type of average used most frequently. It is derived by totaling the values of individual items in a particular group and dividing that total by the number of items. The arithmetic mean is often referred to as simply the "mean" or "average." The *median* of a group of numbers is the number or value that falls in the middle of a group when each item in the group is ranked according to size (from lowest to highest or vice versa); the median generally has the same number of items above it as below it. If there is an even number of items in the group, the median is taken to be the average of the two middle items.

Average annual percentage change. A figure computed by using a compound interest formula. This formula assumes that the rate of change is constant throughout a specified compounding period (one year for average annual rates of change). The formula is similar to the one used to compute the balance of a savings account that earns compound interest. According to this formula, at the end of a compounding period, the amount of accrued change (for example, employment or bank interest) is added to the amount that existed at the beginning of one period. As a result, over time (for example, with each year or quarter), the same rate of change is applied to an even larger figure.

Charitable contribution. A gift to a charitable cause that is allowed by the IRS as a deduction from taxable income. Both individual taxpayers and corporations can deduct contributions for charitable causes from their taxable income.

Community foundation. A public charity supported by combined funds contributed by individuals, foundations, nonprofit institutions, and corporations. A community foundation's giving is limited almost exclusively to a specific locale, such as a city, a county or counties, or a state.

Constant-dollar estimates. A computation that removes the effects of price changes from a statistical series reported in dollar terms. Constant-dollar series are derived by dividing current-dollar estimates by appropriate price indexes, such as the Consumer Price Index, or by the various implicit price deflators for GNP. The result is a series as it would presumably exist if prices remained the same throughout the period as in the base year—in other words, if the dollar had constant purchasing power. Changes in such a series would reflect only changes in the real (physical) volume of output. *See also* **Current dollars** *and* **GNP.**

Contributions deduction. Taxpayers can deduct from their taxable income contributions made to certain religious, charitable, educational, scientific, or literary 501(c)(3) organizations. These could be in the form of cash, property, or out-of-pocket expenses incurred while performing volunteer work.

Corporate contributions. A general term referring to charitable contributions by a corporation. The term is usually used to describe cash contributions only but may also include other items, such as the value of loaned executives, products, and services.

Corporate foundation. A private philanthropic organization set up and funded by a corporation. A corporate foundation is governed by a board that may include members of the corporation board and contributions committee, or other staff members, and representatives of the community.

Corporate social responsibility program. A philanthropic program operated within a corporation. The program may be managed through a department of its own or through a community affairs (or similar) department.

Current dollars. The dollar amount that reflects the value of the dollar at the time of its use. *See also* **Constant-dollar estimates.**

Current operating expenditures. All expenses included the Statement of Revenue, Expenses, and Changes in Net Assets on Form 990, except for grants and allocations, specific assistance to individuals, and benefits paid to or for members. Among current operating expenditures are such components as wages and salaries, fringe benefits, supplies, communication charges, professional fees, and depreciation and depletion charges. *See also* **Total expenses** *and* **Form 990.**

Durable goods. Goods that have an average life of at least three years. Automobiles, furniture, and household appliances account for most expenditures for durable goods. Because expenditures for durable goods can generally be postponed, they are the most volatile component of consumer expenditures.

Earnings. All cash income of $1 or more from wages and salaries and net cash income of $1 or more from farm and nonfarm self-employment.

Employment. *See* **Labor force.**

Endowment. Stocks, bonds, property, and funds given permanently to nonprofit entities, primarily to foundations, hospitals, or schools, so that the nonprofit entities may produce their own income for grantmaking or operating purposes.

Form 990. The annual tax return that tax-exempt organizations with gross revenue of more than $25,000 must file with the IRS. The Form 990 is also filed with the appropriate state offices. This tax return includes information about the organization's assets, income, operating expenses, contributions, paid staff and salaries, names and addresses of persons to contact, and program areas. *See also* **Form 990-PF.**

Form 990-PF. The annual information return that must be filed with the IRS by private foundations and nonexempt charitable trusts that are treated as private foundations by the IRS. This form replaced Form 990-AR circa 1981.

Foundation. A nongovernmental nonprofit organization with funds and a program managed by its own trustees and directors, established to further social, educational, religious, or charitable activities by making grants. A private foundation receives its funds from, and is subject to control by, an individual, family, corporation, or other group consisting of a limited number of members. In contrast, a community foundation receives its funds from multiple public sources and is classified by the IRS as a public charity. *See also* **Community foundation** *and* **Public charity.**

Full- or part-time employment. Full-time workers are those who usually work thirty-five hours or more in a given week. Part-time workers are those who usually work less than thirty-five hours per week (at all jobs), regardless of the number of hours worked in the reference week.

Full-time-equivalent volunteers. A figure derived from an estimation procedure used to transform total hours formally volunteered to an organization into a figure equivalent to the value of full-time paid employment. The total annual volunteer hours are divided by 1,700 (which is a reasonable approximation of actual hours worked by a full-time worker during a year).

GNP. Gross national product. GNP is the total national output of final goods and services valued at market prices. *See also* **National income.**

Independent sector. The portion of the economy that includes all 501(c)(3) and 501(c)(4) tax-exempt organizations as defined by the IRS, including all religious institutions (such as churches and synagogues) and all persons who give time and money to serve charitable purposes. The independent sector is also referred to as the "voluntary sector," the "nonprofit sector," and the "third sector." *See also* **Section 501(c)(3)** *and* **Section 501(c)(4).**

Index numbers. A measure of difference or change, usually expressed as a percentage, relating one quantity (the variable) of a specified kind to another quantity of the same kind. Index numbers are widely used to express changes in prices over periods of time but may also be used to express differences between related subjects for a single point in time. To compute a price index, a base year or period is selected and then designated as the base, or reference point, to which the prices for other years or periods are related. A formula for calculating a price index is:

$(P_t/P_b) \times 100 = index\ number$
Where $P_t = price\ of\ an\ item\ for\ any\ year$
$P_b = price\ of\ an\ item\ for\ a\ chosen\ base\ year$

When 100 is subtracted from the index number, the result equals the percentage change in price from the base year.

Labor force. The civilian labor force is the sum of employed and unemployed civilian workers. The total labor force is the sum of the civilian labor force and the armed forces. "Employed" persons are all persons sixteen years of age and older in the civilian noninstitutional population who, during the reference week, worked at all (as paid employees, in their own business or profession, or on their own farm) or who worked fifteen hours or more as unpaid workers in an enterprise operated by a family member. For purposes of this profile, the full-time-equivalent employment of volunteers has been added to the traditional definition of the labor force. Also included are workers who were not working but who had jobs or businesses from which they were temporarily absent because of illness, vacation, bad weather, labor-management dispute, or personal reasons, whether or not they were paid for the time off or were seeking other jobs. Each employed person is counted only once. Workers holding more than one job are counted in the job at which they worked the most hours during the reference week. *See also* **Full-time-equivalent volunteers.**

NAICS. North American Industry Classification System. NAICS was the basis used by the 1997 economic census. Earlier censuses had used the SIC system. Although many of the individual NAICS industries correspond directly to industries in the SIC system, most of the higher-level groupings do not. As such, data comparison between the two systems should be done carefully. *See also* **SIC.**

National income. The earnings of the private sector plus compensation (wages, salaries, and fringe benefits) earned by government employees during a specified period of time. Earnings are recorded in the forms in which they are received, and they include taxes on those earnings. Earnings in the private sector consists of compensation of employees, profits of corporate and incorporated enterprises, net interest, and rental income of persons. National income is a component of GNP and is less than GNP mainly because it does not include capital consumption (depreciation) allowances and indirect business taxes. *See also* **GNP.**

Noncash (in-kind) contributions. An individual or corporate contribution of goods or commodities as distinguished from cash. Noncash contributions from individuals can include such items as clothing, works of art, food, furniture, and appliances. Noncash contributions from corporations may also take a variety of forms, such as donation of used office furniture or equipment, office space, or the professional services of employees. Although noncash contributions from individuals are tax deductible, noncash contributions from corporations generally are not. *See also* **Corporate contributions.**

Nondurable goods. Goods that have an average life of less than three years. Food, beverages, clothing, shoes, and gasoline are predominant in the nondurable goods category.

Nonprofit. A term describing the IRS designation of an organization whose income is not used for the benefit or private gain of stockholders, directors, or any other persons with an interest in the company. A nonprofit organization's income is used to support its operations. Such organizations are defined under section 501(c) of the Internal Revenue Code. Nonprofit organizations that are included in the definition of the independent sector are nonprofit, tax-exempt organizations that are included in sections 501(c)(3) and 501(c)(4) of the code. *See also* **Section 501(c)(3)** *and* **Section 501(c)(4).**

NTEE-CC. National Taxonomy of Exempt Entities—Core Codes. A classification system for tax-exempt nonprofit organizations, consisting of twenty-six major groups under ten broad categories. (See Resource A for further details.)

Operating foundation. A private foundation that devotes most of its earnings and assets directly to the conduct of its tax-exempt purposes (for example, operating a museum or home for the aged) rather than making grants to other organizations for these purposes.

Operating organizations. Operating organizations engage in a variety of activities, producing information, delivering services and products to their members and the public, in contrast to other entities that function as sources of financial support by raising funds and delivering them. Examples of operating organizations are museums, colleges, universities, and social services agencies.

Out-of-scope organizations. Organizations identified as being either foreign in origin or governmental or supporting government entities (such as public or state colleges), which have been excluded from the IRS file of tax-exempt organizations for purposes of this book.

Payout requirement. The Internal Revenue Code requirement that all private foundations, including corporate foundations, pay out annually in grants and related expenditures the equivalent of 5 percent of the value of their investment assets.

Per capita. A per capita figure represents an average computed for every person in a specific group (or "population"). It is derived by taking the total of an item (such as income, taxes, or retail sales) and dividing it by the number of persons in the specified population.

Percentage of pretax net income. The percentage of net income, before calculation of income taxes, that a corporation earmarks for philanthropic use. (Percentages based on domestic income and worldwide income differ greatly for some corporations.) This is the most common measurement used in analyzing corporate giving that is devoted to charity. It is also used by many companies to establish a contributions goal. *See also* **Pretax net income.**

Personal consumption expenditures. Expenditures for goods and services purchased by individuals; operating expenses of nonprofit institutions; the value of food, fuel, clothing, and rental of dwellings; financial services received in kind by individuals; and net purchases of used goods. All private purchases of dwellings are classified as gross private domestic investment. Per capita personal consumption expenditures are total personal consumption expenditures divided by the appropriate population base. Per capita components of personal consumption expenditures are derived in the same way. *See also* **Per capita.**

Personal income. Income received by persons from all sources. Personal income is the sum (less personal contributions for social insurance) of wage and salary disbursements, other labor income, proprietors' income, rental income of persons, dividends, personal interest income, and transfer payments. Per capita personal income is total personal income divided by the appropriate population base. *See also* **Per capita.**

Pretax net income. A corporation's annual net income before it has paid taxes. The IRS allows corporations to deduct up to 10 percent of the corporation's taxable income as contributions to charitable organizations and to carry forward such contributions in excess of 10 percent over a five-year period. Corporations do not usually release information on their taxable income, however, and data collected by groups such as The Conference Board are based on income before calculation of income taxes. Taxable income and income before taxes may be similar or very different, depending on the industry and the corporation's tax structure.

Public charity. The largest category of 501(c)(3) organizations, which serve broad purposes, including assisting the poor and the underprivileged; advancing religion, education, health, science, art, and culture; and protecting the environment, among others. A public charity that is identified by the IRS as "not a private foundation" (as defined in section 509[a] of the Internal Revenue Code) normally receives a substantial part of its income, directly or indirectly, from the general public or from government sources, which a private foundation does not. The public support must be fairly broad and not limited to a few individuals or families. Only public charities and religious organizations can receive tax-deductible contributions.

Reporting public charities. Public charities that report to the IRS on Form 990. Charities that do not have to file Form 990 are religious organizations and congregations and charities with less than $25,000 in annual gross receipts.

Section 501(c)(3). The Internal Revenue Code section that defines tax-exempt organizations organized and operated exclusively for religious, charitable, scientific, literary, educational, or similar purposes. Contributions to 501(c)(3) organizations are deductible as charitable donations for federal income tax purposes. These organizations make up a large part of the independent sector.

Section 501(c)(4). The Internal Revenue Code section that defines tax-exempt organizations organized to operate as civic leagues, social welfare organizations, and local associations of employees. They are included in the independent sector.

SIC. Standard Industrial Classification. The classification system and definition of industries in accordance with the composition of the economy. Although this classification is designed to cover all economic activity in the United States, government statistical collections emanating from this classification system do not distinguish between private nonprofit organizations and private for-profit organizations. This system was replaced by NAICS starting in 1999.

Support organizations. Support organizations collect funds and distribute them primarily to operating organizations. Support organizations usually do not operate service delivery programs. Examples include federated fundraising organizations such as United Ways or Catholic Charities. *See also* **Operating organizations.**

Tax-exempt. A classification granted by the IRS to qualified nonprofit organizations that frees them from the requirement to pay taxes on their income. Private foundations, including endowed company foundations, are tax-exempt; however, they must pay a 1 or 2 percent excise tax on net investment income. All 501(c)(3) and 501(c)(4) organizations are tax exempt.

Total expenses. All current operating expenditures plus grants and allocations, specific assistance to individuals, benefits paid to or for members, and payments to affiliates. *See also* **Current operating expenditures.**

Volunteer. A person who gives time to help others for no monetary pay. *Formal volunteering* is defined as giving a specified amount of time to organizations such as hospitals, churches, or schools. *Informal volunteering* is performed on an ad hoc basis and involves helping organizations as well as individuals, including neighbors, family, and friends.

Volunteer hours. The average number of hours per week volunteered and the total number of hours volunteered by the population in a particular year. To calculate the average hours volunteered per week, volunteer hours are estimated by using information on volunteering reported for the most recent time period in a particular survey (such as three months or one week) by activity area (such as health or religion). These hours are then totaled and multiplied by the percentage of persons in the population in that period who reported volunteering in that area. Total volunteer hours are calculated by multiplying the percentage of the population volunteering in each of the activity areas specified in Gallup surveys (health, education, and so on) by the average volunteer hours worked in each of the areas. Then all the figures for these areas are summed to get the total number of hours per time period. If the particular time period is three months, these totals would then be multiplied by 4 in order to arrive at the total hours volunteered in a particular year. *See also* **Volunteer.**

Index